SPARKS OUT OF THE
PLOWED GROUND

*The History of America's
Small Town Radio Stations*

by Bob Doll

COMMEMORATING THE
75TH ANNIVERSARY OF AMERICAN RADIO

Cover and Book Design: Practical Graphics, Inc.

ISBN: 1-886745-05-6

Publisher's Cataloging in Publication
(Prepared by Quality Books Inc.)

Doll, Bob.
    Sparks out of the plowed ground : the history of America's small town radio stations / by Bob Doll.
    p. cm.
    Includes index.
    ISBN: 1-886745-05-6.

    1. Doll, Bob. 2. Radio stations--United States--History. 3. Radio broadcasting--United States--History. I. Title.

TK6557.5.D65 1996   384.54'53'0973
                       QBI96-20045

Printed in the United States of America

STREAMLINE
≡PRESS≡
A Division of
Streamline Publishing, Inc.

Streamline Publishing, Inc.
224 Datura Street, Suite 718
West Palm Beach, Florida 33401
(407) 655-8778   1-800-226-7857

To Barbara and the family
for their tolerance and
for their support of this effort.

table of contents

Foreword ....*i*

Chapter 1: The Beginning
            1920/1927..1

Chapter 2: Radio's Golden Age
            1928/1945..33

Chapter 3: The End Of Radio's Golden Age
            1946/1950..71

Chapter 4: Reinventing Itself
            1951/1960..103

Chapter 5: Small Market Radio's Golden Age
            1961/1980..137

Chapter 6: The Challenging Years
            1981/1995..171

Epilogue 241

Small Market Radio Table 255

Resources 261

Snapshots Out Of The Plowed Ground 267

Index 281

f o r e w o r d

In setting out to write this book, I remember the admonition of a Lions Club speaker almost 40 years ago. He advised: "You should never talk about your family or your work. You can't be objective about either." I hope that's not entirely true.

Like many of you readers, I've thought about writing a book for years, but never had the time or opportunity to do so. Furthermore, I didn't know what I wanted to write about.

When I sold the *Small Market Radio Newsletter* in 1993, the new publisher was, I think, "sandbagging" when he called to say that he'd like to interview me for his first issue. I had decided, after 10 years, that the publication and I needed a change. I was delighted when Iowa-based consultant Jay Mitchell enthusiastically agreed to buy it — assuring its continued existence and, I think, improvement.

During the interview, one of the questions he asked was: "What are your plans?" I told him I was thinking about some long trips, continuing my consulting and program and seminar business, on a more limited basis, — and "Maybe I'll write a book about small market radio."

I set out researching the venture a month later. I found the research interesting — even compelling. After nearly 45 years in this business, I knew a lot of radio people — particularly small market people. During my years with the newsletter, I met thousands more on the phone, at industry meetings and at programs and seminars I conducted all over the country. I am pleased to call many of them close friends.

One of my longtime friends, George Allen, former owner of KLGA-AM/FM, Algona, Iowa, called the other day to ask: "How's your book coming? Is it autobiographical?" I said: "No." He then said: "All writers do so to talk about themselves or to espouse a point of view."

Clearly, this book "espouses" a point of view. My view is that there is a widely held misconception that small town radio people are there because they didn't have the "stuff" to make the "big time." Most are not. They are there because they know people flourish living in a small town and raising a family there. Communities based on the traditions and habits of the family, the church and "township" nourish trust, intimacy and cooperation.

What's more, you don't find many "choir singers" among small town radio folks — they're "soloists." Like most of their customers, they're small-business people who everyday bet their future and their families' futures and their reputations on the skill and energy they put into their businesses.

They operate with small staffs, without benefit of highly paid outside consultants, home office support or high-priced specialists within the business. Furthermore, what they say and do is not "filtered" through any high-priced public relations people. They run their own show — warts and all.

To run a good small town station well, it's necessary to have a mission similar to that of a good pastor or school principal. And, as Mel Goldberg of WHJB/WSSZ, Greensburg, Pennsylvania, says: "for a small market man or woman to die rich is almost a miracle."

Along with much broadcast history and the history of the times in which it occurred, we've included a lot of personal stories, because this is, above all, a "people business." I wish we could have written about more people. Being overlooked is not a matter of not doing something worthwhile, it's simply the space limitations of an undertaking like this. I think the story of this unique part of the radio business, so often overlooked, deserves to be told and permanently recorded. I hope you find this effort worthy of your time.

⚡

c h a p t e r   1

THE BEGINNING

1920/1927

*"I've been in this business a lot of years.
I wish I could do it all over again — every day!
I'd gladly take the bad times along with
the good times."*

*Ray Gardner, Retired Owner-Operator,
KELK/KLKO, Elko, Nevada*

THE BEGINNING:

KGCX — 1920/1927

T he equipment to build the radio station was probably bought in Minneapolis. Joe and Marcellous Jacobs owned a manu-facturing plant there.

A half-dozen radio stations had started up, then left the air in the Twin Cities during the 1920s. In 1925, four stations that would survive were operating: WLAG (WCCO), by the millers of Gold Medal Flour; WDGY, from the living room of an optometrist; KSTP, by the Twin Cities Barber College, and WRHM (WWTC), by the Rosedale Hospital. It was in 1925 that the Jacobses moved their transmitting equipment to a ranch they owned 500 miles away in northeastern Montana. Broadcasts were made regularly from the ranch — without benefit of a license.

In the fall of 1925, the transmitting equipment was moved from the ranch to the back room of the First Bank of Vida. To escape the mundane duties of running the bank, co-owner Ed Krebsbach front-ed a band he called The Vida Syncopators. The Jacobses' radio equip-ment was being used to broadcast the Sunday afternoon perfor-mances by the Syncopators. In addition to the radio audience, a good number of locals were on hand in person to witness the broad-casts — an exciting event in an age when most Americans had never traveled more than 50 miles from their homes.

During one of the Sunday broadcasts, a stranger showed up. He was a traveling inspector from the Bureau of Navigation of the U.S. Commerce Department, regulators of the new radio industry. The Secretary of Commerce was Herbert Hoover. The inspector ordered the unlicensed station off the air.

The following Sunday, the bank phone rang steadily with callers from across Montana and North Dakota, wanting to know where the broadcasts were. Customers coming in to the bank told Ed how much they missed the broadcasts.

The First Bank of Vida applied for and was granted a license to operate KGCX. The Jacobses' equipment was purchased for $125. The first legal broadcast was made on October 5, 1926. In addition to the Syncopators' program, Ed slipped away from the banking counter each day at noon to broadcast for an hour from the back room — unheated in frigid winters, uncooled in the sweltering summers. KGCX remained in Vida until 1929 — the smallest town ever to have its own radio station. The population was just 27.

The First Radio Station

It is generally held that radio broadcasting, as we know it, started in 1920 in a Westinghouse manufacturing plant in Pittsburgh, Pennsylvania. A Westinghouse engineer built the station, 8XK. It was part of the company's research and development program.

The engineer, Dr. Frank Conrad, regularly broadcast sports scores, recorded music and other fare. Although WEAF (now WFAN), New York, is generally credited with broadcasting the first commercial, Dr. Conrad probably deserves the credit. Rather than buy records for his program, he obtained them at no cost from a local music store. In return for the favor, he "thanked" the store on the air — so, radio's first ad was a trade out.

Horne's Department Store made a major contribution to the establishment of radio. Dr. Conrad's broadcasts were attracting a wide following of listeners, not just the engineers and amateurs who had listened for a decade. Looking for a new line of merchandise, Horne's began stocking radio receivers. The receivers were given prominent space in the store's newspaper ads, along with a schedule of the programs to be presented on radio station 8XK. The ads told readers that radio receiving sets could be purchased for a little as $10.

Encouraged by Horne's activities, Westinghouse executives decided to begin manufacturing radio receivers. To create a market for the sets, they upgraded their radiotelegraph transmitter to a radiotelephony transmitter and requested a new license. KDKA started broadcasting on November 2, 1920. The first evening's broadcast on KDKA featured returns of the Harding-Cox presidential election.

KDKA did not have the airwaves to itself for very long. By the end of 1920, 30 more licenses had been issued. Two hundred were issued by mid-1921. The number reached 576 in early 1923. The early broadcast station licensees included radio equipment dealers, department stores, newspapers, churches and schools, chambers of commerce — even a Jaycee chapter. Most were inadequately financed and quickly left the air.

Americans were soon clearly caught up in radio. In his chronicle of the 1920s, *Only Yesterday*, Frederick Lewis Allen recalls: "In the winter of 1921-1922, everybody was talking about radio. A San Francisco newspaper said: 'There is radio music in the air, every night, everywhere. Anybody can hear it at home on a receiving set, which any boy can put up in an hour.'" President Harding had a radio set installed in his study in the White House. On Broadway, Allen said: "In *The Ziegfeld Follies of 1922*, a song about a man who hoped his love might hear him as she was 'listening to the radio' was one of the show's biggest hit songs."

Who's Going to Pay for This?

Early radio station owners were generally content to use their stations to promote their businesses or further the mission of their college or church. But it soon became obvious that building and operating a station was not practical as a promotion vehicle solely for the entity that owned it. There were not enough frequencies to accommodate every business or group that wanted one.

AT&T looked upon its radio station, WEAF (now WFAN), much as it did its telephone service. It decided to lease time to businesses for advertising purposes.

It made its first sale in August 1922. The buyer was a New York-area real estate developer, the Queensboro Corporation. The object of the 10-minute commercial, radio's first, was the sale of apartments at Jackson Heights, Long Island. The price of the commercial was $50.

Response, according to research by radio sales trainer Jim Williams, was good enough to prompt Queensboro to buy additional talks at $50 each and an evening spot at $100 during the weeks that followed. Williams says his research shows that the sponsor was not overly excited by the results of his WEAF investment — even though it generated several thousand dollars' worth of apartment sales.

Nevertheless, advertising on the radio quickly spread across the country. By 1923, 476 of the nation's 523 stations were carrying advertising.

While the Queensboro commercials on WEAF are generally thought to be radio's first commercials, Bob Shulberg, author of *Radio Advertising — The Authoritative Handbook*, believes old-time bandleader Vincent Lopez broadcast the first radio commercial. A few evenings before Christmas in 1921, Lopez, on his dance band remote from the Hotel Pennsylvania, asked his listeners to call the hotel to make reservations to see his band during the holiday season. The flood of calls in answer to Lopez's request knocked out one of midtown Manhattan's major telephone exchanges.

The spread of advertising across the airwaves had a lot of detractors — most notably the man who was shepherding the infant industry, Commerce Secretary Herbert Hoover. In 1922, shortly after the radio ads came on the air, he said: "It is inconceivable that we should allow so great a possibility for service, for news, for entertainment, for vital commercial purposes, be drowned in advertising chatter."

An equally outspoken critic of radio advertising was the man credited with being "the father of radio," Dr. Lee De Forest.

The Chicago Tribune quoted De Forest in a 1946 speech to the NAB as saying: "You have cut time into tiny segments called spots — more rightly stains — wherewith the occasional fine program is periodically smeared with impudent insistence to buy and try!"

Advertisers went into radio commercials timidly. Early buyers of time on WEAF, according to Shulberg, had to adhere to a long list of restrictions. Not only was the offering of merchandise samples prohibited, but packages or containers could not be described as to size, shape or color, and prices could not be quoted.

Early sponsors sought the good will of listeners by tying their business names to the acts they sponsored on radio, such as The Ipana Troubadours, The A&P Gypsies or The Cliquit Club Eskimos. The announcer on *The Browning King Orchestra* broadcast made no mention that the New York store sold clothing.

A 1927 book titled *Using Radio in Sales Promotion* told its readers: "The radio listener regards any attempt at radio advertising as an affront." The author saw radio only as a supplement to "direct advertising." He said: "Clearly, it is not an advertising medium useful in disseminating sales arguments and selling points."

According to Bob Shulberg and others, the first singing commercial was broadcast on WCCO, Minneapolis, Minnesota, in 1926. A barbershop quartet appeared on the radio for what would later become General Mills. Their jingle opened with the line:

"Have you tried Wheaties, the best breakfast food in the land?"

Commercials in the Small Towns

The Nebraska station owned by the *Norfolk Daily News* went on the air on July 26, 1922, operating out of the newspaper office. The first program, a newscast from 12:15 to 12:30 p.m., is an institution that continues to this day. The station used the air slogan "The World's Greatest Country Daily." The announcer was a newspaper employee, 42-year-old Karl Stefan, who identified himself on the air as "The Printer's Devil."

The station did not sell time until 1930. Its first manager was Arthur Thomas, who would be succeeded first by his son, Bob, then his grandson, Rob, who now manages the station. WJAG has not only been managed by members of the same family for 65 years, it has been owned by members of the same family, the Huse family, for all of its history — more than 70 years — which is the industry record.

The business history of KFVN, a short-lived station located first in Welcome, Minnesota, then in Fairmont, Minnesota, is probably typical of most early small town radio stations.

According to a history of broadcasting in the state, published by the Minnesota Broadcasters Association: "An advertiser could buy time for an entire evening for $25.

"The station got a $250 grand piano for $35. But it never stayed in tune, probably because an earlier concert artist screwed the strings too tight and took all the zing out of them.

"When we got to Fairmont, thanks to (a) Mrs. Meyer, we got smart and got a new piano when we found out all it took was a little plugging of her store," a man close to the station, C.G. Gaarenstroom, told a service club luncheon in Fairmont. His remarks were picked up by the *Fairmont Sentinel*, which sent them to the MBA.

The station left the air in 1927 when it needed a $27.50 tube. Its founder-owner, Carl Bagely, "didn't have that much money in his treasury."

According to Gaarenstroom: "While the station was on the air, he lived on crackers and milk. After the station went off, he moved to North Dakota, where he lived until he died."

"The Small Towns in the '20s"

In addition to the dangers inherent in any new business, the small towns were not generally sharing in the prosperity the big cities were enjoying. They were not climbing aboard the economic wagon that fueled 1920s' prosperity. In the words of historian Frederick Lewis Allen: "The growers of staple crops like wheat, corn and cotton were in a bad way. Their foreign markets dwindled under competition from other countries. Women were wearing less cotton. Few agricultural raw materials were used in the new economy of automobiles, radios and electricity. And the poor, efficient farmer became poorer as the more machines he bought to increase his output, and thus to keep the wolf away from his door, the more surely he and his fellows were faced by the specter of overproduction."

The index number of all farm prices, which had coasted from 205 in 1920 to 116 in 1921 was, according to a prominent economist of the time: "the most terrible toboggan slide in all American history." By 1927, the index stood at only 131.

Allen recalls: "There were other industries unrepresented in the triumphal march of progress: coal-mining suffered, and textiles, and shipbuilding and shoe and leather manufacturing. Whole regions of the country felt the effects of depression in one or more of these industries. The South was held back by cotton, the agricultural Northwest by the dismal condition of wheat growers, New England by the paralysis of the textile and shoe industries."

During the 1920s, the U.S. population rose from 106.5 million to more than 123 million. The growth was largely in the metropolitan areas, which grew from 54 million to 69 million. The rural areas grew hardly at all, from 52 million to 56 million. The farm population shrank from 30 percent of the overall population in 1920 to 25 percent by 1930.

11 to 1 Odds

The chances of survival of a radio station in the early 1920s were slim at best. Of 543 radio stations on the air in 1923, fewer than 50 survive to this day. Of the small town stations, only three are still on the air from their original community of license: KFJB, Marshalltown, Iowa; WJAG, Norfolk, Nebraska; and WNAX, Yankton, South Dakota. KFNF, Shenandoah, Iowa, which was put on the air in 1922 by Henry Field, principally to promote his seed business, became a non-commercial station in 1967.

Other small town stations moved to larger cities: WCBD, Zion, Illinois, became WSCR, Chicago; WTAX, Streator, Illinois, moved to Springfield, Illinois; KFLZ, Atlantic, Iowa, became WOC, Davenport, Iowa; KFKB, Milford, Kansas, (owned by Dr. J.R. Brinkley) ultimately became KFDI, Wichita, Kansas. KFGZ, Berrien Springs, Michigan, became WKZO when radio pioneer John Fetzer moved it to Kalamazoo in 1930. KFEQ, Oak, Missouri, moved to St. Joseph, Missouri; KFLU, San Benito, Texas, moved to Weslaco as KRGE; WSAZ, Pomeroy, Ohio, moved to Huntington, West Virginia, where it operates now as WTKZ; WTAQ, Osseo, Wisconsin, moved to Green Bay and currently operates as WGEE. KFJI, Astoria, Oregon, traded small towns by moving to Klamath Falls, where it became KAGO.

A Big Hand in the Infant's Pocket

Even in those very lean, early day of radio broadcasting, ASCAP was on the prowl for revenue from the struggling, infant industry. ASCAP, formed in 1914 to collect royalties for composers when their works were performed in public, was less than 10 years old when it started pursuing radio revenues.

In the fall of 1922, a group of early broadcasters met in an empty courtroom in Chicago's Federal Building. The single purpose of the meeting was to set up a united front to resist ASCAP's demands for payments from their stations.

The meeting turned out to be the organizational meeting of the National Association of Broadcasters (NAB). The first NAB convention was held shortly after, in New York, in conjunction with the National Radio Show, primarily an exhibit for dealers in radios and radio parts.

ASCAP and the newly formed NAB went to court in 1923. A federal judge ordered stations to pay copyright holders for music played on their stations. It is interesting to note that the contentious relationship between ASCAP and broadcasters would last all of their lives.

Earl and Henry

In 1924, a remarkable American business story started to take shape in a most unlikely place — Shenandoah, Iowa, a town of only 5,000 near the Nebraska border.

The town was home to two mail order seed companies: the Field Seed Company, owned by colorful entrepreneur Henry Field, and the May Seed Company, owned by equally colorful Earl May. Both companies did business over a wide area of the U.S.

Henry Field put KFNF on the air in 1922 to promote his business. The station, mainly thanks to Henry's overpowering radio personality, quickly gained a wide following and his business boomed. Henry's success was carefully noted by his competitor, Earl May.

In 1924, Earl rented a bus and took a group of local performers to radio station WOAW, Omaha, Nebraska. The local performers included his wife, Gertrude, a singer.

Response to the initial broadcast was so successful that others followed, and then Earl built a studio on the second floor of his seed company headquarters. He leased a telephone line and began regular remote broadcasts on the Omaha station — 68 miles away. On August 12, 1925, May launched his own station at Shenandoah — KMA.

KMA's inaugural program was the noontime *Dinner Bell* broadcast, conducted by Earl May. It became the centerpiece of the station's programming and remains on the air to this day. The program, over the years, would be conducted by three generations of the May family: Earl, his son Edward W. May and, at this writing, grandson Earl W. May, who serves as chairman of the station's parent company, May Seed and Nursery Company.

The terms of KMA's original license required it to share time, first with KWUC, then a college station located at LaMars. In 1927, it was ordered to change frequencies and share time with its seed and broadcasting competitor, the Field Seed Company's KFNF.

The story of KMA/KFNF was a remarkable tale of cooperation between two competitors. May and Field were both high-profile, intense men, but, during the six weeks they shared the same frequency, they decided for good business reasons to put their audience first. When a major ballgame was played in the area, the two stations agreed to alternate hours covering it.

The KMA/KFNF share-time arrangement ended when the Commerce Department moved KMA onto a frequency also occupied by Shreveport, Louisiana, station KWKH, owned by W.K. Henderson, whose radio trademark was "Hello world! Let's have a drink!"

Henderson used his station mainly to promote his political views. He viciously attacked Secretary of Commerce Herbert Hoover and the spreading chain stores. He asked for, and received, great amounts of money to carry on his fight against the chains. His broadcasts were sprinkled with slang and, on more than a few occasions, profanity.

Henderson, like May, was known in broadcast circles as "a wave jumper," often operating at hours, power levels and on frequencies in excess of his license. When May was assigned to share Henderson's frequency, W.K. viciously attacked May and his "seed house."

Remarkably, Earl May put his talents as a master salesman and diplomat to work and forged a friendship and cooperation with the cantankerous Henderson. The two shared technical information and several times visited each other.

Although May from the beginning accepted advertising from other firms, such as the Field Seed Company, KMA was used primarily to promote his seed company and other May enterprises, as evidenced by the radio appearances of the Mayola Orchestra and the May Tire Orchestra.

KMA was a pioneer in early morning broadcasting with a 5:30 a.m. wake up program from its earliest days.

Much of the station's programming, like that of the Field station, was conducted by its owner. First Field, then May, confounded the industry by being voted the nation's most popular radio personality in the mid-1920s. The voting was sponsored by a nationwide radio fan magazine, *Radio Digest*. Thanks to the two radio stations and their mail-order seed businesses, Shenandoah was the smallest town in the United States with a first-class post office.

Henry Field and Earl May were not only great radio personalities and salesmen extraordinary, they were broadcasters with vision, both quickly increasing their stations' power and facilities.

Henry Field built an auditorium in 1926 from which to originate KFNF radio programs. The following year May built a larger, more elaborate structure he named the Mayfair Theatre. The May auditorium seated 1,000 people and cost $100,000 (equal to $800,000 in mid-'90s dollars). It featured a giant plate glass wall that could be lowered at the front of the stage so broadcasts could be conducted free of noise from the viewing audience. The glass was 6-feet-high and 24-feet-long and weighed 3 tons. A screen could be lowered for the showing of motion pictures which, along with the booking of traveling entertainer's roadshows, was a source of extra income.

During the 1930s, the Mayfair Theatre was also the scene of numerous meetings of farm organizations formed to address the problems brought on by the tumultuous farm economy that devastated the Midwest. At its peak, the Mayfair Theatre brought 400,000 people annually to the town of 5,000 residents. The theater was a

Shenandoah landmark until 1963, when it was razed.

May financed the building of the Mayfair Theatre with seed company profits, which increased 14-fold the first year KMA was on the air.

The two-station Shenandoah radio market got an early demographic appraisal from a traveling federal radio inspector. He reported to his superiors that KMA appealed to "higher-class farmers," while KFNF appealed to "lower-class farmers."

Other Farm-Related Small Town Stations

It was no doubt the success of Henry Field and Earl May that prompted the Gurney Seed and Nursery Company at Yankton, South Dakota, to buy a part interest in WNAX in 1927. Gurney put up $2,000 to buy into the station, which had been put on the air by the Dakota Radio Apparatus Company in November 1922.

In 1929, Gurney took full control, moving its studios to the seed and nursery company headquarters. It was from there that Lawrence Welk and his band made their first radio broadcasts. Welk would go on to national fame, first on network radio, then on TV. WNAX also launched the political career of Chad Gurney, who would become a United States senator.

Grain broker James F. Bush began broadcasting grain reports from his grain elevator at Tuscola, Illinois, in 1922. The WDZ station transmitter was near his desk at the elevator. From time to time, he would turn on the transmitter, play a record of a march, give his report, then sign off until he had another report.

In the early 1930s, WDZ, a daytimer, came under pressure from the Federal Radio Commission and began broadcasting continuously. Bush made his wife program director. She filled the non-grain report time mainly with live performances by area country bands. They played free for the exposure and the chance to plug their personal appearances. Many brought their own sponsors to pay for the airtime.

The station had a large, loyal audience 100 miles in every direction from its central Illinois location. It had advertisers throughout its area and beyond. Ray Livesay, a WDZ salesman from 1936 to World War II, tells of a St. Louis-area furniture store that spent $1,000 per month (at $2 a spot) — equal to eight times that much in current dollars.

WDZ moved to Decatur, Illinois, in 1948.

Bert Wick was employed in the office of a Devils Lake, North Dakota, farm supply operation. As he often told the story: "I had met Herbert Hoover at a farm convention. When I decided I wanted a radio station license, I phoned Mr. Hoover in Washington, telling him I wanted to build a radio station. He asked: 'Where do you want to build it?' When I told him here in Devils Lake, he said: 'I'm sure you can get one there. I'll send you the papers.' "

Obviously, the federal government was much smaller and cabinet members far more accessible that they would be in later years.

The license was quickly issued to the Radio Electric Company, Bert Wick, technical director. KDLR went on the air on Sunday, January 25, 1926.

Shortly after his station went on the air, Wick sold an interest in it to finance the purchase of a needed piece of equipment. The buyer was a local insurance agency. One of the considerations for the investment was that KDLR would identify itself as "The Williams Insurance Agency Station." The station increased its power, with the help of its investor, first from 10 to 15 watts, then to 100 watts. Two years later, the insurance agency sold its interest back to Wick.

Bert Wick owned his station until 1977 — 51 years. He broadcast a weekly radio program called *Bert Wick Presents* until he was 78.

KDLR stayed in the family until 1988, owned by his son-in-law and daughter, Mr. and Mrs. Paul Lange. Wick died in 1984. The Langes still live at Devils Lake.

The Electric Farm

J.F. Forrest, proprietor of the Electric Farm, received a license to operate WIBU, Poynette, Wisconsin, in July 1925. Its authorization called for 20 watts of power, utilizing wind for its electric power and light. Forrest's son, William, was to serve as its manager.

In 1927, a ½ part ownership in WIBU was purchased by *The Wisconsin State Journal*, 20 miles away at Madison. The newspaper's interest in WIBU was prompted by its desire to compete with its rival, *The Capitol Times*, considered a liberal newspaper, while *The Journal* considered itself conservative.

The newspaper sold back its WIBU interest in 1928. J.F. then sold the station to his son, William, who would own the station, and others he would build, until 1969 — 42 years later.

Newspapers in Small Market Radio

A few newspapers got into small market radio in the beginning years. One, *The Daily Courier News*, built KLCN at Blytheville, Arkansas, in 1927. The newspaper had placed an illegal station on the air in 1926, during a period when no enforceable radio law was in effect.

KLCN was located at the Radio Sales Company, a local retail radio and supplies dealer. The retailer apparently supplied space and technical work, in return for the promotional value of the station. Edgar Harris, the newspaper's publisher, was the station's only announcer.

Harris apparently was not happy with the venture, selling it six months after he put it on the air. The buyer was Dutch Lintzenich, formerly a member of the Navy Signal Corps. As he was qualified to handle his own technical work, he saw no reason to continue the deal with the radio shop and moved the station to another downtown location.

The station was managed in the 1940s by Harold Sudbury, who bought it for something like $10,000. The station, still owned by members of the Sudbury family, was the start of the Sudbury radio station group and cable television ventures.

Another small market station with newspaper roots went on the air first in Quincy, Illinois, in 1922. The owners of WCAZ were Robert Compton and the *Whig Journal*.

Compton owned a battery shop in Carthage, Illinois, a small town of 3,000 located 30 miles northwest of Quincy. Compton had operated an unlicensed station at Carthage out of the battery shop in 1919. The station identified itself as "Station BOB." For three years, Compton was heard broadcasting ball scores, recorded music and "bedtime stories" illegally on an amateur station he'd gotten licensed as 9EJ.

In 1922, Compton moved 9EJ to Quincy, where he entered into a promotional tie-in with the *Whig Journal*. A traveling Commerce Department inspector soon ordered the station off the air.

Compton and his newspaper partner applied for a license to operate a station with 300 watts (very powerful in those days). The application was granted.

Legal WCAZ went on the air in late summer 1922. Four months later, the newspaper left the partnership. Compton shut the station down in December 1922 for a move to Carthage. Power was reduced to 100 watts at the new location. Compton transferred the WCAZ license to Carthage College, but continued to operate it.

In 1923, Compton was issued a license for another station at Carthage, the small town's second station. Call letters were WTAD. Compton quickly sold WTAD to his former partners, the *Whig*, who moved it to Quincy.

Meanwhile, WCAZ continued to broadcast from Carthage College, where it was on the air on Wednesday evening with a musical program conducted by students. It came on at other times when special programs were available. The college operated the station primarily to promote itself as "The College with an Ideal." The license expired in 1925 and the call letters were deleted.

A year later, a new license was issued with the same call letters. The station returned to the air from the college campus with less power — 50 watts — less than 20 percent of its original 1922 power. In 1929, the Federal Radio Commission changed the station's frequency and limited its operation to daytime only.

The college sold the station back to Compton in 1930. He died in 1934. His son, Bob Jr., operated the station until his death at 54 in 1950. Robert Compton Sr.'s widow, Zola, operated WCAZ until 1977 — 58 years after her husband first broadcast on unlicensed "Station BOB" in 1919.

Another School-Related Station

The original call letters were KFMQ. The original licensee was the University of Arkansas. The university's Department of Electrical Engineering built and operated it. Sign-on was December 4, 1923. The university had operated an experimental speech station from 1914 to 1923, and the popularity of 5YM prompted the building of KFMQ.

KFMQ's program fare included music programs featuring students and faculty members on Tuesday and Thursday evenings. Extension courses were broadcast at other times.

KFMQ operated without paid advertising until May 1932. The growing expenses of operating the station, coupled with a tight Depression-years' university budget, dictated the leasing of the station to a hotel company, which also owned KFPW at Fort Smith, Arkansas. The hotel bought the station a year after the lease was entered into. Studios were moved from the campus to a downtown hotel. The call letters had been changed to KUOA in 1926, and the new owner maintained them.

The hotel company's ownership of KUOA was a short one. In mid-1933, it sold the facility to John Brown University, which kept the station commercial and moved it to its campus at Siloam Springs.

A 1927 list of radio stations on the air shows that 86 were owned by colleges and universities. Only a handful would survive the Depression. Those college-related small town AM stations that survive are:

Iowa	Boone KFGQ (Boone Biblical College)
	Decorah KWLC (Luther College)
Minnesota	Northfield WCAL (St. Olaf College)
Oregon	Corvallis KOAC (Oregon State Agriculture College)
Pennsylvania	Grove City WSAJ (Grove City College)
Washington	Pullman KWSU (State College of Washington)

As the value of radio licenses increased, the quick profits of a sale were irresistible to the boards of generally hard-pressed institutions of higher education.

When it set up the FM Table of Assignments in 1946, the Federal Communications Commission set up 20 frequencies exclusively for non-commercial use. The University of Arkansas returned to the air with a station on one of those frequencies in 1973.

A Chancy Business

Venturing into a new, untried business is always risky. That was never truer than getting into radio in its beginning years. There were far more losers than winners. Even some early owners whose stations survived did not themselves survive financially.

Roy Waller had been an amateur radio operator since 1913. In 1924, he built a 10-watt station at Cambridge, a town of about 10,000 in southeastern Ohio. The call letters were WEBE.

In 1925, he was broadcasting *Waller's Evening Broadcast Entertainers*, along with other music and talk programs, on Friday evenings from 7:30 p.m. to 9 p.m. On Sunday, a concert was broadcast from 2 p.m. to 3:30 p.m. The programs originated from the living room of his home.

The station closed down in late 1925 for reconstruction and went back on the air in January 1927. Soon it received a visit from a traveling inspector of the newly formed Federal Radio Commission. In his April 1927 report, the inspector described WEBE as "an amateur station, now licensed for broadcasting. Its value to the public is nil."

In May 1928, WEBE was compelled to give up the downtown building where it was located because it wasn't paying its rent. Waller found new studio space on the fifth floor of a local bank building.

In 1930, Waller changed the call letters of his station to WALR. Soon after, he moved his station 24 miles north to Zanesville, a town 2½ times the size of Cambridge.

The move did not appreciably help the financial viability of the station. By mid-1930, he leased the station to the Cleveland Broadcasting Company. The lease called for a monthly payment to Waller of $150 for the station and an additional $100 to him for his personal services. A year and a half later, the Cleveland firm ended the lease, saying: "The station has been losing money." Waller was again in full control of the station.

In November 1931, WALR was again visited by a Federal Radio Commission inspector. This time, the report said: "The station's quarters are decrepit and not very clean." Waller finally lost his station in 1932. The owners who followed included early station group operator George B. Storer. Storer changed the call letters during his ownership to WHIZ. When Storer sold the station to the Littick family (which owns it at this writing), the purchase price was $275,000 — just 15 years after its founder had virtually given it away.

Another small market radio pioneer did only a little better. In 1924, Joseph R. Tate got a license to build WEBQ at Harrisburg, Illinois. Tate soon got into financial trouble.

Tate's 10-watt station billed itself as "The Voice of Egypt," referring to the nickname for the region in which Harrisburg is located. While retaining ownership of the station, Tate entered into an operating agreement with a local, privately owned trade school, Raley's School of Beauty Culture.

The arrangement was not successful. In 1929, the First Trust and Savings Bank took it over. Two other ownerships followed over the years.

As it turned out, Tate's radio venture did not make him rich. It did buy him a job. He was chief engineer until his death in 1948.

To Sell Sets

As related earlier in this chapter, Westinghouse built KDKA to create a market for the radio sets it had decided to build and sell. Many of the early small town station builders had similar motives. Typical was druggist Charles Jaren of Minnesota.

Jaren operated the only drugstore in the town of Barrett — population less than 1,000. The town has since disappeared from the map.

To improve the sales in his drugstore, Jaren decided to take on a line of radio receivers and phonographs. He built the station to demonstrate the radios in his store in isolated western Minnesota.

The station's first antenna was suspended from a telephone pole in front of the Jaren residence on the town's Main Street — not far from the drugstore. The 50-watt transmitter had been homemade by Jaren and an engineer from Webster, South Dakota, named Bill Matmair. The 50-watt stations in those early days of radio could be heard 100 miles from Barrett.

Within the first six months of the station's sign-on, Jaren's fellow Barrett merchants chipped in to buy two 110-foot windmill towers on which 100-foot steel pipes were mounted. The new towers were erected in a vacant lot next to the drugstore. A lean-to was constructed there to house the studio and transmitter.

In addition to recorded music, the early KGDE programming included local small orchestras and soloists. Basketball games were described by the town's depot agent. The most popular "star," according to Minnesota radio historian Charles Ingersoll, was a singer named Nick Lucas. He was announced as "The Singing Troubadour." It was a common practice, in those early days, for people with radios with loudspeakers to get on the telephone party line to invite neighbors to share an evening listening to the station's programs — an event that would repeat itself a quarter of a century later when television first made its appearance.

Jaren's roots as a druggist were in evidence in 1927 when the station slogan was "KGDE — Kills Gloomy Dull Evenings."

It is often said, only half-jokingly, by longtime radio people that radio isn't a trade or profession — it's a disease. Obviously, Jaren got it good. In 1928, he sold his drugstore and left that profession permanently. He picked up the antennas his fellow Barret merchants had donated to him and moved KGDE to Fergus Falls — a town of

10,000 where his station would have better prospects. The station was his sole interest the rest of his working life. He sold it in 1946 — shortly before his death.

It'll Be Good for the Town

Many of the people who built stations in the early years did so out of civic pride. As the stations' losses mounted, the stations were either sold or, in many cases, abandoned. One such station survives to this day, largely because of the dedication to it of a hard-working, civic-minded schoolteacher.

In 1927, a group of Flathead County (Montana) businessmen, farmers and professional men contributed to a special fund to build a radio station at Kalispell, Montana. A local physician, Dr. J. Arthur Lamb, was the organizer.

KGEZ went on the air from offices in the local Chamber of Commerce. The station's transmitter was located in a cupola of the Masonic Temple Building. The chamber, which provided studio space, also provided most of its programming. Donald Treloar was moonlighting from his school teaching job as the chamber executive. Once the station went on the air, he also served as station manager.

In 1931, Treloar and a local businessman formed the Treloar-Church Broadcasting Company to buy KGEZ. In 1932, Treloar bought out his partner and became sole owner. He gave up his job as a high school teacher to devote himself full time to the station. When he built a new home, he moved the station operations there. The station was by then operating from 8 a.m. to 10 p.m.

By 1936, Treloar's station was doing well enough that he moved it out of his home to a downtown office building. He also bought land south of town on which he constructed a 250-foot tower.

By 1944, Treloar was tired. He had worked hard in KGEZ's early days, through the bad times of the '30s and the personnel shortages of World War II. He leased his station to a Seattle, Washington-based broadcaster. The 20-year lease called for three annual payments of $15,000 each, followed by 17 annual payments of $5,000. Treloar agreed to continue to manage the station for a time. The lease was terminated a year later, with FCC records showing Treloar paying $8,600 to get his station back.

For the next three years, Treloar devoted less time to the station, turning day-to-day operations over to a general manager. He again became the station's general manager in 1950. At that time he embarked on a manager upgrade. By 1952, KGEZ, which had operated with power of no more than 250 watts on a Class IV channel, moved to 600 kHZ with 1,000 watts day and night.

By 1954, 10 years after he had first wanted to dispose of KGEZ, Treloar sold his station for $100,000 — equal to a half-million of today's dollars. KGEZ, which had started out as a part-time civic venture for Treloar 27 years before, financed a long retirement in Inglewood, California.

The Exploiters

In the 1920s and into the 1930s, operating alongside the generally high-minded early station builders, was a small but very conspicuous group of broadcasters who exploited the medium for their own interests.

Foremost among these was "Dr." J.R. Brinkley. He want on the air first with 500 watts in the small Kansas town of Milford. The station was located at his "clinic," where he dispensed "miracle treatments," most notably a goat gland operation that he promised would restore the sexual vigor of a man in his 60s to that of a man of 20.

Brinkley found his radio station ideal for promoting his "clinic" and advertising a number of "miracle cure concoctions" he sold through pharmacists across the country.

A pharmacist who wished to dispense the Brinkley "prescription drugs" signed up as an agent. Brinkley then sent him the "secret formulas," which the pharmacist prepared on order. The formulas cost only a few cents to fill. The pharmacist charged the customer $4 — remitting $1 to Brinkley. It is estimated that, at the height of Brinkley's influence, he was getting $10,000 a week in royalties from his widespread army of agents.

Despite his running battle with the Commerce Department and later the Federal Radio Commission, he was successful in raising the power of the Milford station first to 1,000 watts, then to 2,500 watts and, by 1930, to 5,000 watts.

The station was consistently one of the most-listened-to stations in the United States. Brinkley's charismatic radio personality had much to do with this. He appeared in long stretches, dispensing medical advice in answer to letters he received. Most often, he advised a trip to one of his agent-pharmacists for a prescription by number, e.g., "Tell him you want 'Dr. Brinkley Formula #60.' "

In addition to his own on-the-air abilities, Brinkley apparently had a good show business instinct and a sharp business sense. One of the station's top attractions was a two-hour nightly appearance by the Stan Love 12-piece orchestra. Love and his ensemble appeared at no cost to Brinkley. The band used the radio shows to further their paid personal appearances.

In 1930, shortly after the station had gone to 5,000 watts, the Federal Radio Commission refused to renew the KFKB radio license, saying Brinkley was operating the station to promote his business interests — "not the public interest." Brinkley continued to broadcast during his court appeals. (In 1931, the FRC denied the renewal of Dr. Norman Baker for KTNT, Muscatine, Iowa. He was promoting a "cancer cure" and assailing the medical profession.)

With his radio license in jeopardy, Brinkley set out on a new career — politics. He ran as a write-in candidate for Kansas governor. It is generally thought that, although he did not win the election, he probably got the most votes. Some 50,000 write-in ballots were disqualified as "illegible." Brinkley had used his radio station heavily to further his candidacy. He got 30,000 write-in votes in Oklahoma, where he wasn't even a candidate.

Brinkley made another run in 1932, this time on the ballot. He polled more than 250,000 votes, coming in second to the winner, Alf Landon, one of a handful of Republicans overcoming the Roosevelt Landslide. It is certain that he would have lost had it not been a three-man race. Landon would be the Republican candidate for president in 1936 and later the owner of a group of Kansas radio stations — mainly in small towns.

Brinkley made a third try at the governorship in 1934, losing badly. He got far fewer votes than he had in either of his first two races.

The courts upheld the FRC, forcing Brinkley to close KFKB. An insurance company bought the equipment and built KFBI, Abilene. That station would be a stopover in the early career of Paul Harvey. It was later moved to Wichita, where it became KFDI, which has been the headquarters station of the Great Empire Group since 1966.

Brinkley, precluded from ownership of a U.S. station, built a 50,000-watt station on the Mexican border, across the Rio Grande from Del Rio, Texas. Over the years, Brinkley would increase his Mexican-based station to 500,000 watts (with a directional antenna beamed over the United States, giving it the equivalent of a million watts in the U.S.).

Initially, Brinkley leased a telephone line from Milford, Kansas, to his Mexican station, but, as a contemporary said later: "The line charges were eating him up alive." Then, the state of Kansas revoked his medical license when it was discovered he had only three years of undergraduate training.

Brinkley had his building at Milford demolished to relieve himself of the tax burden and to keep employees from setting up a "medical" operation on their own. In 1934, Brinkley moved his wife and then grade school-age son, and his "medical practice," to Mexico.

Brinkley's Mexican-based radio operation on XER (later XERA) operated for a time on a frequency between KOA, Denver (an NBC affiliate) and WWL, New Orleans (a CBS affiliate). His audience was enhanced by people tuning between the two leading networks during radio's Golden Age.

In 1940, faced by the increasing heat generated from several quarters, the Mexican government canceled Brinkley's radio license. Brinkley, whose radio-generated "medical" enterprises earned millions in the 1920s and 1930s, died in the 1940s — penniless.

Regulate Us

The early days of radio broadcasting were conducted with a minimum of government oversight. Secretary of Commerce Herbert Hoover had hoped that the radio industry would be able to discipline itself without government regulation.

Between 1922 and 1925, Mr. Hoover had called four radio conferences. As related in *Broadcasting in America*, the first conference, in 1922, attracted only 22 people (there were 536 stations on the air). By 1925, the number of stations grew to 571. More than 400 people attended Hoover's radio conference.

Each conference brought more suggestions for government regulation from the attendees. Mr. Hoover seemed surprised that this industry actually wanted more government regulation.

Things came to a head in 1926, when Zenith Radio Corporation was sued for operating its Chicago station, WJAZ, at times and on frequencies different from those authorized in its license. A federal court found in favor of Zenith. The court said that "administrative ruling cannot add to the terms of an act of Congress and make criminal which such laws leave untouched."

In less than a year, 200 new radio stations took advantage of the government's inability to enforce its rules. Meaningful reception became impossible in many places. Sales of radios decreased from $506 million in 1926 to $426 million in 1927.

In December, 1926, President Calvin Coolidge sent a message to Congress: "The whole service (radio broadcasting) of this most important public function has drifted into such chaos as seems likely, if not remedied, to destroy its great value. I most urgently recommend that this legislation should be speedily enacted."

Coolidge thus gave his endorsement to the legislation that would be passed in late February 1927 creating the Federal Radio Commission.

The writers of the legislation creating the Federal Radio Commission were sensitive in the wake of the government scandals that had occurred during the Harding administration just a few years earlier. They took pains to assure that there wouldn't be a chance for chicanery in granting radio licenses.

The stated purpose of the FRC was "to maintain the control of the U.S. government over all channels and provide for the use of channels, but not the ownership thereof, by licensees for limited periods. No such license shall be construed to create any right beyond the terms, conditions and periods of the license." The guiding standard was to be "the public interest, convenience and necessity."

Originally, the Federal Radio Commission was to be a temporary agency. It was hoped that the FRC could clean up the mess in two years. As those two years drew to a close, it was obvious to everyone that broadcasting would need continuing attention. Congress then made the FRC permanent.

Cleaning up the "mess" was no easy matter. Licensees of stations causing interference could not be canceled. Instead, the FRC shortened license periods from the previous three years to six months. Daytimers were created — allowing some station to operate during daylight hours only, when their signals did not reach as far as they did at night and therefore didn't interfere with other stations. Minimum daily broadcast hours were established. Zones and quotas within them were created to create a fair distribution of radio stations. Portable radio stations were closed down.

A Station Finds a Home

One of the portable radio stations operating in the mid-1920s was WBBZ. The Commerce Department had issued six such licenses to Charles E. Carrell, operator of a Chicago theatrical booking agency. He toured his portable radio stations much as he did traveling vaudeville acts.

The provisions of his portable radio station licenses specified that they could not create interference with stationary stations, would be located in a community for only one or two weeks and could not appear in towns that had a radio station.

In May 1928, WBBZ was broadcasting from Ponca City, Oklahoma. It was scheduled to operate in Ponca City for one week, and its license was scheduled to be terminated three months later, in August.

Instead of moving on to another town, Carrell made application to locate WBBZ there permanently. The FRC granted the application. The Oklahoma town not only got its first radio station, it got new citizens. Carrell sold his Chicago booking agency and, with his wife, Adelaide, moved to Ponca City.

Carrell owned and operated the station for six years, until his death in 1934. His wife became manager then, operating the station until 1949.

WBBZ, which began life as a "gypsy," has had a remarkably stable ownership. In its almost 70-year history, it has had just two owners — the Carrells for its first 23 years, then the Muchmore family, owners of the *Ponca City News*, since 1949. Tom Muchmore, publisher of the newspaper and president of the radio station, a Class IV AM stand alone, says the station is and always has been a good investment — and he says: "In WBBZ, we own a piece of unique history. You can't put a monetary value on something like that."

Radio and Show People

Early radio attracted many show people, not only as performers but as station owners. One of the earliest small market station owners was E.E. Marsh in Astoria, Oregon.

In July 1923, the Liberty Theatre, E.E. Marsh, manager, received a license to build a 10-watt station at Astoria, Oregon. KFJI went on the air from the theater. The initial schedule was from 7 p.m. to 8 p.m. daily except Sunday, when the station broadcast from 9:30 p.m. to 10:30 p.m. Programming consisted primarily of musical selections performed on the theater's organ.

Marsh sold the radio station in 1928 to George Kincaid, who

moved it out of the theater to the mezzanine of a local hotel, installing its tower on the hotel roof. In 1931, Kincaid moved the station to Klamath Falls, where it operates as KAGO.

Unlike Marsh, who stayed in radio just five years, a Manitowoc, Wisconsin, movie theater operator "came to stay." Radio broadcasting seemed to be just right for Francis Mangain Kadow. His principal business was the Makadow Theatre. Like Marsh, he located his station in his theater. The audacious Mr. Kadow got the call letters WOMT, "World's Only Makadow Theatre." He coined the word "Makadow," which included the first two letters of his middle name and his last name.

Kadow's station quickly got a reputation for its extensive news coverage. If not the first, it was one of the earliest stations with "News Every Hour on the Hour" in the late 1920s. The growing importance of the radio station to Kadow was evidenced in the mid-1930s, when he changed the name of the Makadow Theatre Building to the Radio Building.

In the 1950s, he persuaded the city fathers to change the name of the street on which his transmitter was located from Marshall Street to Easy Street. In the mid-1960s, Kadow got nationwide press coverage when he announced that his station would accept hard liquor advertising, violating an unwritten rule voluntarily established by broadcasters and distillers at the end of Prohibition. Nothing came of it, because Kadow decided it was time to retire from broadcasting. In 1966, he sold WOMT to a subsidiary of a local utility. In 1970, the utility sold it to Don Seehafer, who headquarters his station group there.

Love Story

Dana McNeil was a conductor on the Great Northern Railroad when he built an amateur radio station at Pierre, South Dakota, in 1916. That was a year before the U.S. entry into World War I. The call letters were 9ZP. It was "Special Land License #12." The government ordered it and other amateur stations shut down at the outbreak of war. McNeil relicensed it in 1921 as 9CLS.

Ida McNeil married Dana in 1916. She was a multitalented young lady whose several accomplishments included designing the South Dakota state flag in 1909, 20 years after the state was admitted to the Union. When they married, Dana was 55, Ida was 26. The couple had two sons, born in 1923 and 1925.

Ida, whose broadcasts would later make her one of the state's best known and most universally loved citizens, made her first broadcast on the amateur station in February 1922. The broadcasts were beamed primarily to her husband on his Pierre to Rapid City run. She made the broadcasts almost daily, bringing him up-to-date on what was going on at home and, beginning in 1923, the condition of their firstborn, then their second child.

Over the years, the broadcasts would evolve to include items about people and happenings outside the McNeil household. It was a "party line" type broadcast. During the summer and in the fall, emergency messages were broadcast to outdoorsmen. In the wintertime, vital weather and road condition announcements were beamed across the prairies to residents of the largely isolated farms. Pierre is eight miles from the geographic center of the state.

Ida's broadcasts earned her national recognition and honor over the years, including the prestigious Golden Mike. She was the subject of numerous articles in national magazines like *Readers Digest* and *Ladies Home Journal*.

In 1927, Dana McNeil received a commercial license with call letters KGFX. The station went on the air in August, using much of the equipment employed in the operation of 9ZP and later 9CLS. The programming, conducted by Mrs. McNeil, was about the same as she'd been doing on amateur station 9CLS. The station was located in the McNeil home in a residential section overlooking the state Capitol.

Although KGFX held a commercial license, it did not carry a paid commercial until 1930. When it began operating on an "expanded schedule" (9:30 a.m. to local sunset), KGFX began soliciting advertising.

Dana McNeil died in October 1936. Mrs. McNeil took over full management of the radio station and the rearing of their two sons, who were 11 and 13 at the time of their father's death.

The sons did not follow their parents into radio. Both received appointments to the military academies, and both served in World War II.

Mrs. McNeil operated the radio station until 1961, when she was 71 years old. Dean Sorenson, now a small market group owner, got his first managing job when Bob Ingstead bought KGFX from Mrs. McNeil for $50,000. Sorenson would also be the station's first morning man, signing on at sunrise, rather than the 9:30 a.m. instituted by the McNeils back in the early 1930s. Since 1972, Dean

Sorenson has owned KGFX's competition, KCCR.

Sorenson recalls vividly Mrs. McNeil's last day at the station: "She finished her program, picked up her parasol and skipped down the front walk, where a relative was waiting in an automobile to take her to retirement with kin in Sioux Falls." That was 39 years after Ida McNeil had done her first broadcast on 9CLS.

End of the Beginning

Eddie Cantor, George Burns and Gracie Allen, Al Jolson, Jack Benny, Fred Allen, Groucho Marx, Bing Crosby and Jimmy Durante all made their first appearances on the newly formed National Broadcasting Company in 1926. They would rule the network airwaves for the next 20 years — Radio's Golden Age.

The increasing popularity of radio and its dizzying financial growth were well-covered by the nation's press in 1927, this last year of radio broadcasting's beginning. The nation was breathless during the first coast-to-coast broadcast of the Rose Bowl game in 1927.

By 1927, radio had changed from a hobby pursued by engineering types to an industry of business people who saw it as a promising investment. In the small towns, outside the metropolitan areas, it was still a chancy business.

The September 1927 issue of a nationally circulated radio-fan magazine, *Radio Digest*, carried a log of the radio stations then operating. The total number was 757.

The magazine commented on the actions of the then-newly seated Federal Radio Commission, saying: "The Commission has renewed the lease of life to the large majority of radio stations that have complied with its dictates and otherwise comported themselves in a way believed to be best for the general welfare."

It continued: "A few have fallen by the wayside, and some of these were considered doomed to fail anyway — Commission or no Commission."

The creation of the FRC gave investors confidence in the new radio broadcast industry. They were assured that their investment in a radio station would not be wiped out by interference that nearly killed the industry in 1926.

Of the 757 stations on the air in September 1927, 87 were owned by universities, colleges and even high schools. (The small town school-related stations that survive are listed earlier in the chapter). Of the 628 stations that could be expected to earn their revenues from the sale of advertising, 99 were located in small communities. Many of these stations would migrate to cities, or at least larger towns. Some of their communities of license would disappear from the map.Communities with local stations in 1927 that no longer appear on the map are Alma, California; Cedar Grove, Louisiana; Barrett and Shipoc, Minnesota; Olneyville, Rhode Island, and Oldham, South Dakota. Many of the 1927 radio towns that still exist lost their stations in the late 1920s and early 1930s.They would wait into the 1940s and 1950s to get another station of their own. Others that lost their stations never got another.

September 1927 "Small Market" stations and owners from *Radio Guide*, which claimed 99 percent accuracy and GUARANTEED IT!

ALASKA:	Ketchikan, KGBU — Alaska Radio and Service
ARKANSAS:	Blytheville, KLCN* — Edgar G. Harris Hot Springs National Park, KTHS** — Arlington Hotel Newark, KGCG — Moore Motor Company
ARIZONA:	Prescott, KPGM — Frank Wilburn
CALIFORNIA:	Alma, KFQU — W.E. Riker LaCrescenta, KGFN — Frederick Robinson Lower Lake, KGEU — Lotowana Lodge Yuba City, KGFM — George W. Johnson
COLORADO:	Durango, KOLO — Gerald K. Hunter Trinidad, KGFM — Trinidad Broadcasting Co.
IDAHO:	Jerome, KFXD — KFXD, Inc.
ILLINOIS:	Atwood, WLBQ — E. Dale Trout Belvidere, WLBR — Alford Radio Company Harrisburg, WEBQ* — Tate Radio Company La Salle, WJBC** — Hummer Furniture Company Streator, WTAX** — Williams Hardware Company Tuscola, WDZ** — James F. Bush Wenona, WLBI — Wenona Legion Broadcasters
INDIANA:	Brookville, WKBV** — Knox Battery & Electric Co Crown Point, WLBT — Harold Wendall
IOWA	Atlantic, KICK**— Atlantic Automobile Company Burlington, WIAS — Home Electric Company Clarinda, KSO** — Barry Seed Company (1927 slogan: Keep Serving Others)

Cresco, KGDJ — R. Rathert
Decorah, KGCA — Bar Bear Clothing Company
Fort Dodge, KFJY — Tumwall Electric Company
Marshalltown, KFJB* — Marshall Electric Company
Muscatine (2-station market), KPNP — Central Radio Co.
    (1927 slogan: "Home of the caliophone and
    the Iowa Farm Union");
    KTNT — Dr. Norman Baker (conducted an
    operation like Dr. Brinkley for several years)
Shenandoah (2-station market), KFNF*** — Henry Field
    Seed Company;
    KMA* — May Seed & Nursery Company

KANSAS:

Concordia, KGCN — Concordia Broadcasting Company
Lawrence, WREN** — Jenny Wren
Milford, KFKB — Dr. J.R. Brinkley (1927 slogan: "Kansas
    First — Kansas Best")

KENTUCKY:

Hopkinsville, WFIW — Acme Flour Mills (1927 slogan:
    "Whitest Flour In the Word")

LOUISIANA:

Cedar Grove, KGGH — Bates Radio & Electric Co.

MAINE:

Foxcroft, WLBZ — Thompson L. Gurney

MASSACHUSETTS:

Chelsea, WRSC — The Radio Shop
Lexington, WAGS — J. Smith & Carl S. Wheeler
South Dartmouth, WMAF — Round Hills Radio
    Corporation
Webster, WKBE — K and B Electric

MICHIGAN:

Escanaba, WRAK — Economy Light Company
Iron Mountain, WLBY — American Electric
Ludington, WKBZ** — Karl L. Ashback

MINNESOTA:

Barrett, KGDE** — Jaren Drug Company
Fairmont, KFVN — KFVN Broadcasting
Hallock, KGFK — *Kitson County Enterprise* (1927
    slogan: "Away from the Maddening Crowd")

MISSOURI:

Cape Girardeau, KFVS — Hirsh Battery & Radio
    Company

MONTANA:

Havre, KFBB — F.A. Battery Company
Kalispell, KGEZ* — Flatwoods Broadcasting Assoc.
Kellogg, KFEY — Hill and Sullivan Mining
Vida, KGCX** — First State Bank of Vida

NEBRASKA:

Central City, KGES — Central Radio Electric Company
Clay Center, KMM — M.M. Johnson Company
Columbus, KGBY — Thelen and Ladd
Humbolt, KGDW — Frank J. Rist
Norfolk, WJAG* — *Norfolk Daily News*
Ravenna, KGFW** — Otto F. Sothman
Wayne, KGCH — Wayne Hospital
     (1927 slogan: "Remember Us When You're Ill")
York, KGBZ — Dr. George R. Miller, veterinarian (1927
     slogan: "Keep Your Hogs and Poultry Healthy")

NEW JERSEY:

Union City, WBMS — Julius Showerer

NEW YORK:

Auburn, WMBO — Radio Service Laboratories
Cazenovia, WMAC — J.B. Merideth
Coteysville, WRNY — Experimenter Publishing Co
Jamaica, WMRJ — Peter J. Prinz
Kenmore, WKEN — John Wilburn Jones

NORTH DAKOTA:

Aneta, KGFN — Haroldson & Thingstad
Brookings, KGCR — Cutler Radio Broadcasting
     Service
Devils Lake, KDLR* — Radio Electric Company
Mandan, KGCU — Mandan Radio Assoc.

OHIO:

Ashland, WJPW — J.P. Wilson
Ashtabula, WLPN — Robert A. Fox
Bellefontaine, WHBO — Chamber of Commerce
Cambridge, WEBE** — Roy W. Waller

OKLAHOMA:

Alva, KGFF — Earl W. Hampshire
Picher, KGGP — Dr. D.D. Connell

OREGON:

Astoria, KFJI — Liberty Theatre

PENNSYLVANIA:

Oil City (2-station market), WHBA — Schaeffer Music
     House;
     WLBW — Petroleum Telephone Company
Parkersburg, WQAA — Horace A. Beale, Jr.

RHODE ISLAND:

Olneyville, WCOT — Jacob Conn

SOUTH DAKOTA:

Dell Rapids, KGDA — Home Auto Company
Mitchell, KGFF — Mitchell Broadcasting Company
Oldham, KGDY — J. ALbert Loesch
Pierre, KGFX* — Dana McNeil
Yankton, WNAX — Gurney Seed & Nursery Co.

TENNESSEE:	Lawrenceburg, WOAN — James D. Vaughn
TEXAS:	Breckenridge, KXYO — Kirksey Bros. Battery and Electric Company
	Dublin, KFPM — C.C. Baxter
	Greenville, KFBM — New Furniture Company (1927 slogan: "Greenville — where you find the blackest land and the whitest people")
	Union City, WOBT — Titworth Music Shop
WASHINGTON:	Aberdeen, KXRO — KXRO, Inc.
	Walla Walla, KOWN — Frank A. Moore (1927 slogan: "The Valley They Liked So Much, They Named It Twice")
WISCONSIN:	Fond Du Lac, KFIZ* — *Commonwealth Reporter*
	Manitowoc, WOMT* — Makadow Theatre
	Omro, WJBR — Gensch and Stearns
	Poynette, WIBU — The Electric Farm and *Wisconsin State Journal*
	Sisiht, WBAR — Kopp Radio Company

* Remains on air in original community.
** Remains on air from different community.
*** On the air. Became non-commercial in 1967.
**** On the air until August 1993.

By 1929, there would be 50 fewer radio stations on the air. By 1932, the total would be another 50 fewer, as the Depression exacted its toll. Not until 1938 would the 1927 radio station total be reached again.

Two news items about "firsts" in 1927 were recorded in Lois and Alan Gordon's *American Chronicles*, and they would profoundly shape radio broadcasting's future:

First, the first simultaneous television-voice phone transmission was made. The carrying of picture and sound would be an early step toward the reality of television broadcasting. As a result, the coming Golden Age of Radio would be of little more than 20 years' duration.

Second was the first appearance of a car radio, which would be central in the re-inventing of radio in order to claim a place in a media world that 20-plus years hence would be shared with "radio with pictures" — television.

PROGRAM SCHEDULE

KMA, Shenandoah, Iowa
Wednesday, September 29, 1926

5:30 to 7 a.m.	Talk — G.H. Van Houton
	Music — Louise McGlone
	Morning News and Farm Talks — Earl May and others
7 to 9 a.m.	SILENT
9 to 10 a.m.	News — D.S. Ullrick
	Flower Talk — Lina Ferguson
	Markets and Weather
10 to 11:30 a.m.	SILENT
11:30 to 12:30 p.m.	"Dinner Bell" Markets, Weather, Farm News with Earl May
	Music — Ira Cummings
	Vocal Solos — Frena Ambler and Lillian Paul
12:30 to 5:30 p.m.	SILENT
5:30 to 7 p.m	Horticulture Talk — G.H. Van Houten
	Markets, News, Weather
	Baseball Scores
7 p.m.	SIGN OFF

chapter 2

RADIO'S GOLDEN AGE
1928/1945

*"Believe it or not, radio in small towns was a lot
harder to sell in those days. Nobody knew much about
it. Usually, just one station was calling on prospects.
Now, there are several in every place. Remarkably, we
did some businesses a lot of good."*

*Galen Gilbert, who got into radio before World War
II, Community Service Radio headquarters,
Sulphur Springs, Texas*

RADIO'S GOLDEN AGE:

KGCX — 1928/1945

In 1928, as radio's Golden Age began, KGCX was still operating from tiny Vida, Montana (still population 27). Its broadcasts were still emanating from the back room of the bank that owned it. It was still principally the project of bank co-owner Ed Krebsbach.

Broadcasting was undertaken for an hour each day at noon, as Ed spent his lunch hour away from the banking counter doing the KGCX broadcast. Also, Ed's band continued to broadcast on Sunday afternoons.

Things changed quickly. In late November 1928, the newly seated FRC changed the station's frequency and increased its power tenfold, to 100 watts.

A year later, the station got another power increase, to 250 watts. Ed, with agreement from his banking partner and brother, Paul, decided that the radio station might become "a real business."

In 1929, KGCX moved 27 miles to the Roosevelt County seat, Wolf Point. Its population was about 1,900, and the county population was around 10,000.

Ed moved cautiously into the upgraded station, keeping his job at the bank and playing dates with his band, The Vida Syncopators. He apparently got his Wolf Point studio space free in a spare room at his in-laws' gas station. In the early days at Wolf Point, KGCX identified itself as the "Westland Oil Station."

In the early 1930s, the station was programming nine hours daily: 6 a.m. to 9 a.m., noon to 3 p.m. and 6 to 9 p.m.

In 1941, Ed Krebsbach made two important decisions about KGCX. His station was now 15 years old. During the 1930s, he had experienced a high turnover of hired managers, a problem that has plagued most absentee owners of small stations. Ed decided he would leave the bank and become his own general manager.

The second decision was to move his station for the third time, this time 60 miles away to Sidney, Montana. As Charles Scofield, one of KGCX's first announcers at Sidney, recalls: "Sidney was bigger than Wolf Point — a much livelier business town. I think Ed would have liked to move to Williston, North Dakota, an even bigger and better business town, but taking a radio station from one state to another was a tough sell at the FCC in those days."

Scofield also recalls: "There was nothing fancy about the Sidney station — just a couple of rooms on the second floor of the town's hotel on the main street, Central Avenue.

"The station was on the air 12 hours a day, from 8 in the morning 'til 8 at night. I was the only announcer and usually the only person in the station. Ed was out selling. He'd usually come in after sign-off to do his 'book work' and write copy.

"There was a high school girl who came in on her lunch hour and gave me a break from the board. We had an engineer who was on duty all the hours the station was on the air and had to do some of the maintenance after hours. The transmitter for the now 1,000-watt station was two miles out of town. The engineer and his wife lived in a small house near the tower. One afternoon a week, I'd go out to the transmitter so he could take his wife to town shopping."

Scofield continues: "Most of the day, we played LangWorth transcriptions (16-inch discs which ran at 33⅓ rpm). The music was especially recorded for broadcast. LangWorth provided scripts for introducing the songs.

"Ed couldn't get a U.S. network," Charles continues. "Sidney was so small and remote that the line charges were prohibitive. He made a deal with the Canadian CBC network to pick up their programs. A receiver was set up in the studio to pick the programs 'off the air' from CKRC, Winnipeg." (That arrangement continued until 1945, when the Mutual Network started its drive to affiliate the largest number of stations of any U.S. network.)

"I spent about a year with Ed in Sidney, Montana. I don't remember what he paid me. It wasn't much, but — I never told him — but I would have done it for nothing. I'd wanted to be in radio as long as I could remember."

In addition to the experience he'd gotten at Sidney, Scofield says it gave him a pretty good idea of what his career path in radio should be. Like many other young people who have broken into radio at a small station in a little place for long hours at low pay, Charles not only polished his natural talent, but, by doing a little bit of everything, he got a good idea of what he liked:

"I decided I had little interest in or ability for sales. I loved announcing — and I guess I was pretty good — but most announcers have never made a lot of money or enjoyed much security in this business."

Charlie decided to go back to school and get an engineering license. That license got him a job as a "combo man" — an announcer-engineer at the Miles City, Montana, newspaper-owned station, now KATL. He went through the ranks there, ultimately becoming general manager. By 1950, he was owner of a KGCX competitor.

As 1945 and the Golden Age drew to a close, Ed Krebsbach's 20-year-old station was exacting a lot of hard work from him. The financial returns were modest, but things would get better — a whole lot better.

1928 — The First Year of Radio's Golden Age

Herbert Hoover, who, as Secretary of Commerce, had shepherded radio through its start-up, was elected president, promising "a chicken in every pot — two cars in every garage." His opponent, Gov. Al Smith of New York, gave radio new stature during the campaign by speaking regularly about what he'd heard or said on the "rad-ee-oh."

In 1928, less than two years before the start of the Great Depression, Mr. Hoover had told the country: "We in America today are nearer the final triumph over poverty than ever before in the history of any land. The poor house is vanishing from among us."

There had never been so much good feeling and optimism in the country. It was an ideal climate for a young business like radio. Radio historians record that William Paley, a wealthy young man of 27, bought a controlling interest in what would become the Columbia Broadcasting System (CBS), and NBC launched its second network, the Blue Network (later ABC). Radio time sales rose from $4.6 million to $10.8 million in 1928 — a dizzying 235 percent increase. The enthusiasm for radio spread into the small towns as three new stations, which survive to this day, went on the air:

First was WMMN, put on the air by the Holt-Rowe Novelty Company, dealers in office supplies and radio receiving sets at Fairmont, West Virginia. Two years later, even though the Depression had come, they were doing well enough with the radio station that they sold their retail business to devote themselves full time to broadcasting.

The Fairmont station gave a man who would become a historic figure in broadcasting his first radio job. Herbert Morrison would stay with WMMN until 1935, when he got a job at WLS, Chicago.

WLS sent Morrison to broadcast what was expected to be a triumphant landing of the world's largest dirigible, The Hindenburg. Instead, he emotionally described the crash, ensuing fire and deaths of the crew and 98 passengers. The network suspended its longstanding rule of not broadcasting recordings to carry Morrison's account. The recording has been a part of hundreds of sound histories.

Morrison's life ended in obscurity at age 83 in 1989 in a nursing home at Morgantown, West Virginia.

WMMN has had many owners over the years, including George Storer and Nationwide Insurance. At this writing, it is part of an AM-AM-FM duopoly owned by Nick Fantasia. It had been in Chapter 11 and off the air when Fantasia bought it in the early 1990s.

The second startup came in 1928, the beginning of one of radio's longest ownerships, when Hugh Shott, owner of the *Daily Telegraph*, put WHIS on the air at Bluefield, West Virginia. Now, 67 years later, WHIS is still owned by the Shott family, along with other broadcast properties they have since acquired. The president of what is now known as Adventure Media is Hugh's grandson, Mike.

Third was WTBO in Cumberland, Maryland. Its builder, Cumberland Electric Company, operated it for less than a year. In 1929, they leased the station for five months. In contrast to WHIS' long ownership, WTBO had five owners during its first five years.

Limited Opportunities

Many early ownerships were hampered not only by the untried status of radio station operation and local economic problems, but also by early FRC regulations. Those regulations included a system of quota units in each state. Some stations were limited to daytime only. Others had to share time with other stations:

In 1928, WEBQ, Harrisburg, Illinois, shared time with KFVS (now KZIM) Cape Girardeau, Missouri. That continued until 1941.

KMA, Shenandoah, Iowa, was sharing time in 1928 with WGBZ at York, Nebraska. It would do so until 1936, when the York station surrendered its license.

From 1932 to 1935, WHIS, Bluefield, West Virginia, shared time with WRBX, Roanoke, Virginia. WHIS bought that station and closed it in order to go full time.

The surviving share-time facilities, dating back to the 1920s, are in Chicago, where WCRW, WEDC and WSBC divide time on 1240 kHZ.

Daytimers

Daytimers were created to cut down on interference between stations. Signals travel much farther during non-daylight hours because of the skywave, which lengthens in non-daylight hours. Daytimers were created to keep their signals from infringing on other stations sharing the same frequency.

In its earliest days, WJAG, Norfolk, Nebraska, was licensed to operate day and night, but shared time with another station. In 1928, the FRC licensed it to operate daytime only on the frequency also used by WBAL, Baltimore, Maryland, and WTIC, Hartford, Connecticut. It was later moved to a frequency occupied by WBBM, Chicago. It still operates sunrise-to-sunrise on that frequency.

WCAZ, Carthage, Illinois, operated daytime only beginning in 1928, and did so until 1989, when it got non-daytime power of 9 watts.

KUOA, Fayetteville, Arkansas (now Siloam Springs), has been a daytimer since 1928.

WCCY, Houghton, Michigan, went on the air in 1929 as a daytimer. It went full time in 1932. The FCC stopped granting daytime-only licenses in 1989.

Moving Around

As small town radio became a real but generally struggling business, a number of stations looked for new communities where the venture had a better chance (more population from which to draw an audience and more businesses from which to derive revenue). In addition to KGCX, these surviving small market stations undertook what came to be called "move-ins" in the 1980s:

KGDE (later KOLT, now KBRF) moved from Barret, Minnesota, to Fergus Falls, Minnesota, in 1928.

WEBE (later WALR, now WHIZ) moved from Cambridge, Ohio, to Zanesville, Ohio.

WCCY went on the air in 1929 in Calumet, Michigan, and was moved to Houghton, Michigan, in 1941.

KHSN (later KQEH, then KOOS) started in 1926 at Eugene, Oregon. It was moved to Marshfield, Oregon, on Coos Bay in 1928. The city of Marshfield was renamed Coos Bay in 1949.

KFJI (later KAGO) started in Astoria, Oregon. It was moved to Klamath Falls, Oregon, in 1931.

Two of the most unusual moves involved small market stations in Colorado and Washington state:

In February 1929, the Trinidad Creamery was granted a license to operate KGIW in Trinidad in southern Colorado. The creamery owner built the station to replace one that operated in 1927 and 1928. That station, KGFL, moved 20 miles south to Raton, New Mexico. It ceased operation in the early 1930s. Raton would get another station, KRTN, in 1948.

The creamery's owners started a second station, KIDW, at Lamar, Colorado, 130 miles northeast of Trinidad. The two commonly owned stations shared time. The Lamar station went out of business in 1942, in the early months of World War II. Lamar was without a station until 1948, when KLMR went on the air.

In 1933, because of very bad local economic conditions, the creamery's owner moved KGIW 120 miles west on what is now Highway 160 to Alamosa, Colorado. The station is still located there.

A Move Out

In Washington state, Louis Wasmer was granted a license for KGCL (later KPQ) to operate at Seattle. He had just moved another Seattle station he had built 250 miles east to Spokane. He quickly sold the station to a local sporting goods store that changed the call letters to KPQ.

The sporting goods store sold the station to a broadcasting company, Westcoast Broadcasting, which had several other Washington state stations, including another one in Seattle. Westcoast moved KPQ 150 miles east to the small town of Wenatchee, where it still operates.

1929 — The Second Year of Radio's Golden Age

On September 3, 1929, the bull market, as measured by Dow Jones, peaked at 381. On November 23, "Black Tuesday," it dropped to 198. Within a few weeks, unemployment rose from 700,000 people to 3,100,000 — and that was just the beginning.

Volumes have been written about the Depression. No description is more vivid that that by Dr. Norman Vincent Peale in *This Incredible Century*. Dr. Peale, who would soon become one of radio's great communicators, was 31 years old on the day of The Crash. He recalls it and the Depression that followed:

"The Great Depression came with a roar on 'Black Tuesday.' It was the most disastrous day in Wall Street history in total losses, in total turnovers and the number of investors ruined financially."

He continues: "Seemingly everyone was speculating in the market 'on margin,' and when the call came for payment, many suffered ruinous losses. All attempts failed to restore the market to a stable condition." Peale quoted the noted economist John Maynard Keynes, who, when asked if he could point to any historical period that equaled the Great Depression, replied" "Yes, it was called the Dark Ages."

Dr. Peale continued: "More than a quarter of the work force was out of jobs, and never for 10 years did unemployment drop much below 15 percent. Hundreds of thousands of farmers lost their land. Millions of families accustomed to security, even affluence, experienced deprivation and terrifying fear for the first time.

"Businesses closed, shop windows were boarded up, thousands walked the streets futilely looking for jobs. Soup kitchens to feed the hungry were set up and, often, in the long lines of those waiting to be fed, were well-dressed persons who obviously had seen prosperous days."

As 1930 arrived, unemployment had risen from 3.2 percent to 8.7 percent, the gross national product dropped by 13 percent and the stock market during the year would drop to 157 — 41 points less than "Black Tuesday."

The International Apple Shippers Association gave 6,000 jobless men surplus apples on credit to sell for 5 cents each on street corners. One of the year's hit songs was *Bidin' My Time*. A popular boardgame was called Sorry.

There was one business success recorded in 1930: Interest in miniature golf was at a fever pitch, and 30,000 miniature courses were built. One of them was developed by Earl May next to the KMA Mayfair Theatre. He called his course May Fairways.

Starting at the Bottom

In 1931 and 1932, unemployment had reached 15.9 percent, then 23.6 percent. In 1931, payrolls were down 40 percent, and many women earned just 25 cents an hour. Admissions to mental hospitals were up 75 percent over 1922-1930. The Dow Jones Average dipped to 50.

But, as bad as economic conditions were generally and in small towns particularly, a dozen small town radio stations that survive to this day started in the depths of the Depression — 1930, 1931 and 1932:

In 1930 — KGGF, Coffeyville, Kansas; KGNO, Dodge City, Kansas; WPAD, Paducah, Kentucky; KODY, North Platte, Nebraska; KOLT, Scottsbluff, Nebraska.

In 1931 — WKZX, Presque Isle, Maine; WJMS, Ironwood, Michigan; WDMJ, Marquette, Michigan; WWSR, St. Albans, Vermont; WDEV, Waterbury, Vermont.

In 1932 — WAML, Laurel, Mississippi; KADS, Elk City, Oklahoma.

The 1930 to 1932 stations are listed by their current call letters. Some do not have a continuous lineage. The Elk City station was built on a frequency previously occupied by KGMP, which reportedly operated in 1930 and 1931. The St. Albans station (originally WQDM) operated from 1930 to 1940, when its license was assigned to a new owner. He bought the WQDM equipment.

Lum and Abner

The year 1930 marked the first broadcast of *Lum and Abner*. Some 65 years later, it's still on three dozen radio stations — mainly in small markets. Initially a network program, it is currently syndicated by Program Distributors, Jonesboro, Arkansas.

Radio's Greatest Political Star

It is ironic that the man who steered radio through its infancy and reluctantly supported efforts to rein it in, and thus preserve it, would be its first victim.

When Herbert Hoover was nominated for re-election by the Republican Party, the Democrats chose a paralyzed New York governor whose two most obvious assets were a very winning smile and an unequaled radio personality. Hoover, one of radio's "fathers," had what came across as a colorless radio delivery. Over time, Franklin Roosevelt and his advisers and talented speechwriters would use radio not only in their crushing defeat of Hoover, but equally skillfully in selling the Roosevelt administration's radical programs for recovery to the American people.

Booming

Many national and regional advertisers were finding radio a useful medium for selling low-priced consumer items. The national networks, NBC's Red and Blue Networks and their rival, CBS, were rolling up impressive profits. Their owned-and-operated stations (generally the best facilities in the largest markets) were also great financial successes, as were many of their affiliates.

Poor Kinfolks

Just how bad things were for small market radio in the first years of the Depression is evidenced by these figures:

12 new small town stations had come on the air between 1930 and 1933, but 57 of the 99 small town stations on the air in 1927 (almost 1 in 6) had gone out of business.

In 1935, the newly seated Federal Communications Commission conducted its first financial survey of the nation's radio broadcasting industry. It showed that radio advertising sales had grown in the seven years between 1928 and 1934 from $10.8 million to $72.9 million — more than seven times in seven years.

NBC's Red and Blue networks and the CBS network accounted for 57.5 percent — $42 million. National amounted to $13.5 million, 18.5 percent of the industry total. Regional networks did something over $1 million.

In 1934, local business amounted to less than 25 percent of radio advertising sales — $16 million.

1934 Small Market Radio Station Revenue

Population of
Community of License:

	10,000 & under (20 stations)	10,001 to 25,000 (34 stations)
Average Billing:		
Local Channel		
(Full-time)	$17,788	$26,840
(Daytimer)	$13,198	$15,120
Regional Channel		
(Full-time)	$47,592	$56,585
(Daytimer)	$27,162	$21,629
Source of Business:		
Network	1.8%	2.1%
National Spot	2.1%	12.0%
Local	96.1%	85.9%

(Source: *1935 Broadcasting Yearbook*)

Note: To translate 1934 dollars to current 1990s dollars, multiply the 1934 figures by 8. Example, the average full-time station on a local channel in a town of 10,000 or under billed a sum equal to $118,288.

In looking at those 1934 station grosses, it is interesting to note that a Roosevelt administration agency, the National Recovery Agency (NRA), had set minimum wage levels for radio station personnel at $40 per week for technicians and $20 per week for announcers and other production people ($15 per week in stations employing 10 or fewer people).

At the urging of the NRA, broadcasters adopted a code of good practices, outlawing rate cutting, per inquiry (P.I.) business, excessive commission payments, excessive coverage claims, and advertiser- and station-conducted lotteries. Within a year, that code was ruled unconstitutional by the Supreme Court and promptly dropped.

Working in Small Town Radio in the Depression

KGDE and its owner, druggist Charles Jaren, had forsaken Barret, Minnesota, for a move to Fergus Falls, Minnesota. Isolated from big cities, it was a trade center for a considerable part of west-central Minnesota. The town's closest big city competition for retail business was Fargo, North Dakota, 60 miles away over bad roads.

Jaren moved his two 110-foot towers to the west side of Fergus

Falls. Studios were established in what was then the Kaddatz Hotel. Someone got the bright idea that KGDE stood for "Kaddatz Girls Do Everything." Whether an irate hotel owner ordered the station out of the hotel for that reason, or whether Jaren simply wanted to cut expenses by locating his station under one roof is a matter of speculation. Nonetheless, a studio building was constructed at the tower site in 1930.

KGDE would be the second stop in the long career of Jim Ebel, now of Lincoln, Nebraska, and Mesa, Arizona. He had gotten his engineering license in 1928 and his first job at KFJB, Marshalltown, Iowa. Ebel remembers answering an ad in a trade paper. He was hired over the phone by Jaren to be the KGDE chief (and only) engineer. The pay was $100 per month.

Ebel arrived at KGDE in 1930. As he recalls: "The Depression was getting worse by the day. Things were even worse at KGDE because of Jaren's strained relations with the community. He had little to do with the townspeople.

"Soon after Jaren came to Fergus Falls," Ebel says, "Jaren's wife died, leaving him with two young daughters in their early teens. Jaren 'scandalized' the conservative town by quickly re-marrying a woman considerably younger than himself.

"Jaren and his family lived in a few small rooms in the radio station building," Ebel recalls. "Keeping the station in business and on the air occupied most of Jaren's attention. The only social life that I know him to have had was gathering a few cronies in the Jarens' small residential quarters to imbibe of the 'home brew' he concocted in his small kitchen. Otherwise, it was work."

He continues: "Jaren was not an engineer, but he had made a lot of his own equipment. When the FRC mandated frequency monitors, Jaren built one. Every time the FRC inspector visited the station, there was a big argument between the two as to whether Jaren's contraption was capable of the monitoring that was required. The monitor was kept in service over the inspector's objections.

"The transmitter," Ebel recalls, "was also a homemade affair, built by Jaren and one of his earlier engineers. There was a design defect that Jaren or I could never isolate. When I left, he was still looking for it. That defect would cause one of the biggest, most expensive tubes to fail often."

KGDE broadcast from 7 a.m. to 9 p.m. seven days a week, says Ebel, and "I was on the premises every hour the station was on the air (a government requirement)."

In the 1930s, KGDE had no network or news service. Ebel says news was read out of the newspaper and from releases supplied by various government agencies and public relations offices.

Most of the music on the station was from a transcription library. "That library," Ebel says, "was sold to the station by C.C. Pyles, who had become a national celebrity by running coast-to-coast. He did something similar to that in Europe. When he got back to the United States, he capitalized on his celebrity to sell his music service to radio stations.

"As the Depression got worse, Jaren cut my salary to $60 a month. To make matters worse, paychecks were often late and, in some cases, there was no paycheck at all."

When Ebel found employment at a bigger station in Fargo, "I sued Jaren for pay he owed me. Jaren told me: 'I just can't believe you're doing this. You know I need the money more than you do.' "

Ebel's career would span more than 60 years. His last full-time job was as Vice President and General Manager of KOLN-TV, Lincoln, Nebraska, and its satellite, KGIN-TV, Grand Island, Nebraska.

After Fargo, there would be several other jobs, including several years as Chief Engineer of WDZ, Tuscola, then Decatur, Illinois. It was while he was at WMBD-TV that he met John Fetzer, a minority owner in that station. "He told me he needed somebody to straighten his stations in Nebraska. You mean, chief engineer there? 'No,' he said, 'I mean General Manager.' I told him I wasn't a manager, just as engineer. Fetzer replied: 'That's all Carl Lee (Fetzer's righthand man) and I are. You'll do all right.' "

Ebel was there 30 years. Retired, he is, at this writing, in his 80s and on the NAB HDTV Task Force.

A KGDE Star

It's estimated that during the early 1930s there were about 1 million vagabonds traveling the United States — 200,000 of them were teenagers. The numbers were so large that the railroad police made little effort to stop the "boxcar hoppers." One of those teenagers was 17-year-old Harry Sedgewick from Cincinnati.

He had graduated from high school, then taken a night school course in bookkeeping. "Jobs were scarce but, more important, I wanted to go out and see the country. My dad didn't like it, but I left on my great adventure. I traveled to close to 40 states in just a few months, picking up odd jobs along the way to make a few dollars for food."

In the Fred Harvey Restaurant in one of the Chicago railroad terminals, Harry met a fellow vagabond. The young man was from Fergus Falls, Minnesota. Harry remembers: "He wanted to go home to see his family. He asked me to go with him. The plan was to stay a few days and then start out again together."

When Sedgewick and his companion arrived in Fergus Falls, a carnival was unloading for a week's stay. Needing a little cash, Sedgewick approached the man in charge, asking for a job. "What can you do?" The brash 17-year old replied: "I can do anything."

After helping the carnival set up, he was put to work doing a couple of jobs, including "barking the midway." During his week with the carnival, he made friends with several of the town's young people. At week's end, they were eager to have him stay and suggested: "You could probably get a job as an announcer at the radio station. You sound better than anyone on it."

The carnival packed up on Sunday morning. Harry found the station. Charles Jaren and the engineer were in the building. He told Jaren he wanted an announcing job.

Harry recalls vividly Jaren handing him a 15-minute news commentary script, provided by the *Christian Science Monitor*. "He told me to go to a little room next to the control room and read it aloud. 'We'll see what you sound like,' Jaren told me."

Harry says he'd never thought about being a radio announcer. In high school, he'd done some public speaking and was in some plays, and he was on the high school newspaper. "I must tell you," he says, "I was a good reader, mainly because I had an early fascination with words. If I came upon one I couldn't pronounce, or if I didn't know what it meant, I'd look it up in the dictionary. I didn't have any reason for doing that. I was just intrigued by words."

When Harry finished reading the commentary, Jaren, a cold man by nature, matter-of-factly said: "You sound all right. I'll pay you $9 a week — and if you can sell some advertising, you can earn a little more."

Harry spent the remainder of the day at the station. When he looked up his friends after the station went off, they told him of hearing him read the "commentary" on the radio. Unknown to Harry, Jaren had put his "audition" on the air live. "If I'd known I was on the air, I'm sure I would have been so scared I would have flunked," Harry recalls more than 60 years later.

The next day Jaren told him Harry Sedgewick didn't sound like a "radio name": "Call yourself Dick Woods."

Harry, now Dick, couldn't get enough radio in those heady days at KGDE. "It's hard to imagine, now that there are so many radio stations and that radio has been around so long, just how glamorous it was to everyday people, particularly in small towns where people seldom came in contact with even lesser celebrities."

Jaren's or his station's finances had changed little since Jim Ebel had worked there. "Dick," as Jaren had suggested, went out and made some sales. "I sold a 'Man on the Street' program to the manager of the local Penney store. He didn't like Jaren, but took me under his wing. He recommended me to some of his friends, who also bought some time. The Penney guys in those days were people other businessmen looked up to in small towns."

Dick's sale to the Penney manager would be one of the last made to a Penney store for many years. It wasn't that radio didn't work. On the contrary, as radio salesmen would be told for many years by longtime Penney managers, who were told about the commercials run by a Penney store in Durango, Colorado, on KIUP. Listeners from as far as 100 miles away were asking for merchandise at stores in their towns. Those stores didn't have the merchandise being advertised on the Durango station. Penney's "home office" management ordered a stop to radio advertising because, unlike print, "you can't control where it goes." The policy would last from the 1930s into the 1950s. When it changed, the local Penney store would become a good customer of many small market radio stations.

A sports fan, and sometime participant, "Dick" decided he wanted to broadcast the local high school football games. The school officials told him they didn't know if that was legal. "What if I set up outside?" "Dick" asked. They didn't see any reason that couldn't be done. With Jaren's help, a telephone line was tapped and "Dick" began broadcasting the game, seated high up on a telephone pole outside but overlooking the field. When basketball season started, school officials told "Dick" that he and his microphone could come inside the gym.

Jaren was still having problems making his tiny payroll regularly, so "Dick," with his boss's tacit approval, set up an arrangement with a local restaurant. "Dick" would broadcast the eating place's daily 50-cent "Blue Plate Special" in return for free meals there.

Harry left KGDE in 1936, when he landed a job with Scripps Howard Newspapers, who had bought WFBE in his hometown — their first station. They changed the call letters to WCPO. The WCPO job would be followed by many more, including top stations in Minneapolis and Seattle, where listeners would hear, and later see on television, Dick Woods. His career spanned more than 50 years, ending with a several-year job as personality/promotion manager at Andy Hilger's WJON, St. Cloud, just 75 miles from where he'd started. Shortly after he left WJON, Hilger told a mutual friend: "He was 70 years old but hadn't lost his touch. I tried to talk him out of leaving." But Dick and his wife, Ginny, decided it was time to go home to Cincinnati — time for Dick to be Harry Sedgewick again.

Making Ends Meet

Two men — Bert Wick at KDLR, Devils Lake, North Dakota, and Hoyt Wimpy at WPAX, Thomasville, Georgia — were augmenting their meager radio station incomes by providing public address systems for major events in their area. Until the day he died, one of Wimpy's prized possessions was a letter from President Franklin D. Roosevelt. The letter complimented him on his proficiency and the clarity of his public address system, which Wimpy operated for a Roosevelt speech during one of the president's frequent visits to Warm Springs in Georgia.

Earl and Henry in the Bad Times

The postage bought at the Shenandoah, Iowa, post office totaled $309,109.11 in 1929. By 1931, it dropped by almost half — $162,212.53. The Field and May mail order seed companies made up the greater part of the small town post office's volume. (It was the smallest town in the U.S. with a "First Class Post Office.")

Henry Field went into politics in 1932, winning the Republican nomination for United States senator. He was swept away in the general election in the Roosevelt landslide.

He soon brought in outside investors at the seed company and KFNF. Not long after, he lost control. Under the new owners, the radio station and the seed company deteriorated. In 1940, one of Henry's sons, Frank, an authority on farming, gardening and the weather, went to work for Earl May, doing two programs a day on KMA sponsored by the May Seed Company.

One of the innovations installed by the new KFNF owners was

the broadcast of weddings, conducted by one of its announcers, who was an ordained minister.

Earl May doggedly held onto KMA and his other enterprises. During the 1933 "bank holiday," he told his radio audience: "Don't be fearful and tremble. Things look a bit gloomy right now, but the banks will be open again and your checks are good with me. Order what you and your family need. I will accept your check." Soon, $47,000 worth of momentarily bad checks came in (more than a third of a million dollars in 1990s money). Customers eventually made the checks good, and all but a few hundred dollars was collected.

May could have solved his financial problems by selling KMA. He was offered handsome sums by big companies that wanted to move it to Omaha. May turned them down, saying he didn't want KMA to lose its unique small-town flavor and the service it provided to small towns and farmers.

KMA, although it had a huge audience, was a modest financial success. In 1939, it grossed about $100,000 — not really much, even then, for a station with a full-time staff of more than 30, including 16 full-time musicians and a 5,000-watt transmitter.

Henry Field and Earl May died just three years apart, Field in 1949 and May in 1946.

Music and News

In 1932, ASCAP shocked the young radio industry by asking for a 300 percent increase in fees, from 1.7 percent to 5 percent of gross revenues.

In the 1920s, the courts had ruled that radio stations had to pay royalties to composers whose music they broadcast. When the 1932 demand was made, the NAB set out trying to make a better deal. ASCAP set out to make agreements with individual stations, offering a three-year contract at 3 percent the first year, 4 percent the second and 5 percent the third year — plus a sustaining fee to cover music played on non-commercial programs. The individual stations refused the ASCAP offer despite ASCAP threats to sue for unauthorized performances. NAB resumed negotiations.

During those negotiations, in a divide-and-conquer strategy, ASCAP offered a reduced rate to stations owned by newspapers (about 20 percent of the stations then on the air). The offer, ASCAP claimed, was "in recognition of substantial contributions made by newspapers to the promotion of music." But the newspapers didn't bite.

NAB's negotiating tactics included filing a suit in a federal court in 1933 to have ASCAP "dissolved" as "an illegal trade combination." The Department of Justice in 1934 filed a suit to have ASCAP disbanded as an "illegal monopoly." In 1935, a court action in Washington state sought to prevent ASCAP from collecting fees.

In 1936, stations were operating with "temporary licenses." ASCAP terminated the temporary licenses that year, asking for five-year licenses, providing less music at no reduction in fees.

The radio industry-ASCAP fight continued. In 1939, NAB hired a copyright attorney to set up an alternate source of music for radio — a competitor for ASCAP. BMI went into business in 1940, funded by NAB but as an independent stock company. Several years later, after a couple of loans to keep it going, NAB separated itself from BMI, which became a full-fledged competitor of ASCAP.

NAB also removed itself from negotiating industry-wide ASCAP contracts. That chore went to an organization operating outside NAB, the All Industry Music Licensing Committee. It also negotiates with BMI. Each time new licenses are up for renewal, negotiations are long, hard and expensive.

ASCAP was not the only music group seeking performance rights. Beginning in 1933, phonograph records started carrying, on their labels, the following "warning": "Not licensed for radio broadcast." The record companies said the "warning" was posted to "protect their property rights." NAB called it a bluff.

The record companies were in bad need of new revenue. A Bing Crosby biography says that between 1929 and 1934, sales of records had dropped from $75 million to $9 million annually. People just weren't spending the few dollars they had on phonograph records.

In 1935, the National Association of Recording Artists was formed with the intention of collecting royalties for member-artists whose records were broadcast on radio. The association's president was Fred Waring, who, with his musical group The Pennsylvanians, was a radio network staple in the 1930s and 1940s.

Waring went to court and got an injunction against a Philadelphia station, banning that station from playing his records. Suits were also brought against three New York stations. A representative of the artists' group, while attending a meeting of radio executives, asked that artists whose records were played get a commission like advertising representatives and outside advertising agencies were getting. The radio industry turned the record people away.

More suits followed: A suit was brought by Paul Whiteman, the legendary band leader. In one suit, a court ruled that recording companies, not artists, held rights to performances of recorded music. Finally, in 1940, a U.S. Court of Appeals ruled that radio stations have the right, without permission, to broadcast phonograph records. The Supreme Court sustained the appeals court decision. Over the years, recording artists have tried to have the copyright laws rewritten, without success.

In addition to music, news had been carried by radio stations, even before 1920, when the stations were experimental. As stations proliferated and with them news broadcasts, newspaper owners were asking: "Who would buy a newspaper to read news they'd already heard on the radio?" "Who would buy advertising in newspapers carrying 'stale' news?"

In the 1920s and 1930s, there were three principal wire services: The Associated Press, a cooperative owned by newspapers; United Press, owned by the Scripps Howard Newspapers, and International News Service, owned by the Hearst Newspapers. Both Scripps Howard and Hearst were investing in radio station ownership.

When Lowell Thomas started a nightly news broadcast on NBC's Blue Network in 1930, the newspapers became alarmed. To stop radio in its tracks, the Associated Press membership voted to stop supplying its service to networks and radio stations.

By mid-1933, the AP membership softened its ban on radio news, allowing local radio stations to broadcast news bulletins at prescribed times after newspapers had been delivered. Additionally, the radio news bulletin-reports were required to carry an announcement advising radio listeners to read the local AP member newspaper for details. The local newspaper was levied a special assessment for permitting the radio broadcasts. Newspapers generally marked up the assessment to realize some profit out of the venture.

By 1934, CBS had set up its own news gathering agency. Three independent news services had also been set up to serve radio stations.

In 1935, AP eased its rules again, this time allowing its member-newspapers (many of whom by then had radio stations) to use AP copy on their stations. AP did not change its prohibition against advertising on newscasts using its material.

Station owners Scripps Howard and Hearst actively sought radio station clients for UP and INS — and there was no prohibition against advertising. It was not until 1939 that AP would sell its service to any station that would pay for it, without banning advertising on the newscasts.

"If You Can't Beat 'em"

During what radio historians would call the "Press-Radio Wars," newspapers were actively following the old adage "If you can't beat 'em — join 'em" by buying up radio stations. By the early 1940s, newspapers owned ⅓ of the nation's stations. In the small markets, they owned 10 percent of the stations then on the air. Many enjoyed a virtual advertising monopoly in their communities.

The small town newspaper-radio monopolies that existed in 1945 included:

Georgia — Cordele (WMJM/*Dispatch*); Indiana — Vincennes (WAOV/*The Sun*); Iowa — Marshalltown (KFJB/*Times Republican*); Kansas — Garden City (KIVL/*The Telegraph*); Michigan — Calumet/Houghton (WCCY/*Calumet News*/*Morning Gazette*), Marquette (WDMJ/*Mining Journal*); Missouri — Hannibal (KHMO/*Courier-Post*); Montana — Miles City (KATL/*The Star*); Nebraska — Hastings (KHAS/Seaton Newspapers), Norfolk (WJAG/*Daily News*); Ohio — Ashtabula (WICA/Ashtabula Newspapers); Oregon — Astoria (KAST/*The Budget*), Roseburg (KRUK/*News-Review*); Pennsylvania — Indiana (WDAD/Indiana Publishing); Texas — Big Spring (KBST/*Herald*); West Virginia — Bluefield (WHIS/*Daily Telegraph*), Clarksburg (WBLK/*News*), Logan (WLDG/*Banner*).

Additionally, the Arrowhead Network — headquartered at Duluth, Minnesota, at WEBC and composed also of WMFG, Hibbing, and WHLB, Virginia, Minnesota, and WJMC, Rice Lake, Wisconsin — was owned by a newspaper publishing firm.

Former Gov. E.D. Rivers built WGOV at Valdosta, Georgia, in 1939. His success prompted his brother, Jim, publisher of the *Dispatch* in Cordele, to build WMJM to pair with his newspaper, as so many other publishers were doing. After World War II, E.D., Jim and other Rivers family members set out on a station-building program that is probably unequaled in any other single state. Just how many stations the Rivers family owned is still a matter of speculation. In the 1950s, people working in Georgia stations were advised, only half-jokingly: "Don't say anything about the Riverses — you're probably working for one of them."

Another newspaper-related story took place in Astoria, Oregon. The town got its third chance at being a radio town in 1935 when the FCC granted a license to the Astoria Hotel to build KAST. There had been two earlier stations: the local newspaper, the *Budget*, operated a station for five months in 1922 and 1923; and in late 1923, KFJI (later KAGO) went on the air from the town's Liberty Theatre. KFJI was moved to Klamath Falls in 1931.

The *Budget* got back in the radio business when it bought KAST. Unlike its earlier five-month ownership, this one would last 41 years — to 1977.

More 1930s Moves

Although the pace slowed down, there were still more 1930s small stations moves:

The First Congregational Church in Springfield, Vermont, obtained a license for WBDX in 1927. The announced purpose was to serve "sick and shut-ins." For much of its early history, it operated only on Sundays, broadcasting the church's Sunday service.

It was purchased in 1932 by commercial interests. In 1940, it was moved across the state line, 50 miles, to Keene, New Hampshire. Its call letters were changed to WKNE. It would become home to the small station group headed by Joe Close.

Bucknell University began operating WJBQ (later WJBU) at Lewisburg, Pennsylvania, in 1925. In 1933, the university sold its then eight-year-old station to commercial interests that moved it to Somerset, Pennsylvania, 25 miles distant. Call letters were changed to WKOK.

From its beginning, the station was handicapped by being forced to share time with other stations. In 1938, the station operated from noon to midnight on Monday, Wednesday and Friday, from noon to 6 p.m. on Tuesday, Thursday and Saturday and from 6 a.m. to 1 p.m. on Sunday. In 1940, after being on the air for 15 years, it got a full-time assignment.

Kearney, Nebraska, population nearly 25,000, was without a radio station until 1932, when KGFW was moved from Ravenna, a town of about 1,000, 25 miles away.

The 1930s station that probably set a record for "communities of license" was WGRM in Mississippi. It was put on the air at

Clarksdale, Mississippi, in early 1935, as WMFN, but it quickly got into financial trouble.

Records show that in September 1935, the station was padlocked. After sorting out its legal problems, it returned to the air. The following year, it was moved 50 miles to Grenada, where it apparently got free rent, establishing studios in the music room of Grenada College for Women and setting up its transmitter on a site at the local fairgrounds. In 1937, New Orleans broadcaster P.K. Ewing bought the station.

In 1940, Ewing moved the station for a third and final time to Greenwood, Mississippi, 25 miles away. Call letters were changed to WGRM. Ewing family ownership continues to this day, with P.K.'s grandson, Clay, serving as General Manager.

"Family Treasures"

WEAV in Plattsburgh, New York, was built in 1934 by George F. Bissell, an appliance dealer. Today, 61 years later, the station is owned and operated by his son, George F. Bissell Jr. George Jr.'s wife, Judy, who serves as the station's Sales Manager, says: "We've had a lot of chances to sell at a big profit, but this is a 'family treasure.' "

Another "family treasure" that remains in the family, 57 years after it went on the air, is WHAI in Greenfield, Massachusetts. The founder's daughter, Ann Banash, operates that station. She says: "Growing up around the station, I can't ever remember my father complaining about the station's business. I think it did well from the beginning."

She also says: "We've had a radio station competitor since 1980. They've changed hands several times, but we like this business. I'm sure we're here to stay a long time." Ann credits her success in running WHAI not only to being from a radio family, but also to the face that she spent several years away from the station, selling furniture in a retail store. "That gave me a real insight into what the customer expects from his or her advertising."

Another family ownership that dates back to the 1930s is at Price, Utah. KEUB, now KOAL, was put on the air in 1936. One of the original partners was Jack Richards, who also served as the station sales manager. Another was Frank Carmen, the chief engineer, who would become a legendary station operator in the West. Still another was Sam G. Weiss, the station's original manager.

KOAL is currently owned and operated by Richards' adopted

son, Tom Anderson. Of the original partners, Tom says: "This is a small coal mining town. Sam was, I think, the first Jewish man ever in business here. He was here for four years. You wouldn't have expected it back in those days, but the people here liked Sam and he liked them."

Carmen was first to leave the partnership, in 1938, when he got a license to build a station in Salt Lake City. "There was a lot more opportunity there than in this small town." Carmen made his last radio deal in 1987. He was 78 years old and retired in Newport, Oregon, when the local stations, KNPT/KYTE, went into bankruptcy. Carmen bought them. At almost 80, he went to work rebuilding the stations' run-down technical facilities and tarnished reputation. He died in 1990. David Miller, one of Carmen's young Utah radio friends, who was brought in to manage the stations, operates them for his heirs.

Richards, who bought out his partners in 1940, ran the station until 1966, turning over the management to Anderson. He became owner in 1986.

1930s Small Town Radio Business

WPAX, Thomasville, Georgia, dates back to 1922. The station was put on the air by Hoyt Wimpy, who operated a garage and in the early 1920s sold radios, which he built.

The station apparently did not operate continuously from its 1922 startup. However, Len Robinson, current owner-operator, believes Thomas Drugs, a 100-plus-year-old retailer, was the station's first advertiser. It remains on the air at this writing.

WPAX, according to records at the FCC, has been on the air continuously since 1930.

By the mid-1930s, WPAX was doing well enough to encourage Wimpy to run full-page ads in *Broadcasting* magazine. A 1937 ad tells readers that the station covered more than 1 million people (with 250 watts daytime at 1210 kHZ). It said: "WPAX is well-supplied with local talent, has an INS (International News Service) wire." The ad goes on to say: "WPAX has an outstanding audience and reputation through the broadcast of civic events." The station rates, published in the ad: 60 seconds $1 (52 times, 65 cents). Political talks originating in studio — two times regular rates.

The Networks

NBC's Red and Blue and the CBS network sought few affiliations in small markets. They protected their owned stations and metropolitan affiliates to the limits of the stations' usable signals. Furthermore, in isolated markets, the cost was prohibitive for telephone lines that carried the network programs to affiliated stations. In 1935, WCOA, Pensacola, Florida, took AT&T to court, seeking to have its $325 per month "line charge" (equal to $2,600 in current dollars) reduced. The court cut it in half to $162.50 — still a staggering amount.

Building a rival to NBC and CBS was tried unsuccessfully by early radio comedian Ed Wynn in 1933. His venture lasted just six weeks before going bankrupt. A 1934 network venture launched by station group owner George B. Storer lasted only a little longer than Wynn's.

A later 1934 network entry survived. The Mutual Network was formed by WOR, New York, and WGN, Chicago, the only two clear channels without a network affiliation. They were joined in the venture by WLW, Cincinnati (a primary NBC affiliate) and WXYZ, Detroit, a 5,000-watt station.

It was WXYZ, the smallest station in the group, that gave the network one of its hits. The Detroit station fed *The Lone Ranger* to Mutual. Its signature is one of the most memorable in all radio history: "A fiery horse with the speed of light, a cloud of dust and a hearty 'Hi-yo Silver' — the Lone Ranger rides again." Radio legend has it that neither the program's writer, Fern Stryker, nor its narrator, Bruce Beemer, had ever traveled west of Michigan.

Another Mutual hit was *The Shadow*, broadcast on Sunday afternoons. The Shadow was a mysterious figure, actually a wealthy young man-about-town, who aided the forces of law and order "by clouding men's minds so that they couldn't see him." Its memorable opening had the "Shadow saying: "Who knows what evil lurks in the minds of men? The Shadow knows (laughs)." Orson Welles, who would become a radio and later movie and TV legend, was an early Shadow.

Mutual, for the most part, got the leftovers in the major markets — the lowest-powered, shortest-coverage stations. It was, from an advertiser's standpoint, the least desirable of the four national networks. NBC Red was a runaway first. CBS was No. 2. The Blue Network (later ABC) was home to some promising new programs, shows of declining popularity and highbrow fare like the

Metropolitan Opera and *America's Town Meeting*. It was also home to Don McNeill's *Breakfast Club*, which would remain on the network until 1971.

(McNeill had come to NBC in Chicago from WHAS, Louisville, Kentucky. Network executives in 1933 saw 9 a.m. (Eastern time), and earlier in other time zones, as being of little value. In giving McNeill the one hour of morning time, they said: "Do what you want with it.")

During the pre-television years, radio listeners' favorite types of programs were: comedy/variety, music/variety, crime, drama and audience participation. After 1938, when war broke out in Europe, world/national news was of high interest.

Obviously, in those pre-television days, securing a big audience required affiliation with a network. Producing locally the kinds of programs the audience wanted most was impossible. Mutual, with no owned-and-operated stations to protect and with lower-coverage stations in major cities, stepped in to provide small market stations with network programming.

By 1945, there were 314 radio stations in small markets (communities under 25,000). Only one in five operated without a national network. Of the 80 percent of small stations on networks, 62 percent were on Mutual, 15 percent on NBC Red, 12 percent on NBC Blue and 10 percent on CBS. Small town stations received little or no network compensation. Many paid the line charges.

Something Like *WKRP*

Network fare in the 1930s and early 1940s included something akin to the '70s TV series *WKRP in Cincinnati*. It was called *Uncle Ezra's Radio Station*.

The station, "a powerful 5-watter in the small town of Rosedale," was the mythical location. Comedian Pat Barret played Uncle Ezra, owner of "Station EZRA." Fran Allison, of radio's *Breakfast Club* and TV's early hit *Kukla, Fran and Ollie*, co-starred.

In those days, before disc jockeys, listeners associated live music with radio. The Sons of the Pioneers and later the Hoosier Hot Shots provided music and were worked into the program's story line.

Hard Times

The 1930s were not only subjected to the worse economic

conditions in the nation's history, but a series of natural disasters also struck wide areas of the country.

In the early 1930s, a deadly drought blighted the prairies and the Great Plains. During 1934 and 1935, thousands of acres were laid waste by dust storms. The area stretched from the Texas Panhandle up to the Canadian border — from just east of the Rockies into Montana and North Dakota, through Kansas and Nebraska, from eastern Colorado into western Oklahoma and northern Texas.

In 1936, there were widespread floods in the Northeast. Then, in January 1937, the weather turned unseasonably warm. The Ohio River produced what was then the worst flood in American history. A half-million families were driven from their homes. A month after the floodwaters receded, almost 300,000 people were still homeless.

The swirling water rose until the Ohio River was like a great, rushing muddy lake of floating wreckage. Railroad tracks and roads washed away. Towns darkened as the electric-light plants became submerged. Business halted, food supplies stopped, fires raged out of control. The radio was the sole means of communication to direct rescue work and issue warnings and instructions to residents of the flooded area.

The Brothers

Paducah, Kentucky, is several hundred miles downstream from the Ohio River cities of Cincinnati and Louisville. In January 1937, Pierce Lackey was nearing 40 and his prospects were not good. He had left high school before graduation to go into the west Kentucky coal mines, 100 miles from his hometown.

He later spent time as a logger, an auto mechanic and a Navy man in World War I and worked a couple of years in his father's insurance and real estate business. He was known around his hometown as a man of considerable talent "who didn't stick to things."

In the late 1920s, Pierce became fascinated with the infant radio business. He rounded up a couple of investors and set out to build a radio station.

In the late 1920s, as the Federal Radio Commission was getting started, obtaining a radio license was a complicated process. To apply for a station at Paducah, Pierce had to obtain affidavits from community leaders in a 50-mile radius to support his contention that such a station would "serve the public interest, convenience and necessity." His application was granted in 1930. WPAD went on the air later in that year.

Another radio station, WIAR, had operated a short time in the 1920s in the western Kentucky river town. WPAD struggled to avoid the fate of its predecessor.

Early records, in possession of Pierce's heirs, show that on more than one occasion in WPAD's early years, an entire day's revenue was no more than $1.50.

By 1937, Pierce's investors had left the venture, leaving him to fend for himself. Pierce devoted himself full time to the radio station: selling time, writing copy, announcing and whatever else had to be done.

As the floodwaters came downstream, Pierce and his small and, of necessity, low-paid staff, moved the station's studio equipment from the ground floor to the second floor of the building that housed the station. As the floodwaters rose more, it became obvious that the second floor would not be safe from the rising tide. Pierce secured a barge. He asked his listeners to remain tuned during a period of silence until the station would resume broadcasting from higher ground.

The equipment was loaded onto the barge and floated to the west side of town. There it was met by a truck, which hauled it to the home of Pierce's father on high ground overlooking the town. It was moved into a garage, the antenna mounted high up on a nearby telephone pole. Broadcasting resumed in just three hours.

The calm voices of Pierce and his few but dedicated staffers were heard around the clock telling rescue workers to row to such and such an address to take a family off a roof, to row somewhere else to help an old woman out of a second-story window. The broadcasts included locations where homeless could get food and shelter. It was high drama.

When the water receded and the cleanup got under way, WPAD and Pierce Lackey emerged as local heroes. WPAD began to show a handsome profit. Pierce Lackey was elected first to the school board and two years later as mayor, by the largest margin in the town's history.

The 1939 elections were not so kind to a Lackey brother, Hecht, three years Pierce's junior. Hecht had spent most of his working life in his father's business.

He had been active in numerous civic groups and in Democratic politics. In 1939, he was one of 13 candidates in the

Democratic primary for lieutenant governor. He came in third.

When he returned from his grueling, unsuccessful campaign, it was generally expected that Hecht would return to the family insurance and real estate business and then, in 1943, make another race for statewide political office in Kentucky. Brother Pierce had other ideas.

Pierce, by now, had become so successful at the Paducah radio station that his brothers had lately nicknamed him "Kingfish" after the central character on the *Amos and Andy* radio program. "The Kingfish" wanted to build more radio stations. He talked Hecht into a partnership to build a new radio station, 100 miles away at Hopkinsville. Hecht was to move to Hopkinsville to manage the new station.

In 1940, WHOP went on the air. Like Paducah, there had been an earlier radio station there, WFIW. That station had gone on the air in the 1920s in a flour mill. The mill had burned down and, with it, the radio station. WFIW returned to the air from a downtown furniture store.

In 1933, a member of another milling company, George V. Norton, had decided he wanted to build a station in Louisville. He approached the Hopkinsville company about buying their radio station. As the Hopkinsville station was losing money, it was eagerly sold. The station became first WAVE, then WAVG.

The Lackeys' 1940 Hopkinsville venture caught on much more quickly than had WPAD. Aside from the fact that radio had become a more acceptable advertising medium in the 10 years since WPAD had gone on the air, the early days of WHOP had the benefit of not just one, but two more Lackey brothers.

"Dutch" Lackey in 1940 was 34 years old. He had spent his working life as a civil engineer, first with a railroad, then a Kansas City engineering firm and finally with the federal government. He had risen to district engineer at Louisville with the WPA.

During the flood, and the cleanup work after it, "Dutch" had come into contact with, in his words, "radio's powerful potential for doing good." He also was well aware of Pierce's financial success in the late 1930s with WPAD. "When I heard what he and Hecht were planning at Hopkinsville, I told them I wanted to be part of it."

He "hired in," without an equity stake, as a combination salesman/copy writer/newscaster/sports announcer. As he looks back on his early days at WHOP, he says: "For a fellow without training or experience, I guess I did pretty well." Family members say: "He did very well." He caught on fast enough that a year later, when Pierce and Hecht got a license for a third station at Henderson, 60 miles from Paducah, it was decided Hecht would move there and "Dutch" would become manager of WHOP.

Pierce served just one term as mayor of Paducah, then was defeated in a second election. During his term, he helped locate an atomic energy installation at Paducah. The project got immeasurable assistance from a fellow townsman and longtime Lackey family friend, Alben Barkley, then a senator, later vice president. That plant sparked postwar growth that changed the face of Paducah from a sleepy river town to a busy small city.

In addition to the Paducah, Hopkinsville and Henderson stations, Pierce built, operated briefly, then sold a half-dozen other small town radio stations in Kentucky, Illinois and Indiana.

Although he never again sought elective office after his unsuccessful mayoral re-election bid, he remained active in Paducah civic affairs and his Paducah radio station until his death at 69 in 1967. He had a large family, but none of his sons or daughters was interested in radio as a career.

WPAD (and its FM station) were sold after Pierce's death to Edward M. Fritts, father of the later president of NAB, Edward O. Fritts. The elder Fritts operated the WPAD stations for 15 years, selling them for more than 10 times the $150,000 he had paid Pierce's heirs.

WSON went on the air at Henderson just 10 days after the outbreak of World War II — December 17, 1941. Hecht quickly involved the new station and himself in the war effort of his newly adopted hometown. He headed both the USO and Civil Defense there.

After World War II, the Lackey stations were among the first in the country to add FM facilities. Those were operated at losses for more than 20 years.

Hecht bought Pierce's interest in WSON-AM/FM in 1949. During the '50s, he expanded his business interests beyond the radio stations. He organized an application for TV at Henderson, which would become the Evansville, Indiana, market's CBS affiliate. It went on the air in 1953. He and his partners sold it in 1956.

He also, in 1955, organized a real estate and insurance firm that grew to be one of the largest in the area.

He served two four-year terms as mayor, beginning in 1953. Until his death in his 80s, he continued his interest in the radio stations and the real estate-insurance businesses. Most of all, he continued his active civic life, including a term as chairman of the state school board. His honors were many, highlighted by being awarded an honorary Doctor of Laws degree by the University of Kentucky, a singular accomplishment for a man whose formal education had ended with high school graduation.

WSON-AM remains in the family after 55 years. It is owned and operated by Hecht's son, Henry. Like his father and uncles, Henry's enthusiasm for radio is shared with civic enterprise — and, most importantly, politics. At this writing, he is a member of the Kentucky State Senate.

During World War II, "Dutch" operated WHOP with the help of his wife, Bonnie, and just two other full-time staff members. Although radio broadcasting was classified as an essential industry and deferments were available, few radio people took advantage. More than 25 percent of the nation's broadcasting personnel were in the service during the war.

The WHOP wartime news programming, much of it broadcast by "Dutch," focused on Hopkinsville people and people connected with nearby Fort Campbell. "Dutch" and his listeners quickly forged an important bond.

In 1945, after living in Hopkinsville just five years, "Dutch" was elected mayor. He would serve two other terms in the mayor's office in the late 1950s and the early 1960s.

"Dutch's" terms as mayor would be marked by significant expansions of city services and the building of major city facilities. While continuing to take an active interest in WHOP-AM/FM, which he bought from his brothers in 1949, he developed strong management to allow him to spend increasing amounts of time on city business and state and national broadcast issues. He founded and for years headed the effort to raise the power of Class IV stations from 250 to 1,000 watts.

He and Bonnie hired Katherine Peden out of high school. She came up through the ranks, ultimately becoming station manager.

In 1962, when the local state representative, Edward T. Breathitt, announced for governor, both "Dutch" and Katherine signed on to play major roles in his upset victory over Kentucky political legend A.B. "Happy" Chandler. (Breathitt was a radio competitor to WHOP, owning ⅓ of a station at nearby Fort Campbell.)

When Breathitt won, he named Lackey the Commissioner of Urban Affairs and Katherine the Commerce Commissioner. They left the radio station in the hands of Lackey's son-in-law, Roger Jeffers, a onetime football coach.

When the Breathitt term ended four years later (Kentucky governors cannot succeed themselves), "Dutch" and Bonnie retired to Florida. Katherine opened an industrial consulting business in Louisville. Roger still manages the WHOP stations at this writing.

Roger's wife, Sherrie, would, like her father, serve a term as Hopkinsville mayor. "Dutch," now in his 80s and a widower, has not lost his interest in public service. He serves part time as an aide at a facility for disabled veterans, located near his Florida home.

World War II

When World War II came, all new radio station construction came to a halt. A freeze was enacted on station building for the duration.

As a 1994 issue of *Smithsonian* magazine recalled: "It was a time of scanning the skies for enemy planes, of 'Rosie the Riveter,' women rolling up shirtsleeves to do a man's job, of gathering around the radio for FDR's onerous, grave accounts of the latest turns in the world. But, above all, it was a time of waiting for news from distant battlefields of the safety or the grievous loss of husbands or brothers or sons."

World War II sparked a dramatic growth in radio listening. In 1930, 40 percent of the nation's households had radios. By 1940, the number had grown to 70 percent. From 1940 to 1945, radio households would become nearly universal, rising to 91 percent. During the war, about 300 communities of 25,000 and under had their own radio stations.

The small town radio stations served their communities in unique ways. In Minnesota, KYSM broadcast the induction of 13 young men from Mankato, joining the Navy fliers on the first anniversary of Pearl Harbor, December 7, 1942. The broadcast was picked up coast-to-coast by NBC on the Fred Waring program.

During the war years, WDEV, Waterbury, Vermont, inaugurated the *Green Mountain Ballroom*. The station broadcast the Saturday night program from the local high school gym. Relatives of local servicemen gathered to listen and dance to the popular songs of the day, such as *Don't Get Around Much Anymore, As Time Goes By* and

We'll Meet Again. Attendees recorded greetings to their servicemen. Lloyd Squire, owner of the station, sent the recordings to Armed Forces Radio, which broadcast them around the world.

Like the Lackey brothers in Kentucky, most small town broadcasters and their stations served in leadership positions in the war effort on the homefront.

Station staffs were small because of the number of radio people in the service. Furthermore, the small stations were not in a financial position to compete with the high-paying jobs in war work going on in factories in almost every area. High school boys, too young for service, as well as girls, were heard widely on small stations. Some stations, like KNEL in Brady, Texas, were given FCC emergency permission to broadcast limited specified hours for the duration.

Business in small town radio stations wasn't very good. It had taken M.L. "Luke" Medley almost 10 years to get a license at Cookeville, Tennessee. The war broke out a year and a half after WHUB went on the air in July 1940. A Medley associate, after looking at old WHUB logs, says the war years were lean. The station started making money when the war ended. (M.L. Medley, in his 80s at this writing, still owns WHUB and takes an active interest in it.)

The war years were also lean at WLDS, Jacksonville, Illinois, one of the last stations to go on before the freeze (December 17, 1941). It was the "vision of a blind man" that was responsible for the station. Hobert Stephenson, an instructor at the Illinois School for the Blind, talked two local merchants into backing him in the venture. By 1946, it was doing well enough financially for his two partners to buy him out, allowing him to build WILY at Centralia, Illinois, in 1946.

Small stations, unlike most stations in big cities, depended upon retailers for the bulk of their income. With durable goods industries converted to war production, they disappeared from store shelves. Food and clothing were in short supply. Merchants had little reason to advertise.

The government outlawed weather reports and "man on the street" type broadcasts — small station staples.

Right in the middle of the war, the music stopped! Despite actions by no less than President Roosevelt, the president of the musicians union, James Caesar Petrillo, forbade his members to participate in the making of records.

As radio station operators and their audiences increasingly

favored the playing of records, rather than using live musicians, Petrillo believed that by making records, musicians were actually putting themselves out of work. The "recording strike" lasted a year.

Women Managers

Women managers of radio stations became more common during World War II. When Cole E. Wylie, general manager of KPQ, Wenatchee, Washington, joined the Air Corps, his wife, Helen, replaced him. Mrs. Wylie remained in the post until 1945.

When the war ended, Cole and Helen left Wenatchee. In their 40s, the couple set out on a station-building career that included startups KREN, Spokane, Washington; KREW, Sunnyside, Washington; KLER, Lewiston, Montana, and ZBM in Bermuda.

Mrs. Aurelia Becker was another wartime manager. She took over at WTBO, Cumberland, Maryland, after the death of her husband, Frank B. Becker. During her tenure, she upgraded from daytime-only to full time and affiliated with NBC, then the No. 1 radio network. She sold the station at a handsome profit in 1951.

The End of the Golden Age

In 1936, regular television broadcasting began in England. Later that year, a TV demonstration was featured during NBC's 10th anniversary celebration. An RCA exhibit at the 1939 World's Fair gave millions of people their first look at the "sight and sound" medium.

In 1940, experimental commercial TV operation began at two stations in New York City and one each in Schenectady, Philadelphia and Chicago. Sun Oil Company, which had sponsored Lowell Thomas on radio's first network radio newscast 10 years before, became television's first customer, sponsoring a daily newscast with Thomas on a New York TV station in 1940.

The FCC commissioners witnessed the first demonstration of FM radio in 1937. It established FM in the 42-50 mHZ portion of the VHF band in 1940. Some 30 stations had gone on the air by 1942, when station building was halted for the duration of World War II. By 1945, 50,000 FM receivers had been purchased, just 1,666 for each station on the air. Those FM receivers became obsolete when the FCC moved FM to 88 to 108 mHZ.

The FCC had expanded the AM band above 1500 kHZ in 1935. There was little activity there until the nationwide frequency re-allocation took place on March 29, 1941, when 777 of the country's stations changed frequency simultaneously. Several long-established stations moved "up" to the high end of the dial to increase their power to the maximum 50 kW.

The earliest surviving station in the frequencies above 1500 kHZ is WQXR, New York City. In 1936, it came on the air at 1550 kHZ. That station's early struggle on the high end of the dial is recorded by one of WQXR's founders, Elliot Sanger, in his book *Rebel in Radio*.

Many of the stations established in the post-World War II station building boom would be built on the high AM frequencies. Most would do well because, by then, most receivers were built to pick up stations from 1510 kHZ to 1600 kHZ.

As radio broadcasting neared its 25th anniversary, it was becoming obvious that it wasn't really one kind of business, but several. In 1936, the stations on regional frequencies organized. The clear channel stations formed their organization in 1941.

The clear channel stations' major initiative in the mid-1940s would be a proposal that the FCC create 20 750,000-watt facilities (five each for the then four national networks). Twenty long-established clear channel stations were proposed to be lifted to "superpower." The idea never materialized.

At the end of radio's Golden Age, about 32 percent of the nation's 979 radio stations were located in small towns. Their numbers would swell in the five years to follow — five years that would see radio audiences and radio revenues hit their historic highs (in 1948).

Unbelievably, two years after its peak, radio would be written off by many as an endangered species.

The 1945 FCC Radio Financial Report

The war years had been good to radio broadcasting financially. Industry revenues had more than doubled since 1940, to $299 million. The networks and their 28 owned-and-operated stations accounted for more than 50 percent of all industry revenues — 27 percent of the industry's pretax profits. Some 901 stations had reported. The 28 network "O and Os" (3 percent of stations) accounted for 12 percent of all local and national spot business. Industry-wide, national spot revenue equaled 27.5 percent of revenue, and local equaled 33.4 percent. Average station profit: 31 percent.

1945 Small Market Financial Data

A total of 873 non network-owned stations reported in 1945. Some 314, about one-third, were in cities of 25,000 and under. Of these, 169 would grow to more than 25,000 in later years:

1945 Grosses and Pretax Profits

		Number of Stations	Average Revenue	Profit
Market Size: Less Than 5,000				
Regional	Fulltime	5	$71,985	31.5%
	Daytime	5	63,852	12.3%
Local	Fulltime	13	32,065	17.9%
	Daytime	2	39,952	2.7%
5,000 to 9,999				
Clear Channel to 25 kW	1		64,988	44.8%
Regional	Fulltime	6	260,325	31.5%
	Daytime	3	76,873	12.3%
Local	Fulltime	56	41,188	10.3%
	Daytime	2	17,504	2.7%
10,000 to 24,999				
Clear Channel to 25 kW	1		148,551	25.2%
Regional	Fulltime	52	163,649	21.6%
	Daytime	15	96,331	22.9%
Local	Fulltime	142	59,332	24.3%
	Daytime	5	32,514	18.9%

Although the formats for FCC Reports had changed considerably since 1934 (see Page 44), the average full-time station on a local channel in a town of 25,000 or less in 1934 was doing $23,856. By 1945, it was doing $55,130 — 231 percent of its 1934 revenues. (Inflation for the 10 years averaged 1.5 percent per year.) The eight daytimers operating on local channels averaged an estimated $36,402 in 1945 — 55 percent more than its billing in 1934 of $23,473.

For all the romanticism of The Golden Age of Radio, it was not so golden for the stations in small markets. The networks (NBC Red and Blue and CBS) got the lion's share of the revenues. In 11 years, their revenues grew from $42 million to $126.7 million — a three-fold increase. Add their owned-and-operated stations and you add a lot more money: In 1945, the 29 AM and FM stations owned and operated by NBC, CBS and ABC (successor to Blue) accounted for ¹/₃ of all business done by the nation's then 901 reporting stations.

Radio came into its own during World War II. Total revenues doubled 1940-1945, from $155.7 million to $310.5 million. National spot grew, accounting for about 25 percent of total revenues in both 1940 and 1945. The 1940 report includes the following average weekly wages being paid to radio station personnel in that year:

Manager	$118.24
Chief Engineer	55.45
Program Director	56.80
Sales Manager	88.91
Staff Engineer	40.17
Announcer	34.53
Salesman	55.01

The average station in 1940 was grossing $152,598 per year, but 20 percent did less than $25,000 a year. By 1945, those stations dropped to 4 percent (141 of 705 reporting stations in 1940, 35 of 901 stations in 1945). Again, to compare figures in the 1940 and 1945 reports with 1990s money, you have to multiply them by 8.5.

PROGRAM SCHEDULE: KWLM, Willmar, Minnesota, 1945, Morning/Early Afternoon

	SUNDAY	MON thru FRI	SATURDAY
6:00		Rise n Shine	Rise n Shine
:15		County Agents	Rise n Shine
:30		Polka Music	Polka Music
:45		Polka Music	Polka Music
7:00		Dr. Michealson T	Polka Music
:15		Newstime	Newstime
:30	On the Mount	Farm Front	Farm Front
:45	On the Mount	World NewsA;Song	World News;Song
8:00	Baptist Hour T	Breakfast Club A	TommyBartlett A
:15	Baptist Hour T	Breakfast Club A	TommyBartlett A
:30	Voice of T	Breakfast Club A	Mankato
:45	Prophecy T	Breakfast Club A	High School
9:00	Covenant Hour	News; Serenade	Mankato
:15	Covenant Hour	Betty Crocker A	High School
:30	Gospel Hour	Hymns A	Turntable Time
:45	World News	Listening Post A	Turntable Time
10:00	Bible Speaks	Breakfast Sardi's A	Turntable Time
:15	Bible Speaks	Breakfast Sardi's A	Kissie Quiz
:30	Public Service	Galen Drake A	Back to Bible T
:45	Public Service	Exchange Club	Back to Bible T
11:00	Church Service	News; Claudia	Evangelist
:15	Church Service	Claudia;Waltz	Evangelist
:30	Church Service	Waltz Time	Monte American A
:45	Church Service	Back to Bible T	Monte American A
12:00	Noon News	Noon News	Noon News
:15	Local News	Musical Review	Musical Review
:30	Sammy Kaye	Uncle Ezra Sta A	Noon Tunes
:45	Sammy Kaye	Farm Topic Time	Noon Tunes
1:00	Lee Sweetland	John Ford, News	Metropolitan A
:15	Lee Sweetland	Local News	Opera A
:30	Showers Bless'g T	Bride and Groom A	Metropolitan A
:45	Showers Bless'g T	Bride and Groom A	Opera A
2:00	Wings Healing T	Ladies Be Seat A	Metropolitan A
:15	Wings Healing T	Ladies Be Seat A	Opera A
:30	This Week World A	Paul Whiteman A	Metropolitan A
:45	This Week World A	Record Show A	Opera A

A = ABC Network Program
T = Nationally Distributed Transcribed Program

PROGRAM SCHEDULE: KWLM, Willmar, Minnesota, 1945, Early Afternoon/Evening

	SUNDAY	MON thru FRI	SATURDAY
3:00	Our Children A	News; Sons Pioneers	Metropolitan A
:15	Our Children A	Women's News	Opera A
:30	Patti Page A	Man In the Store	Metropolitan A
:45	Patti Page A	Scandinavia Music	Opera A
4:00	Adventure Lance A	Melody Time	Metropolitan A
:15	Adventure Lance A	Melody Time	Opera A
:30	Navy Band T	You Name It	Man In the Store
:45	Navy Band T	You Name It	The Vagabonds
5:00	Drew Pearson A	Nit Wit Club A	Betty Russell
:15	Monday Headline A	Terry & Pirates A	Betty Russell
:30	Greatest Story A	Jack Armstrong A	Betty Russell
:45	Greatest Story	Sky King A	Harry Wismer, Sp A
6:00	Child's World A	News; Sports	News; Sports
:15	Child's World A	Tribune Review	Tribune Review
:30	Explore Unknown A	Lone Ranger T	Modern Music
:45	Explore Unknown A	Lone Ranger T	Modern Music
7:00	Revival Hour T	Prime Time	Deal In Crime A
:15	Revival Hour T	Top Shows	Deal In Crime A
:30	Revival Hour T	Mon. Ted Mack's	Jury Trials A
:45	Revival Hour T	Amateurs A	Jury Trials A
8:00	Winchell A	Tue. High School	Gangbusters A
:15	Hollywood Gossip A	Basketball	Gangbusters A
:30	Theatre Guild A	Wed. Abbott and	Mr. Malone A
:45	Theatre Guild A	Costello A	Mr. Malone A
9:00	Theatre Guild A	Thu. Mr.	Musical
:15	Theatre Guild A	President A	Etchings
:30	Candlelight	Fri. Break Bank A	Hayloft Hoedown A
:45	Candlelight	and Boxing A	Hayloft Hoedown A
10:00	News Tomorrow A	News Tomorrow A	News Tomorrow A
:15	Stardust Lady	Sports	Sports
:30	Dance Orchestra A	Dance Orchestra A	Dance Orchestra A
:45	Dance Orchestra A	Dance Orchestra A	Dance Orchestra A
11:00	News; Orchestra A	News; Orchestra A	News; Orchestra A
:15	Dance Orchestra A	Dance Orchestra A	Dance Orchestra A
:30	Dance Orchestra A	Dance Orchestra A	Dance Orchestra A
:45	Dance Orchestra A	Dance Orchestra A	Dance Orchestra A

A = ABC Network Program
T = Nationally Distributed Transcribed Program

"THE END OF RADIO'S GOLDEN AGE"

1946/1950

"This business has always been long on opportunity
— short on security."

Ray Livesay, The Livesay Stations headquarters:
Mattoon, Illinois

chapter 3

"THE END OF THE RADIO'S
GOLDEN AGE":

KGCX — 1946/1950

As the postwar station building boom began, KGCX, now firmly established in Sidney, Montana, had 20 years of history to build upon. It had just affiliated with the Mutual Broadcasting System. Its listeners were hearing "big-time" radio programming for the first time. KGCX's Mutual schedule included *20 Questions* and *True Detective* in prime time and *The Shadow* on Sunday afternoons. Housewives thrilled when Jack Bailey asked: "Would you like to be *Queen for A Day*?" Youngsters hurried home from school to follow the adventures of *Superman* and *Tom Mix*. Families had a new guest for dinner every night — Gabriel Heatter — who would assure them that, despite what was happening: "There's good news tonight!" In the fall, when everybody was a baseball fan, KGCX listeners were hearing the World Series.

Television, which would soon come on the scene elsewhere, would not make its appearance in eastern Montana and western North Dakota for 10 years — arriving there in 1956 and 1958.

It had taken more than two decades, but Ed Krebsbach had truly come a long way from that Sunday afternoon in 1925 in the back room of the Vida bank. KGCX was now a real business with a certain future.

KGCX got its first competition in the area when radio stations were built at Glendive, Montana, and Williston, North Dakota — each about 30 miles distant. Both stations had faltering first steps. Each was a 250-watt Class IV operation.

Ed Krebsbach quickly decided that KGCX would not only be the area's longest-established station, but would also be its most powerful. He quickly raised his power from 1,000 watts to 5,000 watts, giving him a coverage area almost three times greater than either of the other two area stations.

To get the most out of his big coverage, and to capitalize on the misfortunes of the new station at Williston, which was then, as now, the largest and most thriving community in the area, Ed established a branch office and studios there. (The Williston station's original stockholders included people active in the farmer's co-op movement. Traditional merchants, feeling threatened by the co-op movement, boycotted the new Williston station.)

Two Krebsbach sons joined their father at KGCX, Clair as resident manager of the KGCX Williston operation and Keith at Sidney.

It is estimated that the average small business in the United States fails or changes hands every four years. The Krebsbach radio station didn't really get started until it was 20 years old.

The Country — 1946/1950

The euphoria of winning the war and becoming the unmatched industrial power in the world was, by 1946, being replaced by the earliest stages of friction with the Communist world and concerns about the future economic well-being of the United States. Every war in U.S. history had been marked by a postwar depression.

When wartime price controls were abruptly ended, over the objections of President Harry S. Truman, the country experienced serious inflations. The buying power of a postwar 1945 dollar was reduced by $\frac{1}{3}$ by 1950. Ironically, instead of a depression, the country experienced a boom in consumer goods. There was plenty of pent-up demand — an outgrowth of wartime shortages — and returning veterans eagerly seeking to catch up made purchases of cars and homes. A 1946 newspaper headline graphically caught the condition and mood of the country: "PRICES SOAR! BUYERS SORE. STEERS JUMP OVER THE MOON."

The 1940s would mark the first contraction in the population of the nation's non-metropolitan areas. It dropped by 3 million, while the population of the metropolitan areas grew by 22 million. The farm population decreased from 31 million to 23 million.

Despite the population losses in much of rural America, business was pretty good in many small towns. Many families had savings from World War II. Many of the returning servicemen took advantage of what would become known as the "52-20 Club." The government agreed to pay returning servicemen $20 a week for 52 weeks, giving them a chance to put their lives back together. (The minimum wage at the time was 40 cents an hour, equal to $16 for a 40-hour week.)

By 1946, many of the returning servicemen had gone back to work or taken advantage of government programs to better their lives — V.A. benefits that assisted them in buying a house or starting a small business or, as many did, going to college. Of the 16 million servicemen and women who served in World War II, 25 percent availed themselves of various G.I. Bill benefits. In 1947, it's estimated, 25 percent of the record college enrollment was made up of World War II vets.

Small town businessmen were sharply divided about what the future would hold. Most vividly remembered the hard times of the Depression. One school of thought looked for the inevitable postwar depression. That school was best typified by Sewell Avery, then head of Montgomery Ward. He tightfistedly held onto a hoard of cash to be ready for hard times. His competitor, Gen. Robert Wood at Sears, took the opposite view, borrowing huge amounts of money to expand and create new stores to serve what he accurately saw as a rapidly growing number of new families who would be customers for the goods his company sold. As things turned out, Avery guessed wrong and Wood guessed right. Avery would be turned out in the early 1950s. Wood would be the dominant figure at Sears for almost another quarter century, until his death.

The Station Building Boom

When the owners of the 11 radio stations then in Kentucky decided to form an association, they chose a fellow Kentuckian who had done well to be their keynote speaker at the first convention. He was Paul Porter, then chairman of the Federal Communications Commission.

Porter had grown up in the small Bluegrass town of Winchester. His credentials for the FCC post included several years as an attorney for CBS. Soon after the KBA convention, Porter would become head of the Office of Price Administration, then a more powerful and more prestigious post. He would later become a partner with Abe Fortas in a Washington, D.C., law firm which, thanks to Porter, would have a big radio and television practice.

Porter, in his address, congratulated his fellow Kentuckians on their new association and promised them: "It's going to be a growing organization." He told them that hundreds of applications for new radio stations had been filed and advised them: "We're sure there'll be a whole lot more. We're going to process them as quickly as possible." His comments, an attendee years later recalled, "put a damper on the otherwise festive occasion."

Porter's remarks to the new association enunciated clearly the FCC's new posture on radio station creation. Simply stated, it meant a maximum of choice for listeners, and a local station in hundreds of small communities. Radio would now become a very competitive business. The criteria would basically be engineering. If a new station did not cause interference to existing stations, its license would be granted.

From 1946 through 1950, the number of stations would swell from 925 to 2,352 — 1,395 new stations. Additionally, there were 647 new FM stations, compared with just 55 in 1945.

About ¹/₃ of the building boom era stations would be built in the small towns. Two-thirds went into the metropolitan areas. Station builders, like famed bank robber Willie Sutton, were inclined to go "where the money is." New stations came on the air at a dizzying rate of more than one a day for five years.

(In Kentucky, where Porter outlined the Commission's postwar station creation policy, total AM stations grew from 11 to 28 between 1946 and 1950. Additionally, eight FM stations were built to pair with established AM stations. The greatest flurry of station building was in the state's two largest cities: Louisville went from a prewar total of four stations to eight, and Lexington, the state's No. 2 market with a population of about 50,000, went from one station to four. Fourteen small towns would get their first stations, and four of them got two stations. Three of those second small town stations quickly failed.)

Tough Starts

Clarence "Red" Fleming, a young man locals would recall later as a fast-talking promoter, approached the manager of the local Chamber of Commerce, Sneed Yeager, about building a radio station in Kentucky's state capital, Frankfort, then a town of 7,000 residents. The town was one of the country's smallest capital cities.

The town's economy, largely state government, was not outstanding. The local payroll was made up, for the most part, of state workers — generally low-paying jobs. (The governor was paid just $10,000 by a constitutional mandate.) Many of the state workers were political appointees from across the state. Many left town on the weekend to return to their hometowns. A lot of them made their major purchases "back home." Local industry, at the time, was confined to whiskey distilling — a highly seasonal employer. Farming around the small city was generally hard scrabble because of the hilly terrain. The town's trade area was small, with the state's two largest cities only 60 and 30 miles away. The business community, for the most part, was made up of chains (not good radio advertisers even then) and small independent merchants.

Yeager and the "radio man" enlisted a group of local business and professional people to fund the venture. WFKY went on the air in February 1946.

Perhaps Fleming's greatest mistake was putting the station's tower and transmitting facilities atop a high, rocky hill north of town called Bald Knob. The station, on 1490 kHZ, had serious coverage problems, even in the town below it. Studios were located on the edge of the downtown business district in rented quarters — a costly arrangement.

A year after it went on the air, Fleming was gone and the first of several ownership changes took place. Les Perkins, reportedly the richest man in town, acquired half the stock. The other half was purchased by a Lexington businessman, Garvice D. Kincaid. Perkins would say later: "Garvice stopped in to tell me what a great opportunity the station was and how good it could be for the community. I told him: 'If you feel that strong about it, why don't you buy my share?' He did!"

Kincaid, in his late 30s, already had a reputation of knowing how to make a buck. But radio and WFKY seemed to baffle him.

His first move was getting a consulting engineer to move the station to vacant, low-lying land along the Kentucky River. A half wave antenna was built there, along with a building to house the studios and offices. Coverage improved and expenses declined, but the station was still far short of making a profit.

It was Kincaid's third manager in less than three years who turned the station profitable. It had been on the air six years. Ken Hart was an unlikely choice for success. A Long Island native, his radio experience was light but, as even his detractors said: "He was a fellow with an idea a minute."

Hart had fallen in love with the Kentucky Bluegrass country during his last World War II assignment at an Air Force installation there. He stayed, forming a little ad agency which, he said "never got big enough." Then he tried his hand at radio sales, with, as he said, "a little success."

At the Frankfort station, he quickly put his love of promotion and his imagination to work. One of his most unusual program ideas: When the longtime editor of the local newspaper was fired, Ken hired him to do a daily news program called *Capital Comments*. The former editor had started a cigar counter in the town's hotel, a beehive of activity frequented by state government people and the town's "service club types." The editor did his nightly broadcast from his stand in the hotel lobby. Hart installed high-impact signage on the stand.

During the 1950s, new industry came, state government expanded and wages increased. Hart's high-profile operation of the local station allowed it to grow with the town.

By 1963, Kincaid had expanded his radio investments into larger markets. The Frankfort station was sold to allow him to buy into Louisville.

Station records indicate that Kincaid's investment in the station was limited to a $40,000 loan made by one of his financial firms. The loan had been fully repaid. The 1963 sale price was five times that — all cash.

During Hart's early years at WFKY, friends would say: "He's done well because he's found a home. The other folks who ran it were just guys traveling through town."

In his 50s, Hart changed careers. At this writing, he is 78 and not retired. He is the senior consultant on lobbying for the small coal mining interests in the state and the long-depressed counties where coal is mined. He's still a man with an idea a minute and, he says, modestly: "Some of them turn out to be pretty good."

Big Building! Small Billing!

Lloyd L. Felker was a true small town American success story. By 1946, in 11 years, he had parlayed a gas station, without service bays, into five full-service, high-volume locations, the Shell Oil distributorship for five central Wisconsin counties, a tire-recapping plant, a company that made a product called Penetread, a bottled gas plant and an appliance dealership. Felker decided his town, Marshfield, should have its own radio station. He invited two local doctors and his "old maid" sister-in-law to join him in the venture. The four visited the Marshfield branch studio of WFHR, Wisconsin Rapids. They offered the job of managing their new broadcasting venture to the branch manager, Bob Behling. He declined, saying he didn't have that kind of experience, but said: "I'd like to talk to you about a job selling." Behling remembered years later that one of the doctors remarked: "I guess we'll need one of those."

To get someone with experience, the group approached George Meyer, who had sold his laundry in 1941 to build WIGM at Medford — 40 miles north — a town of 2,000, one-sixth the size of Marshfield. A merger was undertaken, with Meyer trading his station for a 20 percent interest in a new company that would operate both WIGM and WDLB. Meyer would serve as general manager of both stations.

Felker was a big thinker who was known for working hard and driving fast. (He was by then driving new Cadillacs. He didn't have the patience to drive at the slow speeds required then during a car's break-in period. When he bought a new car, it was given to the manager of one of his businesses for six months. By then, it could be driven at speeds more to Felker's liking.)

Felker was also known as a man who did things in a big way. The radio station was no exception.

WDLB went on the air in early 1947 from a huge, two-story building on the main thoroughfare at the town's north end. The building, which Felker "mother-henned" from start to finish, had three studios, including a large one for programs that could be viewed by as many as 100 people. There were private offices for the manager, the bookkeeper, the program director and the traffic manager. There was also a big sales office and an even larger newsroom.

On the lower level, there was a continuity office, a handsomely appointed staff lounge and a huge community meeting room. There was also, in addition to a storage room and the room which housed the heating and air conditioning plant, an office for the custodian. (The building's spacious lawn and size required the services of a full-time custodian.)

The original staff, all experienced radio hands, included three newspeople — and just one salesman, Bob Behling. The entire staff numbered 20.

Most radio stations in towns of 12,000 (like Marshfield was at that time) were housed in small, second-story office building locations. The rule-of-thumb then was one employee for each $1,000 per month gross. WDLB did $68,000 worth of business the first year. As Behling would later recall: "$68,000 was a lot of business for one man to write. I worked morning, noon and night." (WDLB's first rate card carried rates like: 52 half-hour programs, $12.50 each; 60-second "spots," $3; 10-second spots as low as 75 cents. The rates were as high or higher than other small Wisconsin stations at the time.)

WDLB and WIGM "de-merged" after the first year, with Meyer returning to sole ownership of the Medford station. He would own it until 1952.

A man with a long resume, but apparently a short list of accomplishments, succeeded Meyer as general manager. He lasted just a short time. After he and Felker and his associates parted company, they asked Behling to take over on a trial basis. Behling said Felker told him: "If it doesn't work out, you can go back to your sales job."

It did work out. Behling promptly cut back the newscasters to one, who would also do play-by-play sports and four hours a day announcing. When he made that move, he said: "If every newscast on the station had been sold, the news department would still be operating at a big loss."

Behling increased the sales department to three. Long before it was commonplace, Behling put the station into sales promotions heavily, such as an annual invitational softball tournament, an annual station-sponsored beauty contest and a Christmas contest in which children colored the teddy bear on entry blanks, available from participating merchants. He bought a gigantic circus tent from which the station broadcast live music, audience participation shows and fair news and events nonstop from the area county fairs. Fair month was so successful financially that the station, after the fairs were over, threw a lavish party for staff members and their wives or girlfriends.

Behling, who had had some experience traveling with carnivals, was reportedly looked down on by the more traditional broadcasters in central Wisconsin. Paul Olsen, away in the Korean War in 1952, opined on a visit back to the station: "Some of the other guys criticize Bob, but you have to hand it to him, he pays better than anybody else in the area, because he can. I came here because they paid me $10 a week more (25 percent) than I was making down the road."

By 1951, WDLB was billing more than $150,000 a year and making a good, steady profit, despite the heavy, fixed overhead that was built in by the big physical plant and Lloyd Felker's wish to do things first class.

Behling and WDLB would do well until 1954, when television

came to central Wisconsin.

The Wausau TV station was scheduled to go on the air in October 1954. During the county fair late that summer, Behling came up with what at first seemed like a great idea. He announced that "WDLB will be first to bring television to central Wisconsin."

Behling leased a closed-circuit TV system on which he telecast the radio programs originating under the WDLB circus tent at the fair. Monitors were put up at various location on the grounds.

Dick Hanneman, then an engineer at the station, helped set up the television rig. He remembers: "I had never seen anything like the excitement generated when people saw their neighbors appearing over the TV monitors. Unwittingly, I think Bob enhanced the appetite for television around here.

"Initially, the Wausau TV station didn't come on the air until noon," Hanneman recalls. "Within weeks, the salesmen were saying: 'Nobody will buy anything that's scheduled after the TV station comes on.'"

In 1956, with the station's billing at a low ebb and Felker's health deteriorating, the decision was made to sell. Recalls Hanneman: "Bob and some of the employees wanted to buy it, but getting money in those days for a radio station, particularly one that wasn't doing well financially, was an impossible task."

Behling and his two key people, Chief Engineer Gerry Boos and Program Director "Pink" Allen, bought KRFO, Owatonna, Minnesota. The partnership was short-lived. Boos and Allen would later say: "We were equals. Bob couldn't get used to that. He still thought he was boss." Behling would say, with little rancor: "I was never much of a committee man."

Behling would go on to several other radio jobs, but as former employee Howie Sturtz would say later: "He always made his employers money, but he never had the freedom or success he'd had here with Lloyd Felker and WDLB." He died in his early 60s of cancer, in the early 1970s.

Jerry Boos and "Pink" Allen owned the Owatonna station until shortly after Allen's death in the early 1990s.

The 1956 buyer of WDLB was Hartley Samuels, who had other stations in Nebraska and West Virginia. He returned the station to profitability, mainly by cutting staff (including reducing Chief Engineer Hanneman from full time to part time), and by turning in the license of the WDLB's FM station. He sold out in 1965 to

Nathan Goetz, who had built a station in his hometown of Fort Atkinson in 1963 — WFAW. Felker had sold in 1956 for $150,000. Samuels got $233,250 in 1965. Goetz has since acquired stations in Illinois and Michigan. Jack Hackman, who had started at WDLB in 1957 as a sport announcer, has managed WDLB since 1969 and, since 1985, has been chief operating officer of the Goetz group of stations. He also owns several stations on his own.

On Again! Off Again!

Ely, Minnesota, probably has the worst financial history of any small radio market in the United States. The first station was built there in 1936 over a garage. The builder, Bill Strand, was an electrician. Boyd Brownell, a local businessman, joined him in a partnership. They moved the station to a new location over a local drugstore. The partners saw so little future in the venture that they allowed the license for WYEA to expire in 1937.

In 1947, an area advertising man decided to give Ely a second chance at a radio station. Charles Ingersol put WXLT on the air there. By 1949, he decided: "Ely isn't ready for a radio station." He turned the station over to a couple of local businessmen. Another sale followed. In 1950 and 1951, the station was reported on and off the air. It went silent again in 1951.

Ely got its third chance for a radio station in 1954, when Charlie Persons left the Arrowhead Market Stations of Minnesota, Wisconsin and Michigan to go for himself. He had joined Arrowhead out of high school in 1926.

Persons had built numerous stations for Arrowhead and others. With the help of his wife, June, and the couple's $7,000 savings, Charlie built WELY. He says: "June and I made it a pretty good business."

With money from the radio station's cash flow, Charlie built the town's first cable system. Six years later, he sold the station and cable system for $250,000. He invested that money into other cable systems at Marshfield and Merrill, Wisconsin. He and June sold those cable systems and in 1964 built KVBR, Brainerd, Minnesota, which they operated into their 80s.

The out-of-state investors who bought Persons out let the radio station and the cable system deteriorate. The cable system ceased operating. The radio station was put up for sale in 1976. The buyer was Jeanie Larson, who says she "got into the radio business by accident."

Mrs. Larson and her husband, since deceased, were owners of a small retail business in Michigan. David Kelly, then owner-operator of WTIQ, told her he needed someone to do a radio program on his station. She says: "I was hooked on radio immediately." So, the retail business was sold.

She was offered the Ely station by a broker in Colorado. "When I drove over here to look it over, I was enthralled with the beauty of the area. And, the station was in the basement of a nice story-and-a-half house. I decided getting a station and a house for one price was a real bargain."

Shortly after Mrs. Larson bought the station, the Ely economy, never flourishing, took a bad turn for the worse. New regulations concerning outboard motors hurt the tourism business, and ore mining in the area suffered a steep decline. Ely's population, 5,200 in 1976, shrank to 3,700 by the 1990 census.

By 1984, Mrs. Larson and her radio station were in deep trouble. She says: "All I could do was go silent." The townspeople were "shook over the loss of the station," she says. She contacted the FCC to see if Commission rules would allow her to operate with a combination of advertising revenues and listener donations. She was told that no rule prohibited her from doing that. The initial fund-raising effort quickly brought in $10,000 cash. "That got my bills caught up and we got back on the air."

When the "80/90" FM list was published, it included an allocation for Ely. "A group of out-of-town speculators with a 'female front' applied for and got a 'CP,' " Mrs. Larson says. They did not build, but kept getting extensions. The extensions ran out. Mrs. Larson built in 1991.

Originally, she went on the air with separate programming — a satellite-fed format. "We found no advertising buyers. In an area like this, businesses have small amounts to spend. What they do spend, they want on a locally programmed station — the old station." She ended up doing simulcasts. "The benefit of the FM is that it reaches three times farther than the AM station."

She operated with just three employees, doing all the selling because, she says: "It's easier for a small merchant to tell an employee 'no' than to say 'no' to the owner — who's working hard, just like them."

She also wrote all the copy, gathered and broadcast four community calendars and four local newscasts every day. "For 10 years, I didn't take a vacation; now I take one every Sunday."

In addition to her station responsibilities, she was manager of the Chamber of Commerce for six years. For a number of years, she also ran the town's wireless cable system.

"The cable system had gone under, leaving the town virtually without any television service. Then, a wireless system replaced it. It got into trouble," she says. "The townspeople, particularly seniors and the poor, had no way to get television. The bank, impressed with what I'd done to keep my radio station going, sold me the system for what was owed on it — on easy terms. I sold it for enough to build the FM. The new owners are strong financially and are doing a good job."

There was a special relationship between Mrs. Larson, her station and the community. Its most unique service was provided thanks to a longstanding FCC waiver that allowed the station to broadcast direct messages, such as "Jim Smith of Minneapolis, please call your office" or "The godparents of Jimmy Jones are notified that the christening has been postponed because of the storm" or "Jack Davis, please call your wife." The messages ranged from two per day to a dozen or more — indispensible to fisherman, hunters and isolated residents.

Mrs. Larson and WELY got into financial trouble again in 1995. The station was forced off the air and into receivership in mid-April 1995. But, Ely got still another chance at its own radio station. Charles Kuralt of CBS Television's *On the Road* and *Sunday Morning* fame has been a longtime summer resident of the Ely area, finding it a perfect place to write and reflect. He bought the little station from the receiver and returned it to the air in July 1995. Mrs. Larson got nothing after the creditors were satisfied. She's left with "just a lot of memories."

They Got It Right — Right From the Start

Gordon Capps

Marshall Cornett had made a lot of money in the lumber and insurance business. When he decided to further diversify, he decided to go into radio broadcasting. He first bought KOVM, LaGrande, then KBKR, Baker, both Oregon. As John Powell, who worked for him 50 years ago, recalls: "He was not only an astute businessman, he was an excellent selector of men." He hired Lee Jacobs, an experienced broadcaster, and made him his group station manager and a minority stockholder.

Jacobs added a third station by building KSRV at Ontario, Oregon, in 1946. The town was about 4,000 and, by the wisdom of the time, too small to support a radio station.

Jacobs sent one of his staff members at the LaGrande station to set up and operate the new venture. Gordon Capps was appointed manager. He, in turn, named John Powell program director. He had broken into radio during the war as a summer announcer at WCED, DuBois, Pennsylvania, then worked on a campus station at Akron, Ohio. In 1942, he moved across the country to WLBM, LaGrande, Oregon. He served six months of World War II military duty, returning to LaGrande.

"I guess the Ontario station was a risky venture," says Powell, "but, as it turned out, it was a textbook example of how to do it right — right from the start."

The Ontario of the mid-1940s was a very unusual small town. Its population was 8 percent to 10 percent Japanese and 5 percent Basque (a mixture of Spanish and French). "It was the smallest community I've ever seen with its own Buddhist temple." About 35 percent of the community was Mormon — "What a mixture," Powell recalls.

"We received a lot of help, support and advice from Lee, but, I must say, the real secret to the station's success was Gordon. He was a remarkable combination of ability and modesty.

"When Gordon and I got there," Powell continues, "Lee told us: 'I'd like you to do $200 a day when you get going.' By the end of the first year, we'd done something over $80,000 — or $220 a day — 10 percent more than he'd asked. I stayed six years. By the time I left in 1951, the station was doing $125,000 a year, or $350 a day." The station grew at twice the rate of inflation over those five years.

"The station was more than a financial success," Powell says. "It served as a common rallying place for the diverse community — and it expanded the town's trading area — bringing new people to town. We built remote studios at Nyssa, Oregon, and in Idaho at Weiser and Payette. Back in those days, you could hire an announcer-salesman to 'work' the branch. You'd pay all the expenses at about $1,100 per month. One of our studios doubled that every month.

"Everybody on our staff, except the engineer and the bookkeeper, carried a 'list.' Nobody was a specialist. We recruited our people from among the returning servicemen who were in broadcast schools on the G.I. Bill. Most of those people stayed with us a little while, then went on to bigger, and maybe better, things," Powell recalls.

Powell believes KSRV was the first station to sell a "Sportscasters Club," instead of selling one, two, three or four sponsors on a game. "We didn't plan it that way. When we went out with the high school schedule the first time, so many people wanted to be on the games that Gordon and I decided we didn't want to make anybody mad. We decided to sell short announcements on the games to as many people as would buy. To keep it from interfering with their regular radio advertising, we spread the cost of being on the games over 12 equal monthly payments. I guest almost everybody does that now."

Capps insisted that everybody on his staff become active in the community. "We were all from out-of-town. He didn't want us to be viewed as 'carpetbaggers.' " Powell, a returning serviceman, was steered into the American Legion with the words: "A lot of those young fellows will be running things around here pretty soon."

It's been almost 50 years and John Powell has been a lot of places, but, he says: "My experience in the Legion there is still one of the high points of my life." He points with pride to being the unofficial campaign manager to elect a Japanese-American veteran of the "442nd" as commander of that post.

Before going to work in Ontario, Powell always considered himself a "programming guy." He left there for his first sales manager job in Kentucky, which was followed by a management job in Missouri. He settled down at Hastings, Nebraska, where he served 30 years as manager of the Seaton Group's home station, KHAS Radio.

After retirement from Seaton, he spent five years as an interim manager. "My father was a Methodist minister. I remembered how the churches would bring in an 'interim minister' while they searched for a good replacement. Over the years, I'd seen many owners hurriedly hiring or promoting people into the vacant spots. Often, the results were disastrous."

Beginning in 1985, Powell served as interim manager (usually about 90 days) at stations in Florida, Georgia, Illinois and Iowa — 10 in all.

After he gave up his career as interim manager, he returned to Hastings. One of his clients said: "After 20 years with my station, I was burned out. I read about John, met and talked with him. Without reservation, I turned things over to him and set out on a nationwide motorcycle trip that I'd dreamed of taking. I didn't call the station once. When I got back, things were fine. I hope 20 years from now, there'll be somebody like John. I'll need another break."

KOVM's founding principal owner, Marshall Cornett, died in the early 1950s. After Jacobs died, the stations were sold to their managers.

Gordon Capps, as owner, continued to expand his business, first raising the power of the AM station to 5 kW D, 1 kW N on a good, low frequency; then, in 1977, building a Class B 50,000-watt FM station. Although other stations have come into the area, KSRV has continued to increase its billings. Capps, though retired, at this writing still takes an active interest in his community and his station, which has served it so well for almost 50 years.

Ben Sanders

It was no secret in Spencer, Iowa, that the local radio station was in tough financial shape. It had been put on the air during the early days of World War II by an out-of-town promoter with the financial help of a half-dozen local business and professional people.

When another out-of-towner showed up to buy it, some of the local folks thought that there might be something in "this thing." Ben Sanders, 33, paced the floor of the anteroom of a bankruptcy court. "I knew one of the lawyers involved was dragging his feet — trying to bring a deal together in which he'd be 'cut in.' " It was after 11 o'clock on New Year's Eve when Sanders decided to bring things to a head. He told the bankruptcy judge: "I've got to close this before midnight. If we can't do it, I'll be on my way." The bankruptcy judge quickly said: "Mr. Sanders has $19,000. I want to be home with my wife to ring in the New Year." Sanders said: "The judge didn't ask me why I was in such a hurry. If he had, I don't know what I'd have told him."

Sanders was born in Brooklyn. He had migrated from his hometown, with his family, to California. He got a job at KQW, San Jose. From there, Sanders went to Chicago, where he interviewed for a sales job with a small Iowa station. After being hired, he boarded a train for his new job. On the train he met another young man, who, Sanders says: "Believe it or not, had been hired for the same job."

Sanders speculates that the station owner thought the two young men would fight it out for the job. Instead, he says: "We divided the town in half, running from the main street. He took one side; I took the other. I think we flipped a coin. By the end of the first week, I hadn't sold anything.

"I had heard that WTAD, Quincy, Illinois, was looking for someone to manage their branch studio at Hannibal, Missouri." It was a fortuitous move for Sanders. He polished his selling skills there and took a bride, Betty, to whom he is still married after 60 years.

After several years, Sanders decided it was time to move up. He answered an ad in *Broadcasting* and landed a job at powerful WNOX, Knoxville, Tennessee.

The station, owned by Scripps Howard Newspapers, assigned accounts to salesmen by category. "Being the new man, I got the 'dog' categories. I also was given the religious accounts.

"With 10,000 watts (the most powerful in east Tennessee), WNOX had the kind of coverage preachers wanted. I quickly ran up some big billing. It was enough that Betty and I bought a house.

"An evangelist, J. Harold Smith, came in one afternoon. He wanted to broadcast the opening of a crusade he was having at Bristol — 100 miles away. I had the chief engineer order a telephone line and gave the traffic manager an order. It was going to be the following Sunday night. I was instructed to go to Bristol with the engineer — and to get cash, before the broadcast went on the air.

"When I got there, Reverend Smith told me he'd pledged the first night's collection for lot rent. He assured me he'd bring the money in the following Thursday. I said OK.

"The next morning, when I told the manager what I'd done, he was fit to be tied. I said, you can hold my check until he pays. If he doesn't, you can keep my check.

"Reverend Smith came in on Thursday as promised," Sanders happily recalls. "He not only paid for the program from Bristol, but he had gotten so much response, he decided to start a church in Knoxville. He signed a year's contract for daily broadcasts and paid the first month in advance. He became one of the station's best customers — and a lot of other religious broadcasters, seeing his success, started running."

In 1944, following the lead of most of the major networks and major stations, Scripps Howard decided its stations would no longer accept paid religious programs. "I guess it was a good thing to do," says Sanders, "but it was going to cost me a lot of commission. I decided it was time to make a change."

Sanders ran an ad in *Broadcasting*, saying he wanted to buy a small radio station. "There weren't many, but I got two replies — one in Texas and one in Iowa."

The choice of the Iowa station was aided by his wife. "Betty had had a job in the claims department of a fire insurance company. The company sustained major losses when a fire had destroyed most of the Spencer, Iowa, business district. Betty advised: "Spencer must have a nice business district. It's almost all new."

Ben planned to sell his house and use the proceeds as a down payment on the station, but the bankruptcy court wanted all cash. Ben told Rev. Smith about his problem.

Smith matter of factly said: "Ben, you helped me get started. Now it's my turn to help you get started." They walked to the bank, where Smith instructed an officer to make out a cashier's check for $19,000. He then handed Sanders the check, saying: "You don't need to sign a note. You trusted me. I'll trust you."

It took the FCC three months to approve the sale. In the meantime, Ben, wearing a mackinaw, went to see the vendors (unsecured creditors) of the station, some in Chicago and New York City. They had given up on the old ownership, so settling the bills with ASCAP, BMI, SESAC, AP, etc. wasn't too hard, he says.

KICD, under Sanders, was an instant hit. "The cornerstone of our programming was radar weather. We may have been the first in the country to install our own radio weather station. I bought surplus government equipment for $850. My engineer got it going. In an area subject to severe weather, where a lot of money is earned and lost because of that weather, and where unforecast bad weather can cause serious injury or even loss of life, dependable weather information was (and is) paramount in people's lives.

"When I put out word that I was looking for a salesman, two young returning servicemen came in. I liked them both — hired them both. I divided our coverage area in half. They flipped a coin to decide which part would be each one's territory.

"There wasn't much radio sales training material available in those days," Sanders recalls. "All I could do is share with them what I had learned on the street for 10 years. They caught on quickly, and so did the merchants."

Another contributor to KICD's almost instant success was Mason Dixon, with whom he'd worked in Knoxville. In Ben's words: "He was an extremely talented man on the air and off. He liked doing the inside things. I liked being out with the customers and the listeners. When he came here, he suffered a culture shock. A small town in Iowa is a lot different from a city in east Tennessee."

Ben indoctrinated him by, one afternoon a week, "taking him out with me. We'd stop for coffee at 'meeting places' in Spencer and the other small towns we served. We'd visit with a farmer in the field. Mason would ask them what kind of music they and their families liked and what kind of other programs they wanted to hear. We asked what kind of news and farm information was important to them. We got good information and made a lot of friends."

Sanders used some ingenuity in answering requests about the size of his audience from agencies placing business for regional and national advertisers. He would have a group like the ladies' guild at a Lutheran church conduct surveys, and make a cash contribution to their organization. "Who would accuse those nice ladies of conducting a crooked survey?" he asked.

And so, 250-watt KICD, thanks to Sanders and Dixon's outstanding program efforts and Iowa's high ground conductivity, built an audience up to 40 miles from the station. They installed Foreign Exchange (FX) services so that listeners could call in news items, lost and found announcements, etc. without paying a long-distance toll. They also allowed the far-flung customer base to make last-minute copy changes toll-free.

By the early 1950s, KICD was the subject of a full-page article in *Broadcasting* magazine reporting the fact that this station, in a town of 9,000, was billing more than $200,000 a year — the country's first big-grossing small town radio station.

Ben Sanders didn't keep many secrets. He traveled 38 states as a panel member of the "Radio Programming Clinics" sponsored by BMI. He often spotted doubting Thomases in the audiences. To them, he'd say: "Come on up after the program. I brought the books with me. Look 'em over." He carried the station's latest yearly operating statements with him.

Sanders operated his station into his 60s, selling it then to his son, Bill, who had spent most of his career in the sales department of WMT, Cedar Rapids, Iowa.

Ben Sanders' long and successful career at KICD was not without crises. After KICD was well on its way to being a success, the FCC got a complaint about the money Rev. Smith had advanced for the purchase. A hearing was held in Spencer to find out whether it was hidden ownership, a gift or in fact a loan. After hearing the evidence, the hearing officer determined with certainty that it was indeed a loan (fully repaid), made by one friend to another "who trusted each other."

In 1950, a Saturday night fire destroyed the station's transmitter. Ben believes baby chicks, stored at the transmitter for an Easter promotion, were the cause. Ben theorizes: "Apparently, an electric light bulb we'd installed to keep them warm overheated."

When informed of the fire, Ben immediately set to work. His engineer was dispatched, and a transmitter and other equipment were found 200 miles away. They were brought to Spencer in a borrowed pickup truck.

Ben and other staff member set about cleaning things up. The station would be off the air all day Sunday. Sanders knew a lot of gawkers would be coming by to view the destruction. Late Saturday night, Ben summoned a local sign painter. A huge sign was put up at the crack of dawn on Sunday. It said: "KICD WILL BE BACK ON THE AIR — MONDAY MORNING AT 6 A.M." It was!

Bob Rounsaville

Bob Rounsaville's first encounter with radio was in the late 1930s. He bought radio ads on his hometown radio station, WRGA, Rome, Georgia. The ads promoted enrollment and recitals at his dance studio.

In connection with the dance studios, Bob, in his very early 20s, was emceeing talent nights at theaters in small towns in northern Georgia. He became fascinated with the network radio program *Dr. I.Q.* He talked to one of his theater operator friends into staging a Friday night event patterned after that program. He called it *Mr. Professor*, with himself serving as quizmaster.

When he'd approached the manager of WRGA about broadcasting *Mr. Professor*, he was told: "Get a sponsor and I'll put it on the air." Bob approached a local furniture store that had not been on the station. Bob's enthusiasm for the project got him a 52-week sponsor.

Bob liked the celebrity of being on the radio. It seemed that everybody he encountered told him: "I listen to you on the radio." Bob was hooked.

He approached the theater operator about going in with him to build a second radio station in Rome, but the theater operator declined, feeling that the town couldn't support two stations. Bob quickly came up with another idea. The man was building a second theater in Cedartown (about a third the size of Rome and located 18 miles away). "If Cedartown can support two theaters," he argued, "it should be able to support one radio station."

The radio station venture would cost $20,000. All Bob could raise, mainly through the sale of his house, was $5,000. He put his money up with the understanding that he could buy another 25 percent later. Bob was paid $35 a week for managing the new enterprise — about half what his partner was paying his theater managers.

WGAA went on the air in mid-1940. The station was an immediate success. Typical of most small stations, then and now, Bob was, in addition to being manager, his own "star" salesman, radio personality, etc. The full-time station had only four other employees. Eighteen-hour days were the rule rather than the exception for Bob. He didn't mind. He loved everything about "his" radio station.

Bob went into the service in 1943, leaving the station in the care of his wife. When he returned, after a medical discharge, his partner had sold the 25 percent interest Bob had been promised to a third party. When Bob protested, the theater man told him: "I'll buy you out." He was given a check for $5,000, the amount of his original investment, even though his interest was by now worth three times as much.

As Bob would often relate later: "We had a handshake deal." That would be the last time that he would make such a deal. His rule henceforth would always be: "Get it in writing."

Bob and his wife then toured area small towns that did not have radio stations — which was most of them in those days. The young couple decided that Cleveland, Tennessee, a little larger than Cedartown, would be a good place for a station. It was 35 miles north of Chattanooga.

When Bob set out on the project, he found out, to his dismay, that someone had beaten him to it. Prior to the World War II freeze, the president of Bob Jones University, located there, had applied to build a station. He turned out to be a distant relative of Bob. The university, typical of many small town schools, had a goodly share of critics. When Bob visited him, he was told: "If you want to build the station, go ahead. I'll withdraw my application. I really didn't want a station. I just didn't want our critics to get it."

Bob filed his application. While it was pending, Bob and his wife rented a small apartment in Chattanooga, where they hired on at the Hercules Powder plant — she in the office, Bob in sales. They kept those jobs until the station was ready to go on the air.

Shortly before the station was ready to begin broadcasting, Bob totaled up his and his wife's assets and found that they were at least $3,500 short. He went to a small bank in his Chattanooga neighborhood and talked the little bank's president into lending him the money, "and a little more, if necessary."

In 1945, when construction began, Bob's meager funds were not the only problem. There was a shortage of broadcast equipment. The equipment companies' output had been devoted to the war effort. Weekends, when he and his wife were off from their jobs at the powder plant, they drove to radio stations throughout eastern Tennessee and northern Georgia, buying equipment that had been taken out of service.

The station's tower was one originally meant for other purposes that had been discarded by the Tennessee Valley Authority. Bob got a farmer with a mule to plow the field around it and lay the ground system. Bob did a lot of the construction himself, on weekends and after hours from the powder plant. He also got "pick up" labor.

WBAC went on the air on June 18, 1945. It was the first radio station license granted to a World War II veteran, records indicate.

Bob hired mostly local people without radio experience. Many, like himself, were returning veterans. Legend has it that they were serving under a government training program called "on-the-job training." The government picked up half their wages.

Bob put in the same long hours and hard work at WBAC that had marked his years at Cedartown. The programming, a lot of which Bob did himself, was typical of what was found on good small town stations in those days — church, club and school announcements; lost and found programs; buy, sell, rent and trade announcements; local news and sports broadcasts.

Bob was alert to every opportunity to put business on the station. An example: Cleveland is the world headquarters of a Church of God denomination. Each year, there was a big weekend series of revival services. Thousands of the church's membership took part. Bob decided to broadcast the services, sponsored by local merchants. In addition to sponsorship credits on the broadcasts, the merchants also got ads during the day, welcoming the visitors to town and inviting them to visit their stores to take advantage of the merchandise and services offered.

Ninety days after he'd borrowed the $3,500 from the

Chattanooga bank, Bob paid off the loan in full. The bank president told Bob that WBAC was doing so well that he ought to build another one and that he (the banker) would like to be his partner.

Bob and the banker built WBEJ at Elizabethton in 1946 and WKSR at Pulaski (both Tennessee) in 1947. Bob told the banker that the station they built together would not be built as WBAC had been built, with used equipment, but rather with state-of-the-art gear. To build them that way would take $20,000 for hard assets and working capital. The banker first suggested that they each put up $10,000. "That's not what I had in mind," Bob Rounsaville said. "You put up $9,000 for 49 percent. You loan me $11,000 for my 51 percent. I'll do all the work." The banker said: "That sounds fair," and they put it in writing.

Bob's reputation as a good small town radio man spread quickly throughout Tennessee. He was given 50 percent of WGRV, Greeneville, and 25 percent of WHAL, Shelbyville, by local business and professional people (non-broadcasters) who wanted to build stations in their communities. They put up the money, and Bob supervised the building, startup and operations.

His first sale of a small market interest was his 25 percent interest in WHAL to other stockholders for $25,000. It had gone on the air the year before with a good, strong manager he had hired. On the station's record, Bob's shares were a bargain at $25,000.

He used the WHAL money, and cash flow from the other four Tennessee properties, to finance his entry into major market radio. He built a daytimer at Buckhead, then a crossroads in the north Atlanta suburbs, in 1947.

Rounsaville believed that if you could make money with little stations in little towns, you could make a lot more money with a station in a big city. He and his wife had long had a love affair with Atlanta, a town that in postwar years maintained much of its Southern charm along with new dynamic growth. He would make Atlanta his home for the rest of his life — even after the 1959 sale of his Buckhead station (by then Atlanta's WQXI) for $2 million.

Another area that the Rounsavilles loved was Florida. A station purchase of what was then WEAT, Lake Worth, turned out to be a disaster from the beginning. Shortly after he bought it, the tower went down in a hurricane.

Despite Bob's sales calls on regular visits, and despite the efforts of a couple of his best managers, there was little if any business on the Class IV station's logs. One of the managers he sent into WEAT would say later: "I doubled the business in just over three months. It was doing $10 a day when I got there. I got it up to $20 a day."

That station prompted the sale of another Tennessee station interest, WGRV, to his partners there to finance the Florida station purchase. Losses there prompted the sale of WKSR, Pulaski. One of the buyers often told of Bob saying at the closing: "Owning WEAT is like buying a Cadillac the first day of the month and driving it off the Lake Worth pier (into the ocean) on the last day of the month."

Bob soon found a New England buyer for the Florida property, one who wanted to "have a deductible reason to enjoy winters there." Bob was happy to sell out at his first radio station loss.

In 1951, with WEAT off his back and WQXI and his remaining small markets in Tennessee producing steady and handsome cash flow, Bob entered a kind of radio in which he would be a pioneer. It also would make him a millionaire many times over. Rounsaville "bailed out" the owner of a daytime station in Louisville, Kentucky, with a $40,000 purchase. He would be one of the first station operators to target exclusively the city's black community. Only a handful of stations were doing it at the time.

The Louisville experiment turned out so well that Rounsaville quickly bought up other struggling stations, aimed them toward a black audience and repeated the success of WLOU in Louisville.

By 1957, with three black-programmed stations, he wanted at least two more, but he had come up against the FCC's seven station limit. To make way for his new acquisitions, he sold WBAC, which he had put on the air for $10,000, for $125,000. WBEJ, put on the air "right" for $20,000 in 1946, brought $85,000. Bob's banker-partner in WBEJ got $41,650 for his $9,000 investment, and in 11 years had drawn about 10 times his $9,000 investment in dividends. Although their business dealings ended with the 1957 sale of WBEJ, their friendship continued until the banker's death.

Sixteen years after Bob had gotten into small market radio as manager-25 percent owner of WGAA, Cedartown, Georgia, he sold his last small market radio station. He claimed, though, until the mid-'70s, when he sold his black-programmed stations, that he really hadn't left small market radio.

The Rounsaville black-programmed stations were in Louisville, Cincinnati, Nashville, New Orleans, Miami and Tampa — all big cities. But, in his view, they were not big city stations; they were small town-type stations that undertook to serve a relatively small community within a city.

As he often did in his small town stations, he employed local people at his black stations and encouraged them to participate in their community's church and civic life. The stations did more than just play the music favored by their black audiences. They carried news, public affairs, sports and special events that didn't mean a lot to a general audience, but meant a lot to his target community.

Bill Summers, a longtime Rounsaville employee, was then the general manager and later became, along with Bob's Washington attorney Vince Pepper, a partner in the Louisville station. He said of Rounsaville: "When he came to town, he'd not only carefully check to make sure that everything and everybody was working and that sales and collections were good, but he always asked: 'What's going on in your community — and what are you doing about it?' "

1947

Although radio was still king and television as a big thing was not yet a certainty, radio was undergoing big changes. It was the year that gave birth to celebrity disc jockeys. Previously, record programs had been conducted by staff announcers, in addition to other announcing duties during their shifts. A New York station announced the signing of Ted Husing, a veteran sportscaster, to host a record show. A competing station promptly announced the signing of Mel Allen, also a top sportscaster, for similar chores. Both reportedly got $50,000-a-year contracts. Bandleader Tommy Dorsey was signed to do a one-hour, five-day-a-week "strip" on transcription. The syndicator would sell the program to stations coast-to-coast.

ABC, like other networks, had resisted playing records. It signed music legend Paul Whiteman to do a daily disc jockey show on that network. Mutual quickly followed by signing "the original disc jockey," Martin Block, originator in the 1930s of the *Make Believe Ballroom* on WNEW, New York.

As more radio stations came on in the mid-1940s, new stations were unable to forge affiliations with the four major networks — they were all taken in most cities. Stations that played mostly music started to show up everywhere, with good audience and advertiser success. The overcrowding also gave birth to two new kinds of stations. For years, stations (mostly small ones) had broadcast music programs aimed at minorities. But 1947 saw the debut of the nation's first two stations programmed exclusively to minority audiences: WDIA, aimed at the black community of Memphis, Tennessee, and KCOR, aimed at the Spanish community of San Antonio, Texas.

Giveaway programs like *Take It or Leave It* (aka *The $64,000 Question*) and *Pot O' Gold* had been on the networks for years. Many small stations broadcast telephone quiz shows. (WLDS started one on the day it went on that air in 1941, and the show survives to this day at Jacksonville, Illinois.) *Dinner Winner*, a copyrighted quiz show generally sponsored by supermarkets, was heard on large and small stations. Man on the Street programs gave contestants theater passes and/or samples of the sponsor's product.

In 1947, Ralph Edwards' *Truth Or Consequences* raised its ratings with the first big giveaway targeting the home audience. A Lock Haven, Pennsylvania, woman won $17,590 worth of merchandise prizes by identifying the recorded voice of "Miss Hush" as retired movie star Greta Garbo.

A year later, third-place network ABC ran veteran comic Fred Allen out of eighth place in the ratings, all the way down to 38th place. The following year, Allen was off the air. Critics were furious, but the audience loved the chance at instant wealth. On that program, the *Stop the Music* orchestra played a song as a listener, called at home, was asked to identify it. When he or she did, the emcee, Bert Parks, would holler: "Stop the music!" and the listener would win thousands of dollars worth of prizes.

At its peak, it's estimated at programs on the four major networks gave away $165,000 a week. The FCC soon stepped in to try to "Stop the Giveaways." A rule passed was soon put on hold by a judge's restraining order. Several years later, an appeals court overturned the FCC rule. Giveaways continue on radio and TV to this day.

In 1949, the FCC passed some deregulation that would be cautiously taken advantage of. "The Mayflower Decision" eight years earlier had forbidden broadcasters to editorialize. In 1949, the Commission said broadcasters could, provided an equal opportunity was given to those with opposing views. Broadcast editorials would not appear widely until the mid to late 1950s.

Television Arrives

As early as 1948, when only 1.6 million families had small-screen television sets (generally 10-inch) and the handful of stations on the air were broadcasting six or so hours a day, the nation's most respected, widely read magazines were prophesying radio's imminent death: "Television will make radio as obsolete as the horse." (*Time* magazine); "Radio's days in the big time are numbered." (*Newsweek*); "Radio is on the way out." (*New Republic*).

Perhaps the most damaging of all was a late 1940s quote in the trade press, attributed to Dr. Frank Stanton, president of CBS, operators of the No. 1 radio network and group of network-owned radio stations: "TV is radio's baby and, right now, the baby is feeding out of Papa's hand — and will eventually bite it (Papa's hand) off."

From 1949-51, television homes increased from 1.6 million to 17.3 million. Advertising revenues grew from $34.3 million in 1949 to $105.8 million in 1950, and to $239 million in 1951. After suffering losses of $25.3 million in 1949 and $7.9 million in 1950, it broke solidly in the black in 1951 with a $43.8 million profit (a margin of 18 percent), although by 1951 there were only 107 stations in 60 cities reaching less than 40 percent of American households. Radio was reaching 96 percent of all homes. Live television network programs would not begin nationwide until 1952.

FM Radio

Of the 647 FM stations that went on the air, only the ones supported by profitable commonly owned AM stations enjoyed any stability. Most duplicated their AM stations. The stand-alone FM stations universally lost their owners money. Newspapers that couldn't find AM frequencies but wanted to get into radio built FM stations.

One of them was WFAH, Alliance, in northeastern Ohio. The station was put on the air by the town's newspaper, *The Review-Republican*. Bob Hansen had gotten into radio after being mustered out of the service in Missouri. He went to work for Oscar Hirsch at KFVS, Cape Girardeau, Missouri. Within a short time, he was looking for more money and a chance to be program director. He was hired on the original staff of WFAH in 1947.

"I had never heard an FM station — only heard that it was static-free and higher fidelity than AM radio. It must have a future, I thought," he later recalled. "I was young, middle 20s, full of ideas. We had great programming but few listeners and even fewer advertisers. There just weren't many sets out there."

He recalled one of his greatest programming feats on the FM-only station. "When the local football team got into a big game a couple of hundred miles away, I made arrangements to broadcast it. To assure the advertisers of an audience, the engineer and I rigged up an FM set to the public address system in the school gym. The newspaper ran an ad telling people they could hear the game by going to the gym. It was packed." Despite good programming and shrewd promotion, the Alliance station lost money until 1953, when the owners "wedged in" an AM directional to pair with the FM.

In 1949, the FM Association, founded five years earlier, folded because of financial problems. It became part of NAB. Most devastating of all for the new medium, upstaged by television, was the decision of WTMJ, Milwaukee, Wisconsin, owners of a legendary AM station and a VHF television station. They surrendered the license for the FM station, on the air since 1940.

The 1949 NAB Convention

Radio operators at the 1949 NAB Convention were clearly on edge, what with the new competition from new stations on the air all across the country. Those on the networks were already seeing signs of network decline. FM was near death's door — and television, even with only a relative handful of TV homes, was now clearly seen as a certain threat. There was a real question as to the survival of the radio medium.

From the floor, delegates demanded that the NAB's small Broadcast Information Office be expanded. That office had, for many years, done audience research and promulgated information about the effectiveness of radio advertising. The delegates demanded more. The NAB renamed the office the Broadcast Advertising Bureau, expanded its staff and resources, and named high-profile radio salesman Maurice B. "Mitch" Mitchell its first general manager.

(Mitchell soon left the post for a better job, president of the Associated Transcription Service, providers of music libraries to radio stations. As a bonus, Associated soon offered one of the first audio radio sales training series, 13 15-minute transcriptions called "Mitch's Pitch" that included some of the best-known sales ammunition of the time.)

Mitchell was replaced as NAB manager by a savvy West Coast broadcaster, William B. Ryan. During his tenure, it was decided that the Broadcast Advertising Bureau should be an independent entity with headquarters in the advertising capital of America, New York City. Ryan stayed behind at the NAB, where he was given a new executive assignment. Hugh M.P. Higgins, vice president and general manager of small market WMOA, Marietta, Ohio, became the bureau's third manager — on an interim basis. BAB's budget was $200,000. In 1951, Ryan returned to Broadcast Advertising Bureau as its first president. Soon, it was renamed Radio Advertising Bureau.

In the 44 years since, RAB would have only five presidents. Ryan, a handsome, smooth and articulate man, was followed by

Kevin Sweeny, a high-profile "idea man" who genuinely thought that "when it came to radio's advertising potential, only the industry's ambition was the limit." He was followed by Miles David, a deep-thinking, precise man with a penchant for statistics and organization. In the early 1980s recession, RAB turned to Bill Stakelin, a group executive and recent NAB Board Chairman. His education at a Baptist college, Georgetown, in Kentucky, was evident when he turned on his high-powered "evangelistic" speaking style.

When the radio business and the RAB's fortunes turned downward in the late 1980s, Warren Potash, a retired Capital Cities station manager, was brought aboard. His tightfisted, no-nonsense management style brought radio and the RAB through a crisis.

At this writing, RAB is headed by Gary Fries, with the most varied resume of any bureau head to date. His 30-plus years in radio includes sales and management posts in every aspect of the industry. He is blessed with a good financial showing being made by the networks and the large groups, who provide much of the funding.

His greatest contribution to date is probably his spoken belief that radio is unique in an increasingly crowded advertising world. "Nobody," he says, "talks about 'my' newspaper or TV station or cable channel; they talk about 'my radio station.' That unique position with its listeners, which has existed from the beginning, makes radio a very special advertising medium."

When the delegates at the 1949 convention demanded an organization to market the medium, they got one. Early on, Ryan coined what would be radio's most enduring slogan: "Wherever You Go, There's Radio." The greatest contribution of all, though, has been the information RAB generated over the years. It told people things they didn't know about radio, enabling them to sell it with more conviction, and disseminated information the bureau has assembled about the customers, enabling the industry to serve them better.

1950 Radio Financial Report

The inflation of post-World War II makes it necessary to multiply figures in the 1950 report by 5 (instead of the 6.5 in the 1945 report). The radio industry had increased its volume by about 50 percent in the five years since World War II, to about $453.6 million. The number of stations reporting had grown 245 percent, from 901 to 2,203 — 1,392 new stations — about one-third in small towns. The 1950 report does not break out station revenues by city size. These figures shed some light on how the newcomers were doing:

Of the 1,797 stations on the air for two years or more, 807 (44.9 percent) were profitable. All FM stations were losing money — an average of more than $500 per week. 1,309 stations that had come on since 1945 were doing 31 percent of the total station business. 901 stations on the air before 1946 (38 percent of the total) were doing 69 percent of the total station business. The average newcomer was doing $81,400 a year and showing a profit of $6,055. The pre-1946 stations were averaging a profit of $62,781 on revenues of $340,400. The networks owned 29 stations. They had earned their owners in three years (1948, 1949, 1950) a total of $54.6 million — more than twice what they'd earned in 1943, 1944 and 1945. Network radio was down 7 percent from its historic high, reached in 1948. The 1950s' star performer was the local business sector. While the total radio business grew by 50 percent in five years, local business was up more than 100 percent — contributing 44.8 percent of radio revenues — up from 33.4 percent in 1945. National spot contributed 25.2 percent of the industry's total revenues.

The arrival of television was impacting the radio networks' revenues. Where they had created more than 40 percent of the industry total ad sales in 1946, they contributed just 27.5 percent in 1950.

Radio station revenues were up across the country in 1950, but the impact of television could be seen clearly: In radio markets outside the reach of television, radio was UP 10.1 percent. In television markets, it was up 6.8 percent.

Program Schedule, KSRV, Ontario, Oregon, 1950, Morning/Early Afternoon

	SUNDAY	MON-FRI	SATURDAY
6:00		Slumber Busters	Slumber Busters
:15		Slumber Busters	Slumber Busters
:30		Slumber Busters	Slumber Busters
:45		Slumber Busters	Slumber Busters
7:00		R.F.D. (Farm)	R.F.D. (Farm)
:15		R.F.D. (Farm)	R.F.D. (Farm)
:30		Songfest(MWF)	Tune Trails(TTS)
:45		News	News
8:00		Best Buys	Best Buys
:15	Waltz Time	Christian Call	Christian Call
:30	Organ Reveries	Music for Today	Music for Today
:45	Baptist Church	Music for Today	Music for Today
9:00	World of Song	Hospitality Time	Music for Today
:15	World of Song	Music for Today	Music for Today
:30	Baptist Church	Weiser(ID)Datebk	Music for Today
:45	Baptist Church	Grocer; News	Music for Today
10:00	March Time	Little Show	Little Show
:15	7th Day Advent	Fash Music (MWF)	Hawaiian (TTS)
:30	Concert Hall	Remember?	Remember?
:45	Concert Hall	Gems Melody(MWF)	Health Talk(TTS)

Time			
11:00	Concert Hall	Time Out	Time Out
:15	Church Service	Nat Brandywine	Nat Brandywine
:30	Church Service	How D Ya Do (MWF)	Sweet M'dY (TTS)
:45	Church Service	Song Style (MWF)	Home Agent (TTS)
12:00	American Songs	Mystery;Shopping	Mystery;Shopping
:15	American Songs	Western; Agent	Western; Agent
:30	News	News	News
:45	Top Pop	Farm Bulletins	Farm Bulletins
1:00	Top Pop	Call for Cash	Call for Cash
:15	Weiser (ID) Hour	Claudia T	Eddy Howard
:30	Weiser (ID) Hour	Church/Wildwood	Church/Wildwood
:45	Weiser (ID) Hour	Church/Wildwood	Church/Wildwood
2:00	Manhattan Music	Vocal Time	Columbia Records T
:15	Weiser Ch Christ	Vocal Time	Columbia Records T
:30	Week's News	Shep Fields (MWF)	Concert Min (TTS)
:45	Talk	Lean Back Listen	Lean Back Listen

T = Nat'ly Distributed Transcribed Program. MWF = Monday, Wednesday, Friday. TTS = Tuesday, Thursday, Saturday

Late Afternoon/Evening

	SUNDAY	MON-FRI	SATURDAY
3:00	Music Hall	Request Hour	Request Hou
:15	Music Hall	Request Hour	Request Hour
:30	Memory Lane	News	News
:45	Memory Lane	Request Hour	Request Hour
4:00	Memory Lane	Request Hour	Request Hour
:15	Valley Serenade	Request Hour	Request Hour
:30	News	Request Hour	Request Hour
:45	Decision Now	Request Hour	Request Hour
5:00	Familiar Melody	Weiser (ID) Pgm.	Weiser (ID) Pgm
:15	Familiar Melody	Weiser (ID) Pgm	Weiser (ID) Pgm
:30	Land of Free T	News	News
:45	Land of Free T	Song Styles (MWF)	Melody Gems (TTS)
6:00	Songs Eventide	Movie Guide	Movie Guide
:15	Songs Eventide	Sports	Sports
:30	Songs Eventide	Call for Cash	Call for Cash
:45	Area News	Area News	Area News
7:00	Singers	Sons of Pioneer	Guest Star T
:15	Church/Wildwood	Singing Sam T	Proudly We Hail T
:30	Church/Wildwood	Barry Wood T	Proudly We Hail T
:45	Here's to Vets T	Dramas T	Serenaders
8:00	Lawrence Welk	3/4 Time	Slim Bryant
:15	Lutheran Hour T	Oak Ridge Quart	Geo. Corliss
:30	Lutheran Hour T	News	News
:45	Concert Stars	Eddy Arnold T	Varieties
9:00	Concert Stars	Smiles/Song (MWF)	Sagebrush (TTS)
:15	Dick Jurgens	Music Manhattan	Crossroad Jamboree
:30	Three Sons	Harmony Lane	Crossroad Jamboree
:45	Jerry Sears	Parade of Bands	Voice of Army T
10:00	News	News	News
:15	Words & Music	10 o'clock Special	10 o'clock Special
:30	Words & Music	10 o'clock Special	10 o'clock Special
:45	Words & Music	10 o'clock Special	10 o'Clock Special
11:00	Waltz Time	Masterworks	10 o'clock Special
:15	Waltz Time	Masterworks	10 o'clock Special

KSRV broadcast Pacific Coast College Football and Snake River Valley High School Football *chapter 4*

"REINVENTING ITSELF"
1951/1960

*"We had to re-think and re-learn this business —
and the new radio was far better than the 'old' radio."*

Bill Warren, WMCR, Oneida, New York

chapter 4

"REINVENTING ITSELF"
KGCX — 1951/1960

As 1951 began, KGCX was operating with 5,000 watts, day and night, dwarfing the coverage of its two closest competitors: KXGN, Glendive, Montana, and what is now KEYZ, Williston, North Dakota. Both of the stations, established in the late 1940s, were Class IVs. There was no television in the area.

In the early 1950s, Ed Krebsbach continued to spend most of his time selling the station's advertising. He was assisted by two sons, Clair and Keith.

The station continued its Mutual Network affiliation. The small communities the station served were enjoying an expansion of their business districts. When television came to the area in 1956, Krebsbach suffered some anguish about the new medium, but radio generally, and his station in particular, were by then doing very well. The arrival of television impacted KGCX and other radio stations in the area, but the impact was nothing like what television had exacted earlier in other parts of the country. Nobody was any longer expecting radio to disappear.

In Williston, KGCX's "second market," what would become KEYZ was off the air. It would return to the air when Charles Scofield, a onetime KGCX announcer, came from his managing job at Miles City, Montana, (now KATL) to buy it.

Scofield put up $3,000 in hard cash and assumed a bank loan, agreeing to relieve investors of their responsibility for payment.

The banker was so concerned about the station's prospects that he told Scofield: "Our bank will be your first customer. We'll spend $303.46 a month for advertising on the station (enough to service the note)." In a few years, Scofield would become a member of the bank's board of directors, on which he still serves at this writing.

Scofield did very well with his station, his employees calling him an excellent engineer, a first-class programmer and a solid business-man. He said: "I am not a salesman," but he knew how to spot one.

Ray David, a former theater manager, had come to Williston to be the town's chamber of commerce executive. Scofield was on the chamber board when he recruited Ray to be his sales manager. David left Williston in 1978 to build his own station at Dickinson, North Dakota (KLTC/KRRB-FM). He was succeeded by Bob Miller, whom Scofield had brought through the ranks from part-time announcer in high school.

At the top of the market, while the oil and cattle businesses were thriving in the late '70s and early '80s, Scofield's station was probably worth near $2 million.

Even though the newcomers at Glendive and Williston were both doing well as the '50s passed, the Sidney station, the area's first, thrived.

Fifties Profile

David Halberstam, in his book *The Fifties*, tells his readers: "Photographs from the period tend to show people who dressed carefully, men in suits, ties — and, when outdoors, hats; the women with their hair in modified pageboys, pert and upbeat. Young people seemed, more than anything else, 'square' and largely accepting the given social covenants. At the beginning of the decade, their music was still slow and saccharin, mirroring the generally bland popular taste. In the years following the Great Depression and World War II, the American Dream was to exercise personal freedom, not in social and political terms, but rather in economic ones."

In 1951, the Korean Conflict was at its peak. By 1952, it was winding down, and by 1953 had ended. Dwight Eisenhower became president. He had grown up in the small town of Abilene, Kansas. Although he had seen most of the world and, during World War II, become one of the world's most historic figures, he was still very much a small town man at heart. Eisenhower's eight years in office would be considered remarkable in peacetime financial terms. They have not, to this date, been repeated:

Average unemployment was 4 percent, compared with 4.65 percent in the Roaring '20s.

The average salary rose from $2,990 in 1951 to $4,743 in 1960 — an increase of 58.5 percent — while prices rose just 11 percent.

The small towns and rural areas were not left behind in the 1950s prosperity boom, as they had been during the 1920s. The negative growth in rural America recorded in the 1940s was stemmed in the 1950s. America's non-metropolitan population had dropped by 4.2 million in the 1940s. The net loss in the 1950s was just 200,000 — a fifth of a million — despite the fact that the decade's long migration from the farm continued. Farm population shrank by one-third, to 15.5 million — one-half the 1940 figure.

Industrialization was coming to the country town, as small start-up manufacturers expanded. Many major corporations were building new plants in the small towns — spreading their investments out of the big cities. The small towns were mostly beyond the areas of influence of big labor unions. Not only were wage rates lower, but land and building costs were lower, as were taxes and other expenses.

Small town life fit the 1950s lifestyle. More than half the adult population attended church every week. Civic clubs and fraternal organizations were recording dramatic membership gains. Many of the young middle managers who were sent in to manage the new small plants liked their new roles as "big frogs in little ponds." They brought with them fresh ideas that would make their new hometowns better places to live.

Although the newcomers were a sign of change and threatened the status quo favored by a lot of longtime small town residents, the newcomers were generally warmly welcomed — whether they were coming to town to run a new factory, to start a business, to manage a chain store — or the town's new radio station. Every town had its own version of the following story:

A young couple coming out of a real estate office stopped to talk to an old man whittling under a shade tree on the courthouse lawn. "What kind of town is this to live in?" the strangers asked. The old man answered by first asking: "What kind of place are you coming from?" The couple answered: "We can't wait to move. The place is hostile and negative. We're glad to get out of there."

"Well," the old man replied, "you'll probably find this place to be about the same."

A few days passed and another couple stopped to chat with the old man. "Would you mind telling us what kind of town this is?" Again, he asked: "What's the town like you're coming from?"

They replied: "We're going to miss it. The people are some of the best we've ever known — kind, caring, considerate. We've made a lot of friends — and we're going to miss them."

The old man replied: "You'll probably find the same kind of people here."

The Radio Business

New TV station licenses were not granted from 1948 to 1952 to allow the FCC to redo its table of TV allocations and settle on a color TV standard. When the freeze was lifted, new stations quickly came on the air, blanketing the country. By 1960, there were 483 TV stations. By 1960, television was reaching virtually every home in the nation — 47 million of the nation's about 50 million homes. Even though only 4 out of 10 American homes had TV sets by 1951, the prime-time TV audience surpassed the prime-time audience of radio.

Most of the small market radio stations that came on the air beginning in 1946, affiliated with either the Mutual Network or ABC, CBS and NBC, were still protecting their long-established metropolitan affiliates' network franchises.

Mutual was not in television. It was a "stand alone business." ABC, the No. 3 radio network, had the weakest lineup of television stations. Even after it was merged with United Paramount Theatre, it was badly outdistanced in financial resources by CBS and NBC.

In 1953, Mutual quit paying compensation to its major market affiliates, substituting programming the station could sell. Its non-compensated stations in small towns got their affiliation fees increased by $100 per month (up from an average of $250 per month.) The plan was not successful.

By December, *The Shadow* and *20 Questions*, two of the network's most popular programs, were canceled. By 1955, the programs for local sale had disappeared from the lineup. Mutual, without benefit of a profitable television network, suffered losses. In late 1955, it laid off 25 percent of its personnel and cut back on its programming. Shortly, Mutual dropped all its programs except news and sports. By 1957, parent company RKO-General, which had TV and radio stations but no television network, decided to sell Mutual.

Between 1957 and 1960, it would have five owners and make a trip to the bankruptcy court. The first sale was in 1957, to a group of California businessmen for $550,000. In 1958, it was sold to Hal

Roach Studios. That company's president, Alexander Guterma, would go to jail in 1960 for stock fraud. The next buyer was Malcomb Smith, who put it into bankruptcy shortly after he bought it. Businessman Al McCarthy rescued it from bankruptcy. It sold to 3M.

ABC did little better than Mutual during the 1950s. The quality and quantity of its programming was steadily cut back. The company's resources, of necessity, had to be focused on its television network owned and operated stations. The ABC television operation was running a poor third to NBC and CBS. By 1957, serious consideration was given to exiting the radio network business.

NBC, amassing huge profits from its television broadcasting activities and the manufacture of television receivers, was struggling to keep its radio network on the air. Its pride in having been the first network no doubt kept it in the business. CBS Radio was also struggling, despite the devotion of its founder and CEO, Bill Paley.

In the 1950s, network radio would launch only one big star attraction, *Bob and Ray*, whose comedy centered around spoofing longtime radio fare like soap operas, the man on the street and letters from lonely hearts. Stan Freberg, who would later give radio some of its most memorable commercials, lasted less than a season on CBS in 1957.

In the mid-'50s, Pat Weaver, then head of NBC Television and Radio, best known for TV innovations like *Today* and *Tonight*, launched a radio series that would endure 20 years. The program was *Monitor*, initially 40 hours each weekend featuring news, special events, features and comedy bits interspersed with music and hosted by pleasant hosts. Ironically, the program left the network in 1975 because the time proved to be more profitable to network affiliates opting for play-by-play sports and remotes.

In 1950, Burns and Allen (on the air since 1932) did their last network radio show. Also leaving were *Dr. I.Q.* (1929) and *Tom Mix* (1939). In 1951, *Superman* (1940), the *Bill Stern Sports Newsreel* (1939) and *Mister District Attorney* (1939) left the networks, followed in 1952 by *Ozzie and Harriet* (1944), *Green Hornet* (1936) and *Inner Sanctum* (1941).

Against The Current

Harold Fitzgerald, who would later spend 30 years with SESAC as a field man, was Hayward Talley's boss, general manager of WOKZ (now WBJZ) at Alton, Illinois, in the St. Louis suburbs.

Fitzgerald recalls: "When I heard Hayward was planning to build a radio station at Lietchfield, Illinois, I had a 'big brother talk' with him. A town of 5,000 people seemed to be far too small to support a radio station, and, I added, I'm not sure that building a radio station now isn't something like starting a blacksmith shop."

Talley had dreamed of owning his own radio station as far back as junior high school. After World War II service in the Signal Corps, he took engineering, with a minor in business and journalism in college, then took the chief engineer post at the Alton station. "I was ready — the business just had to be ready for me."

Talley was going into his new venture with a great deal of confidence. "On my own time, I was going out with a wire recorder, interviewing people around Alton about their views on current issues. Even though Milton Berle, *Kukla, Fran and Ollie* and the *Roller Derby* were being watched by nearly everybody, my little wire-recorded tapes got a lot of comment. I was sure people were still listening to the radio."

Talley pooled his resources with another engineer at the Alton station. WSMI went on the air in 1950, on the cheap. Regrettably, Talley's friend and partner, not yet 30, died less than a year after the start of the venture.

WSMI would be, despite early reservations of others, a big financial success. It was not only the hometown station, but also became the hometown station for the nearby communities of Hillsboro, Carlinville and Greenville, where the station established branch studios. Carlinville and Greenville later got their own stations, but WSMI continues its presence there. "Those are two-station markets now," Talley says.

Forty-five years after WSMI went on the air, Talley, with his wife and two sons, continues to own and operate the station and its companion 50,000-watt FM.

"A Not Very Imposing Man"

He broke into radio during high school, did World War II Navy service, then, at 19, helped build WHUN, Huntington, Pennsylvania. He was its first program director.

For Cary Simpson, the Huntington job was followed by jobs at stations in Ohio and Nebraska. He was just 22 when he approached a Pittsburgh attorney about backing him in building a radio station. Quite a feat for a man so young, who all of his life has described himself as "a not very imposing man."

The first station, WKBI at St. Marys, Pennsylvania, was so successful that Cary built five more stations in Pennsylvania towns of about 5,000 population. Only one of the five stations was not successful — WECZ, Punxsutawney, home of the world-famous groundhog who, each February 2, predicts a long or short winter by seeing or not seeing his shadow.

"We lost some money there, so we sold out." Simpson would not sell another station until the early 1990s. In the 1960s, ahead of his time, Simpson built high-power FM stations near the larger markets of State College and Johnstown.

A Simpson employee during the '50s, Bill Pawley, says of him: "I've known a lot of people who were caught up in this business — none more than Cary. He didn't get married until he was 30. That was awful old in those days."

Of his marriage, Simpson says: "I was able to spend more time with the family that Betty and I would later have. I also broadened my interests." He became active in his church, where he would serve as a lay leader of its statewide organization. He also became active in the Boy Scouts, for years serving as head of his area's Boy Scout Camp.

He also broadened his broadcast interests beyond his group of small stations, serving the state broadcasters association, including a term as president, and with the NAB and the Radio Advertising Bureau. He has, for many years, been on the RAB Executive Committee and serves as its treasurer. Additionally, he has been chairman of the RAB Small Market Committee, formed in the mid-1980s.

At 67, Simpson is still the hands-on head of his station group. Betty serves as the group's comptroller. His daughter, Barbie, for many years served as sales manager of the State College station. When she left to raise her family, son John stepped in at WGMR to fill that post.

Small station group owners — there were 33 of them by 1960 — were often known for "churning" their station investments — selling at a profit to buy bigger stations. Many were also known for their rapid turnover of managers and other personnel. By contrast, Simpson's group has been known for its long ownerships and long-time employees. Observers say that Simpson is devoted "to the towns and his people." The feeling is apparently mutual.

A 1994 article about Simpson in *Radio Ink* tells of a 37-year employee, now only working part time after retirement. Bill Moses, during a hospital stay, sold Christmas greetings for one of the Simpson stations from a phone at his bedside.

Television in the Small Markets

When the 1948-imposed freeze on new television station creation came to an end in 1952, a table of assignments for 2,053 TV stations in 1,291 cities and towns — 617 VHF and 1,436 UHF stations — was issued by the FCC.

It is no wonder that many owners of small market radio stations eagerly looked over the list. Most, at the time, were not sure, in the face of TV, that their radio stations would remain viable — or even on the air.

The spring 1951 radio ratings in New York City, the country's most highly developed television market, showed:

	1948	1951
Jack Benny	26.5	4.8
Arthur Godfrey Talent Scouts	20.3	5.9
Bing Crosby	18.0	3.8
Bob Hope	16.0	3.8
Amos and Andy	13.6	5.9
Groucho Marx	12.0	5.0

Clearly, the kind of radio most Americans had heard for years was at death's door.

Many small market operators quickly filed applications — few built. Economic reality quickly set in. 1950s television economics dictated an initial investment of at least $300,000, and $30,000 a month income (equal to five times that much in 1990s money).

WRAY-TV, Princeton, Indiana

Ray Lankford was the owner of a successful hatchery business in Princeton, then, as now, a town of about 10,000. In 1949, faced with an overabundant inventory of baby chicks, he called WVMI, Mount Carmel, Illinois — 30 miles away — and bought a schedule of ads. He was so pleased with the results that he decided to build a station at Princeton.

WRAY went on the air in 1950 from studios in surplus space

on the second floor of the hatchery. The walls were lined with cardboard egg cartons for acoustics. There was no television in the area at the time. The station was immediately very profitable.

The 1952 allocations list included an assignment for a UHF station at Princeton. Lankford, with help from some outside investors, decided to build WRAY-TV.

Harold Bass, an engineer at WRAY-TV, is still chief engineer for the AM station and later-established FM station. The TV station, without a network, operated for eight months with movies, syndicated programs and some live shows: news, sports, weather and a kids show.

Bass recalls going to St. Louis to buy a UHF television set so he could pick up the station. The dealer told him: "If you can't pick anything up, bring it back and I'll give you your money back."

During the eight months WRAY-TV was on the air, Bass says, "we worked ourselves to death. I think Mr. Lankford almost went broke. On many occasions, he made our payroll out of the hatchery cash register."

After WRAY-TV went off the air, it got permission to go on once a year to conduct a charity telethon, a tradition begun while the station was on the air full time.

Bass continues: "It took years to sell off the equipment. People weren't building UHF stations. I think it was in the early '60s that the last of the equipment was sold."

WRAY-TV left a legacy. The 420-foot tower built for the TV station was used to mount the antenna for 50,000-watt WRAY-FM. The big parking lot in front of the building, where the radio stations are now located, houses another Lankford family business, a successful Kentucky Fried Chicken franchise.

WHIZ-TV, Zanesville, Ohio

WHIZ-TV, Zanesville, Ohio, owes its survival to the hard work and ability of one man — Allan Land.

WHIZ radio (formerly WEBE and WALR) was put up for sale by group owner George Storer to make room in his portfolio for WJBK, Detroit, Michigan. The Littick family, owners of the *Times Recorder*, bought it to keep their competitor, *The Signal*, from getting it. The Litticks were a little short of money for the $272,500 purchase, so they sold a minority interest to their lawyers.

The new owners hired Vernon Nolte to manage the station. Allan Land, who would come from WMRF, Lewistown, Pennsylvania, to serve as news director, describes Nolte as "a brilliant man — an exceptional broadcaster."

Nolte persuaded his owners to file for the UHF allocation for Zanesville. It went on the air in the spring of 1953 — costing $375,000. By doubling up much of the radio station personnel, the operating costs were held to about $20,000 a month.

Although the stations in Columbus, Ohio, and Wheeling, West Virginia, theoretically covered Zanesville, "TV reception before cable wasn't good," Land recalls. But, he continues, "on Channel 50 in this hilly area, our signal wasn't good, either."

In the early days when TV advertising was sold, "the first thing the station had to do was take a UHF receiving antenna to the client's house so he could see his commercials on our station," Land recalls.

After less than a year on the air, the TV station had piled up losses of more than $100,000. In Land's words: "It devastated Vernon. He left to enjoy great success in the radio business — but he never again ventured into television."

With Nolte's departure, the owners seriously considered giving up on the television station. Instead, they decided to give the venture a little more time.

Doing so dictated a move to a more favorable channel, 18, at a cost of an additional $250,000. It also required a replacement for the departing Vernon Nolte. They chose Land, by then not only news director of the AM station but also its program director and the program director-news director of the television station.

In addition to the technical improvements, Land changed the sales operation, installing a separate sales manager and sales staff for radio and TV. All were changed from salary, a staple in the newspaper business, to commission.

Additionally, a separate program director was installed at each station. Talent continued to appear on both stations.

Selling time on TV continued to be a real challenge. There were four TV networks at the time. The DuMont Network was still on the air. WHIZ-TV had arrangements with all four. There was no blanket affiliation. Time was sold to the four networks on a program-by-program basis. "With only about 30,000 homes in our coverage area, and with the maps showing coverage by the outside stations, many advertisers didn't think they needed us. A case in point: We were ordered for the first and last half hours of NBC's *Show of Shows*. We sandwiched a CBS show in the middle.

"Miraculously," Land relates, "the television station showed a profit (small) the sixth month after I took over — and we've been profitable every month since." The station later became a full-time NBC affiliate. Thanks to that network's pioneering move into color TV, WHIZ's superior signal in its market made it a solid success.

That success took it into another small market TV station, at Parkersburg, West Virginia, and a chain of radio stations in Ohio and Michigan. The newspaper and the out-of-town stations were sold over the years at handsome profits. Land had, for a time, served as chief operating officer of both the print and broadcast properties.

In his early 70s, Land continues to operate WHIZ-AM/FM/TV for the Littick family. He doesn't talk about retirement, saying: "I'd have to find something I'd like doing better than this. I don't know what that could be." Of WHIZ-TV, he says: "This is a hybrid. It's never really been done anyplace else — and is unlikely to ever be done again. I'm glad fate made me part of it."

Other Survivors

In 1954, WBOC radio built WBOC-TV, Salisbury, Maryland (TV Market #163). The two stations were sold for $1.2 million. The new owners later sold the radio station.

In 1956, the Seaton family built KHAS-TV, Hastings, Nebraska (TV Market #95). In 1994, they sold their AM station, KHAS. They continue to operate the TV station.

Also in Nebraska, KNOP put KNOP-TV on the air at North Platte (TV Market #208) in 1958. In 1968, the two stations were sold for $216,810. The buying group still operates them.

KAUS-TV, Austin, Minnesota (TV Market #149) was put on the air in 1953 by the owners of the local radio station, KAUS. In 1958, the radio station and the TV station were sold for a reported price of $41,000. There were later several more owners. In 1985, the station, now KAAL-TV was purchased by the Dix family, an Ohio-based small market newspaper and radio group with other TV interests, for $13.2 million.

Ray Eppel was an organist in a downtown Minneapolis hotel prior to putting what is now KORN on the air in 1948. In 1960, he and his investors built what is now KDLT in Mitchell, South Dakota (TV Market #100). He kept the radio stations until 1975, when he sold them to a group of local businessmen. In 1985, KDLT was part of a three South Dakota TV station sale at $15.5 million.

The Mitchell radio station was one of many stopovers in the long radio career of George Blum, now owner of KOLV at Olivia, Minnesota. He remembers the TV station going on the air. "In addition to my duties as radio station engineer and sign-on man, I was given the job of hosting the afternoon kids' show."

Dean Sorenson, now a small market group owner, says: "Ray gave me my first radio job. I learned a lot. When the TV station came on, it was a pretty crude affair. We didn't have very good, even enough, equipment to do a first-class job. I did get a taste of TV and, by the time I left, decided my future was as a 'radio guy' — not a television star."

De-regulation

Some 513 radio stations had been built in 1946, 397 in 1947 and 391 in 1948. The number of new stations fell dramatically between 1949 and 1951 (174, 146, 99). There was a brief freeze in 1951 so that radio station technical equipment could be targeted to the Korean War effort. New station building hit rock bottom in 1952, when only 60 stations debuted. Many radio stations were unprofitable. The radio industry boosterism that was so widespread for much of its history had disappeared. To make matters worse, engineers, qualified or not quite qualified, were in short supply, many leaving radio for better hours and better jobs in the increasing industrial economy.

By 1953, radio station technology dramatically improved. Bill Rust had invented a reliable remote control system that allowed stations to operate their transmitters from studios away from the generally rural transmitter sites. The need was gone for an expensive studio-transmitter building or separate transmitter buildings to house on-duty engineers (complete with FCC rules that said the building had to have running water and sanitary facilities).

Instead, the new, unmanned facility could be a 12-foot-by-12-foot building to house the remote-controlled transmitter. Studios could be located in inexpensive leased quarters near the heart of town. The cost of building dropped substantially.

Furthermore, equipment had become reliable enough that the

Commission backed off on its rule that an engineer (with a first-class license) had to be on duty at all times. One full-time First Class "ticket" holder would be required — but he could handle other duties. Routine monitoring of the station meters could be done by an announcer with a Restricted License. The licenses were obtained simply by filling out a short application that required answering only the simplest questions, such as "Do you speak English?" (Stations had been allowed to operate that way during World War II's manpower shortages without incident.)

In addition to lessening costs of building, costs of operating dropped by $1,000 or more a month. The new, relaxed rules quickly changed small station economics. Stations losing money soon were doing much better, and those new small station economics brought a host of new stations to communities previously thought to be too small.

From World War II until the rules change, it was generally thought that a station needed a home county population of 20,000 and retail sales of about $20 million. Such a station could be expected to do about $6,000 per month ($200 a day). The new math held that a station could be profitable in a county of 12,000 to 15,000 people with retail sales of $12 million to $15 million. Station builders in such communities were often surprised by doing much better, not having daily newspaper competition.

A station-building boom was quickly under way again. In 1953, 130 stations were built, and in the following five years, an average of 160 new stations, mostly in small towns, came on the air each year.

Some of the vendors didn't catch on quickly. The late Shelby McCallum sold his then-struggling theaters and decided to invest the proceeds in a radio station in the small town where he lived — Benton, Kentucky (population then under 3,000 — home county about 15,000). When he wrote to the Associated Press about a news service, he remembered many years later, he received a response saying that they didn't think a station in such a small town could be successful: "If we are in error, let us know, if you've been on the air for a while." He got service from UPI. He was often, after the station proved itself, solicited by the AP. By 1970, his station was doing $125,000 a year and the proprietor was keeping half of it.

"Deregulation Threatened His Job"

Reed Anderson had, on the G.I. Bill, taken an engineering course at a Cincinnati trade school. When he completed the course, he hired in as a transmitter engineer at a station in Lexington, Kentucky. When a new station was to be built 25 miles away at Richmond, he applied for and was given the job of chief engineer (under the new rules, the only engineer) of the 250-watt station. After a little more than two years on the job, he found out that a friend of his owner had hired the operator of a local TV-radio repair shop to be chief engineer. The rules called for full time. The radio-TV repairman, with a first-class ticket, would be listed on the payroll as working 40 hours a week at the then-minimum wage of $1 an hour. It was completely legal and Anderson figured his owner would not be able to resist the $50 a week savings that such a change would make at his station. WEKY was paying him $90 a week — $10 more than the wages at which he'd been hired.

Anderson looked around for a town without a station where he could build one. By selling some real estate he'd bought earlier, and with help from his small town merchant father, he found what he was looking for in Cynthiana, 50 miles south of Cincinnati, a town of 4,900 people in a county of 12,500 with retail sales of $12.5 million. The station was WCYN.

Years later, after he'd made a lot of money out of his little station, as well as a town CATV system and shrewd real estate investing, he would say: "I think I would have gone in business for myself someday, but the change in the FCC rules forced me to do it at what turned out to be the right time."

He would also say: "I think I've done well, because I knew what I didn't know." When he built his station, he hired a 23-year-old co-worker who, in five years, had been, in turn, an announcer, program director and time salesman. When they made their deal, Anderson said to him: "You set up the programming and sales and hire a staff. I'll do the engineering and keep my eye on the money." He was the station bookkeeper.

Studios were established in rented quarters on the third floor of a local bank, which had formerly been the local Elks Lodge. Rent was $50 a month. He took a long-term lease on land on which to construct the transmitter building and tower ($40 per month).

The best facility he could get was a Class IV, limited to 100 watts power. Thanks to installing an expensive "ground screen" and the ground conductivity of Kentucky Bluegrass land, the 100-watt station had amazing coverage — a 26-mile half "mil" coverage.

The Sunday before construction was to begin, he and his young manager met in the dining room of the town's hotel. A prim middle-aged lady approached them, asking: "Why in the world would you want to build a radio station?" His young manager politely answered: "After it's on for six months, you'll wonder how you ever got along without it."

The forecast was accurate. Town leaders would often say: "The station has built a bridge between the folks out in the country and those in town. It's given them a common interest."

The station provided the town's first daily news service and advertising medium. Political candidates spoke on it. Town folk and country folk were heard on the daily *Man on the Street* program.

Hometown talent appeared. The county jailer had a country band that was on for an hour every Saturday night. A gospel quartet from out in the country performed for an hour every Sunday night. At Christmastime, the church and school choirs were heard every evening.

One of the most popular features (which got the highest rates) was a half-hour program every night during the tobacco auction season. Every crop sold was reported, including the grower's name, the pounds per acre, the price per pound and the total amount of money received. "The local credit bureau tuned in each night, having a clerk take the information down in shorthand, to see how some of their problem accounts had done."

When there was a "fire call," the station told listeners where it was, advising them not to go to the fire for the safety of the firemen. The announcements were sponsored by a local insurance agency, which asked: "Is your fire coverage up-to-date?"

WCYN is now almost 40 years old. When Reed Anderson died of cancer in his early 60s, his wife, Ann, who'd spent her life raising the couple's three children and, as she says, "housewifing," became the station's president and general manager.

Mid-'50s Miscellany

Few small stations were taking advantage of their freedom to editorialize. There had been, up to that time, few complaints at the Commission of unfair "station comment." One of the first appeared when the police chief in a small Florida town filed a complaint against his small local radio station.

When the police chief was accused of filling the tank of his personal car with city gasoline, the station, the complaint said, started referring to him on the air as "High Octane." When it was found that the chief's son, a patrolman on the same force, was also filling up his personal car with city gasoline, the station referred to him as "Low Octane."

The chief and his son were soon relieved of their duties. The Commission took no action, but the small station reportedly lowered the "pitch" of its broadcasts.

Stations +5% — Industry Revenue -5%

Although the number of radio stations increased by almost 5 percent, the FCC 1954 Financial Report showed that there was a nationwide decline in radio advertising sales of 5 percent. It was radio's first down revenue year since 1938.

Industry advertising revenues turned up in 1955, but only slightly — less than 1 percent. Revenues in 1956 saw a 7.7 percent gain, followed by a 9.3 percent gain in 1957. The pace slowed in the recession year of 1958, posting a gain of less than just 0.9 percent. Things turned up again in 1959.

Daytimer Trouble

At the end of World War II, there were only a handful of daytime-only radio stations. Of the 314 stations in towns under 25,000 in 1945, only 13 were daytimers.

By the mid-1950s, 900 of the then 2,500 AM radio stations were daytime-only — more than one-third. Most of them were in small towns. The 1941 allocations system had created six Class IV (250 watts or 100 watts unlimited time) channels. The Class IV channels could accommodate about 1,000 stations nationwide. The Class IV channels were quickly filled up in the post-World II station-building boom. When an applicant could not get a Class IV channel in the town where he proposed to build a station, he generally backed off to a daytimer on a frequency that would work. One of those after the war station builders was a 28-year-old returning Navy veteran, Ray Livesay.

Ray had gotten into radio out of high school in 1936 at daytime-only WDZ, then at Tuscola, Illinois. He hired on as an announcer, shortly switching over to sales, "because," he says, "even then, that was where the money was."

In addition to his sales activities and radio announcing, Livesay had a profitable sideline, a photography business. "I picked up quite a bit of money photographing weddings and, after the draft started, taking pictures of girls who purchased them to send to their boyfriends in the service," he happily recalls. "My new bride, Level, wisely insisted that we put the 'photography money' aside. We'd also bank some commission money when I had an especially good month at the radio station."

After he went into the service, studying electronics first, then teaching it, the savings grew, but a smaller rate. When he returned from the service, he and Level had $5,000 in the bank.

WDZ, although just 1,000 watts, had phenomenal coverage, thanks to Illinois' high ground conductivity and the station's middle of the AM dial frequency. The station sold advertising 75 to 100 miles away from its transmitting facilities. A lot of business was done in small towns. One of those towns was Mattoon.

Ray invested his and Level's savings in a station he built there — a 250-watt daytimer. He was joined in the venture by a couple of his pre-war WDZ customers — the owner of a small regional baking company and a retail furniture store. "In addition to our cash contributions, the three of us borrowed a little money at a bank. The new station quickly paid it back."

About his daytimer, he says: "Obviously, I would have liked to have gotten a full-time station, but in 1946, the rules made a daytimer on 1170 the only thing that would work. I was sorry we couldn't do the local high school games at night, but, by 1949, we added a 250-watt FM station. For more than 20 years, sports was the only thing we could sell on the FM station."

In 1954, the Clear Channel Broadcasters Association, representing the 50,000-watt AM stations, persuaded the FCC to open for comments Docket #8333, which would have limited daytimers, operating on clear channels, to operating only during non-critical hours — two hours after sunrise to two hours before sunset. That would mean that stations like Livesay's at Mattoon and the one he'd bought at Clinton, Illinois, WHOW, would be on the air from only 9 a.m. to 2:45 p.m. in the winter months. "That would have put us out of business," Livesay says.

From its beginning in 1941, the Clear Channel Broadcasters Association hoped to raise the maximum power of most of its members' station above 50,000 watts. Only one U.S. station had ever done that. WLW in Cincinnati, in May 1934, on a temporary basis, operated with 500,000 watts on 700 kHZ. By the fall of 1934, CFRB,

Toronto, Canada (on 690 kHZ), and WOR, New York (on 710 kHZ), were complaining about WLW interference to their signals. By Christmastime 1934, the FCC ordered it to operate daytime only with its 500,000 watts, broadcasting at its permanently licensed 50,000 watts in non-daylight hours (or to operate with a highly directional antenna). Powel Crosley, owner of WLW, decided against the directional antenna and went to the separate daytime/nighttime powers. Under increasing pressure from many sources, the FCC reduced its power back to 50 kW in 1938.

By 1954, although it members were few in number, CCBA was formidable. Its stations were owned by the three leading networks, powerful newspapers and rich manufacturing companies.

Opposing CCBA efforts was the Regional Broadcasters Association, formed in 1936 to head off "the superpower" threat, which it saw as jeopardizing its national network affiliations and national spot business.

The only type of stations that did not have an organization looking after their specific interests were the daytimers — more than one-third of the nation's AM radio stations. Docket #8333 alarmed some of them. "Most of them did not realize how much their businesses were being threatened," Livesay recalls.

The first meeting of daytimers was held shortly after "#8333" surfaced. Among those in attendance were Livesay and Ken Patterson, operator of WVEL, Pekin, Illinois. The group elected Patterson president and Livesay secretary. Two years later, Livesay rose to president — a post he would hold for more than 25 years.

"Over the early days of the Daytime Broadcasters Association," Livesay says, "we were successful in heading off the short-hour proposition, but another problem quickly crept up. Most of the daytimers were on regional channels. Their licenses specified operation from local sunrise to sunset but, if a full-time station did not complain that the daytimer was causing it interference, the daytimers could sign on as early as 4 a.m., local standard time.

By the early 1960s, full-time regional stations began filing complaints. Many daytimers, used to coming on at 6 a.m. or earlier year-round, were forced to wait to start their broadcast day until local sunrise (7 a.m. or 8 a.m. in winter months).

DBA obtained a compromise from the FCC. All daytimers would be allowed to sign on at 6 a.m., local standard time, with powers of 500 watts or less, subject to a showing by a consulting engineer that an agreed-to interference level would not be exceeded. The studies, which generally cost a station $500 or less, were filed almost universally. Power levels could be attained by a relatively inexpensive transmitter modification at pre-sunrise levels like 383 watts. In the early 1970s, the powers were set by the FCC at a uniform 500 watts.

The Daytime Broadcasters Association became a passion for Livesay. At NAB meetings, his group met in a separate session. He carried his message to state broadcasters' associations across the country. He piloted his own plane, most often accompanied by his wife, Level.

Livesay was also a regular presence at the FCC and on Capitol Hill. Without paid lobbyists, the effort in Washington was carried on by Livesay and a handful of DBA members.

"All we had to offer was our story about what the daytimers were providing to their communities. In addition to the small town stations, daytimers in cities were providing an exclusive service to minorities and audiences that were too small for the big stations to serve."

Livesay enlisted the efforts of some high-profile directors with daytime station interests, most notably former Gov. Alf Landon of Kansas, as well as one of the few 1960s female radio station owners, Marianne Campbell of WJEH, Gallipolis, Ohio, and a cross section of daytimer owners or managers from minorities.

He recalls: "We had only a few dues-paying members, so nobody got a salary and there were no travel expenses paid." When the association went out of existence, its records were then in the care of Jim Wychor, who succeeded Livesay as president. Those records, he said, showed that in its more than 30 years of existence, no more than 200 of the then 2,400 daytimers had ever made a financial contribution to it.

In the late 1960s and early 1970s, new treaties with Mexico and Canada allowed hundreds of daytimers to sign on earlier or to get unlimited hours.

But, as Livesay would say: "There were still hundreds upon hundreds of daytimers that continued to operate at severe handicaps." The matter came to a head when he attended a late-1970s World Allocations Radio Conference (WARC). Livesay had learned that AM frequencies in the Orient and in Europe were set at 8 or 9 kHZ separation, rather than 10 as in the Western Hemisphere. "I listened," he says, "to the radio stations on my American-made portable and I didn't see any difference in quality from what I'd heard at home."

Livesay then set about redesigning the U.S. radio dial with 9 kHZ separation. His plan called for each Clear Channel station to get a frequency on which only one station would broadcast. The full-time regional stations would continue to operate with their allotted powers and directional patterns, but without daytimers on their frequencies. The plan called for an increase in Class IV channels from 6 to 18, to which all the daytimers would be moved and could broadcast unlimited hours.

Livesay was shocked at the almost universal opposition to his plan. As he says now: "Everybody was going to get something better than they had." NRBA (National Radio Broadcasters Association), then NAB, came out squarely and loudly against it. (Livesay had spent terms on both their boards.) The industry and the Commission had been concerned, since the early-1960s, about AM radio overpopulation. The fear was that 9 kHZ would open the floodgates to even more stations. But, the Ferris FCC staff endorsed the plan. The failure to get agreement from other Western Hemisphere nations stopped the plan cold.

Livesay chuckles when he says: "I dropped a hot potato and, all of a sudden, to head off the 9-kilohertz idea, the FCC, the NAB and just about everybody else jumped in to help the daytimers. I decided it was time to step down. The association wisely replaced me with Jim Wychor, then at KWOA, Worthington, Minnesota."

Wychor immediately put his overpowering abilities to work for the daytimers. The Commission quickly improved their lot by first giving most of them pre-sunrise and an initial two hours post-sunset authority, and finally full time (at reduced power levels). Additionally, DBA was successful in getting a "Daytimer Preference" for daytimers filing for FM stations. By the time it was over, all but 200 of the nation's 2,400 daytimers got something. One of those that got nothing, WJDM, Elizabeth, New Jersey, on its own initiative got a bill passed in Congress to give it a full-time license in the new 1610 to 1700 frequencies.

The final stages of the daytimer effort were costly. Huge amounts had to be spent on engineering studies and legal fees. The organization was folded into the NAB, in return for NAB bailing it out financially. At the NAB, Bud Walters, whose widespread radio interests included two daytimers, became chairman of the Daytimer Committee. It was soon folded because, as Bud would say: "There just wasn't much left to do." In 1989, the FCC stopped accepting applications for daytimers permanently.

Ray remained active in the operation of his small station group, including broadcasting a daily editorial (a staple since 1950) until his death at 78 in May 1995. "In the beginning, we hoped every day-timer would become a full timer," he recalled before his death. "We didn't get that done, but hundreds of those daytimers did. Some of those little stations, particularly in little towns, wouldn't be in business today if they couldn't carry local night ballgames and early morning local news programs."

Ironically, Livesay's own stations got little or nothing from the effort: WLBH at Mattoon got one watt during non-daytime hours; WHOW, Clinton, got no extra hours; his Florida property, WBAR, Bartow, got 156 watts. He said: "That's not important. I've done pretty well in this business. I'm glad I could do something for some folks who weren't doing well."

The New Beat

The introduction of transistor radios in 1955 (at $49.95 each) greatly increased the medium's circulation. It also aided in developing a powerful new constituency — teenagers. The teens of the late '50s were different from any of their predecessors. They had more free time and more money than any other generation of teenagers to date. They were not satisfied with the "musical hand-me-downs" of their parents' generation.

A music type, foreign to most American ears, made its appearance on the top 25 best-selling record list in 1954 — Bill Haley and the Comets' recording of *Shake, Rattle and Roll*. Haley came back in 1955 with another top 25-selling record, *Rock Around the Clock*. By 1956, two such songs made the top 25 — Elvis Presley and *Hound Dog* and Fats Domino's *Blueberry Hill*.

By 1957, this "strange" to most people's ears music dominated the best-selling record lists with more than half the entries. It combined the beat of what had earlier been called "race music," heretofore appealing primarily to black listeners, and hillbilly music, appealing primarily to the working classes of Southern cities and to rural residents.

The stars on the new hit records were not the established ones, many of whom had dominated popular music during the '30s, '40s and '50s. Most were new to national audiences.

One such act, The Everly Brothers, had their first million-selling record in 1957. The young men, Don and Phil, had appeared only five years before with their mother and father, Ike and Margarite, on KMA and KFNF in Shenandoah, Iowa. The family had settled there in the 1940s to get off the road. Ike and Margarite hired on as staff musicians at KMA. The boys often appeared with them. The boys might, in the senior Everly's words, never have left for Knoxville Tennessee, where the Everly Brothers were discovered, if it had not been for the changes in radio programming. KMA dropped live musical programs in 1953; KFNF in 1955.

Radio's First Big Scandal

"Song pluggers" dated back to the early 1900s. A composer with a song often hired a promoter to take his songs to producers or stars, persuading them to include his song in their show or repertoire. Such exposure enhanced first the sale of sheet music, then later phonograph records.

When Pat Weaver, then head of NBC Television and Radio, said: "Television would never 'make' a hit song," the record promoters, successors to the old-time "song pluggers," caught on fast. Disc jockeys, by repeated playing of a record on their programs, could help the sales of records. Most of the disc jockeys selected their records in the early days.

The record promoters, in the course of business, often treated the disc jockeys on whom they were calling to lunch or a drink after work. Over time, the entertainment became more lavish. Next, inexpensive, then more expensive gifts appeared — including sums of cash — payola.

By 1959, the practice became so widespread that there was a Congressional hearing. Alan Freed, whom historians credit with introducing rock 'n' roll on his Cleveland, Ohio, program in the early '50s, was payola's first casualty. After being convicted in a New York court of racketeering, his radio career ended.

Most disc jockeys who took payola were dismayed by the uproar. They looked upon the gratuities from the record promoters as something similar to tips a waiter customarily receives.

Station managements, at FCC urging, enacted tighter controls on the records that were played. Most stations began broadcasting an announcement several times a day telling listeners: "Many of the records heard on this station are supplied free by the record companies for promotional purposes."

Payola was not a big issue in small market stations. The record promoters, like most large national advertisers, felt that the small audiences were not worth expending a lot of effort on — the records were national products.

One young Cajun disc jockey on a small station in Louisiana reportedly wrote a letter to the FCC confessing that he might be guilty of payola. He said that requests for songs on his Cajun record program were often accompanied by jars of homemade Cajun food delicacies. He said he had accepted them.

Rebirth

It is truly amazing that a medium largely written off as an endangered species just 10 years earlier had become so successful, that the news of a few employees "taking bribes" could make the front pages of newspapers, get major play in the big newsmagazines and be the lead story on TV. Radio had come back from near-death.

Small town radio's fortunes had never deteriorated as badly as had the fortunes of the networks and the big metropolitan stations. The small town stations were offering a unique service, one that couldn't then, or can't now, be duplicated by television.

Guglielmo Marconi, Lee De Forest and Edwin Armstrong were its fathers; David Sarnoff and Bill Paley were the midwives of the Golden Age and three men were its godfathers during its rebirth.

Elmo Ellis

"Get out of television to get into radio in 1951? It's insanity." That was the consensus among Elmo Ellis' wide circle of friends, gathered during seven years as a radio writer-producer from 1940 to 1947, then four years in a similar job at WSB-TV.

Ellis was intrigued to find out what was going on — and, more importantly, not going on in his years away from radio. He quickly decided that "one obvious mistake was that radio was clinging to the pragmatic philosophy that if you work hard enough, everything will come out all right." But, he thought: "Radio had to realize its audience was living an entirely different kind of life than it had in previous decades. What was 'right' before wasn't necessarily 'right' in the 1950s."

In an article, "Removing the Rust From Radio," written for *Broadcasting* magazine, he said: "Broadcasters should find out what listeners want, and the broadcasters should dare to be different." He urged stations to get involved in their communities and to feature local interests. He suggested attention to small details, like "sharpening up interviews by having the guest do more talking and the announcer less." He advised stations to take their microphones out to the people, covering the sounds of the community, "listening and talking with people from all walks of life."

As blocks of non-productive programming opened up, as the network cut back its schedule, he increased music programming. Contests were developed in which the audience could participate in station activities. Eighteen entirely new programs were started during his first 18 months in the radio job.

Every idea wasn't a smash hit, he would often recall. When the organist didn't show up for *It Pays To Listen* to play "mystery songs on the organ," Ellis told the announcer: "Let's see what happens if you just hum the songs."

After the program was over, everybody involved, including Ellis, agreed: "It was unbelievably bad."

In 1955, the station created *Nightbeat* to compete with prime-time television. It attracted national attention. Ellis described it as a "Town Crier" format. It told about people — what people were doing, saying and thinking. Often, the interviews were offbeat, such as plumbers making night calls and a safecracker who agreed to talk about his profession. A local newspaper columnist called the program "the heartbeat of our town."

Ellis spent a lot of his time traveling to talk to broadcast groups all over the country. He didn't mind sharing his secrets, "because I think it's good for the radio industry." During a lot of his appearances, he'd refer to WSB as a "small town station that just happens to be in Atlanta and just happens to have 50,000 watts."

His boss, J. Leonard Reinsch, Cox Broadcasting's CEO and author of books on broadcast station management, said: "Television was a blessing for radio. The transfer of star-studded shows to television was the best thing that could have happened to radio. It melted off the fat and lethargy and created a streamlined, robust new type of broadcasting, in tune with the times and the people it had to serve."

Ellis would say of "the new radio": "Rather than being backed up to the wall by television, radio got off its podium, dropped its pomposity and put on its roller skates. It became mobile and started rolling around the country, mingling with citizens, collecting and reflecting reactions and opinions. Radio fought for its life successfully by taking off its tie and tails and slipping into sportsclothes."

Todd Storz

Todd Storz passed up a career in his family's Minneapolis brewery to venture into the radio business. KOWH, Omaha, Nebraska,
had gone on the air in 1922. It was a daytimer with no network. Its
four competitors were all full-time stations and all had networks. The
station had never really made much of a mark.

KOWH, of necessity, played music all day long — all kinds of
music. The often-told story has it that when Storz and his tiny staff
finished the workday, they generally stopped off to enjoy what for
some time has been called an "attitude adjustment hour."

They noticed that, although there were dozens of songs on the
bar's jukebox, patrons generally played just a few of the most popular songs — over and over. With little to lose, in 1949, Storz and his
staff embarked on a new kind of radio — "Top 40," 40 of the most
popular songs played over and over, all day long.

The format was successful enough that Storz bought more stations at what would turn out to be bargain prices. Many radio station managements were very critical of the format, calling it repeti-
tious, tiring, etc. But when the results in the rating books in Storz
markets became widely known, something like a Storz station
showed up in almost every big market. *Time* magazine did a piece
on Storz programming, before rock 'n' roll had become widely popular. The early Storz stations didn't play rock — it wasn't in the Top
40. When it arrived on the charts, it arrived on the Storz stations.

Broadcasting in America recalls that "In the early 1950s, a typical
hour on a Storz station included 125 program items" — 73 time signals, 58 repetitions of call letters, a $3\frac{1}{2}$-minute newscast featuring
accidents and assaults — each news item averaged two sentences in
length." The news was always scheduled five minutes before the
hour, so the Storz station could claim it was first with the news —
and so that the Storz station would be playing music while its competitors were doing news. The overall effect, the book says, "was
loud, brash, fast, hypnotic — and memorable."

Years later, the station group's advertising in publications targeted to time-buyers would say: "Wherever you live, there is a Storz station near you!" The copy went on to accurately say: "In every market there is a station — probably most stations — that are using program techniques pioneered by Storz."

Gordon McClendon

He was described by some of his radio competitors, and when he made an unsuccessful 1962 bid to unseat Texas Sen. Ralph Yarborough, as "a bankrupt huckster."

Following in the footsteps of comedian Ed Wynn and group broadcaster George Storer in the 1930s, a group of California broadcasters launched The Progressive Network in 1950. Like the others, it failed — in just two months. Another effort would last a little longer, but it too would fail.

Gordon McClendon was the son of a wealthy Texas oilman and theater owner. His venture into network radio was The Liberty Network. It went on the air in October 1950 with 240 stations — marginal properties in cities and small market stations.

The centerpiece of Liberty's programming was the baseball Game of the Day, with McClendon, identifying himself as the "Old Scotchman," doing the play-by-play account. On days when there was no major league baseball game available, the "Old Scotchman" re-created "great games of the past." He was articulate and dramatic. To this day, recordings of his Liberty broadcasts are prized by radio buffs and by baseball buffs as well.

(The idea of broadcasting the major league baseball game of top interest to fans, rather than following one team for a whole season, was an innovation in the late 1940s on WVLK, then at Versailles, Kentucky. The station was owned by the then Commissioner of Baseball, A.B. "Happy" Chandler. Apparently, Chandler just called each of the 16 major league teams, telling them what he wanted to do "on my little radio station." He would say later: "I don't think they asked me for any money."

(The dominant team in the area was the Cincinnati Reds — about 75 miles away. Their games were on a WVLK competitor. O.C. Halyard, then program director at WVLK, would recall: "The idea was a hit. We received telephone calls, telegrams and letters from hundreds and hundreds of fans as far as 100 miles away." He added: "It was a great programming idea. Funny thing, though, we only made one sale on it — a few spots each afternoon to a brewery." When the baseball owners fired Chandler in February 1950, the baseball game broadcasts stopped on his "little radio station.")

After a successful 1951 season of baseball broadcasts, Liberty ran into problems before its second season. Thirteen of the 16 major league teams withheld permission for the broadcasts. Meanwhile, Mutual, noting Liberty's success, started its "Game of the Day," obtaining rights from nine teams. Dizzy Dean, a Hall of Fame former pitcher with a natural bent for humor and unusual descriptions of what was happening on the field, was a nationwide hit, as he had been a regional hit in his early broadcasts in St. Louis.

Less than two months into the 1952 season, Liberty suspended operations and soon after filed for bankruptcy.

One of the assets that survived the bankruptcy court was KLIF, a station in the Dallas suburbs that had been the originating point for much of the Liberty Network programming.

McClendon soon installed the Top 40 format, with even more on-the-air energy than that employed by the Storz stations. McClendon translated his penchant for high drama, a trademark of his Liberty baseball broadcasts, into slick production values on KLIF and the other McClendon stations that would follow quickly.

His stations produced huge crowds at drive-in theaters for "exploitation" motion pictures. His stations would take a share of the gross and then broadcast heavy schedules of compelling radio ads, often voiced by McClendon himself.

The success of the movie ventures prompted McClendon to produce "exploitation" movies on the family's Texas ranch. As one McClendon contemporary said: "The movies were not artistic masterpieces, but I think they made money."

Obviously a radio buff as well as sports buff, McClendon no doubt remembered the 1940s success of the *Miss Hush* and *Stop the Music* prize giveaways. Big giveaways became a central feature of McClendon stations — most noteworthy, the "Treasure Hunts," with a $1,000 bill buried in the market. The audience listened to the station for clues — and the idea quickly spread across the country.

The manager of a conservatively programmed station, with a competitor programming McClendon-style, would say: "When the girls in my office skipped lunch to look for my competitor's $1,000 bill, I knew we had to change what we were doing."

McClendon in the 1960s proved to the industry that he was not a one-trick pony. He modified his Top 40 formula to switch some stations to "beautiful music." The music was different, but with the McClendon touch, softer and more subtle. KABL, San Francisco, and WYSL, Buffalo, New York, both scored huge ratings successes.

Two of McClendon's innovations did not score: His all-news

station (probably because of station coverage limitations) in Chicago was a failure. He got an FCC waiver to try out another of his creations — a station that broadcast nothing but classified ads 24 hours a day. KADS, an FM station, launched its format without success and was soon converted to a then-traditional FM music format — and sold.

McClendon retired in the '70s and lived on his ranch in near obscurity. Fred Welch, a several-year employee at his Shreveport, Louisiana, station, KEEL, said later: "I think the 1962 Senate race was the beginning of the end for Gordon."

A man of strong but, on balance, intelligent opinion, he often delivered editorials on his stations. They were short and to the point and, in Welch's words, "pretty effective."

In 1962, McClendon was, in Welch's words, "a Texas legend. But, he campaigned on television. When he came on TV, he was a lot different than what the people who had heard and heard about him had pictured. He was a man of modest height and modest good looks — not the hero type they expected. If he'd campaigned on the radio only, he might have won. Nobody ever knew as much about radio like Gordon did."

1960

The displaced radio engineers, mainly "chain break" staff announcers on radio network-affiliated stations, along with the live musicians and the management staffs who couldn't compete profitably in the more competitive advertising marketplace, knew that radio had been "reinvented." Radio people functioning well in the business knew it and were making the most of it. Most important, the audience knew it.

A 1938 Roper Poll revealed that radio listening was the fourth most popular leisure time activity. By 1960, it had fallen off the list. "Reinvented radio" was understood by the audience as something you enjoyed in concert with other activities: driving, doing household chores, working, etc.

The 1960 FCC Radio Financial Report

Just how radio had reinvented itself is illustrated graphically in the 1960 report. Network revenue had slipped from $124.6 million in 1950 to $35 million — an $89.6 million drop, or 72 percent. In the 1960 $591.9 million radio market — up 30.5 percent — the network's share dropped from 27.5 percent in 1950 to 5.9 percent in 1960. And the "O and Os," long a cash cow for the networks, had slipped from $110.5 million in 1950 to to $63 million in 1960. Not only were the networks losing money, the "O and Os" had lost a total of $10.7 million in three years (1958, 1959 and 1960).

National spot, by 1960, accounted for 34.1 percent of industry revenue — up from 26.2 percent 10 years earlier. Spot had grown by $83.3 million — +70 percent.

The star in radio's re-birth was local business, rising from $203.2 million in 1950 to $385.3 million — an increase of 90 percent. It now accounted for 65 cents out of every radio revenue dollar vs. 45 cents 10 years earlier and 29 cents just 20 years before.

Of the 3,381 AM stations on the air (an increase of 1,115 during the '50s), 68 percent were showing a profit.

The fortunes of FM stand alones (80 in 1950 — 218 in 1960) were also improving. All 80 stand alone FMs in 1950 reported losses — averaging more than $500 a week. In 1960, 23 percent were profitable (50 of 218).

With television in more than 90 percent of all homes, radio's doomsayers had clearly been proven wrong. Radio had found a way to survive, and even to flourish, alongside its television competitor.

How were all those "little" stations that many experts had advised against building? The FCC reported again on small station finances, including profit before tax figures. Stations in the 1950s had gone into such small places, the FCC included new breakdowns in its "community of license" breakdown:

	1 to 2,499	2,500 to 4,999	5,000 to 9,999	10,000 to 25,000
Revenue (Avg)	$52,899	$51,357	$67,915	$92,308
Pre-Tax Profit (Avg)	2,723	3,776	5,248	6,641

The profit figures look pretty good when you realize that the average small market station, exclusive of a studio/office building (generally leased at low rent), was being built for $20,000 or less in the 1950s — and profit figures generally came after the owner and, in increasing numbers, manager-owners paid themselves and enjoyed perks out of the business.

Program Schedule, WCYN, Cynthiana, Kentucky, 1957
Monday-Friday

6:00 News
6:06 Farm News
6:10 Top O'
Morning
7:00 News
7:10 Weather
7:15 Morning
Parade
(non rock pop)
7:30 5 Minutes to
Live By
7:35 Morning
Parade
8:00 News
8:05 Morning
Parade
8:45 Table Talk
of the day)
9:00 News
9:05 Women's
Club
(women's
features
and standards)

10:00 Hospital Report
10:05 Women's Club
10:30 Mystery Quiz
10:45 Hits for Mrs.
(non rock pop)
11:00 News
11:05 Hits for Mrs.
11:30 Tradin' Post
11:45 Livestock Mkts
11:50 Eddy Arnold
12:00 County Agent
12:15 News
12:30 Sons-Pioneers
12:45 Man On Street
1:00 News
1:05 Good Afternoon
(pop standards)
2:00 News
2:05 1400 Club
(non rock pop)
3:00 News
3:05 Merry Go Round
(Country)

4:00 News
4:05 Merry Go
5:00 News
5:05 Big 6
6:00 News
6:15 Sports
6:20 Dinner Music
7:00 News
7:05 Spinarama
(phone requests -
mostly rock 'n' roll
Headlines and
Sports hourly)
11:00 News and
Sports
11:05 Sign Off

Saturday

6:00 News
6:05 Morning
Parade
7:00 News
7:10 Weather
7:15 Morning
Parade
8:00 News
8:05 Morning
Parade
9:00 News
9:05 Dr Pepper
Silver Dollar
Man

10:00 Hospital Report
10:05 Hi Time (teens)
11:00 News
11:05 Hi Time
12:00 County (PS-ET)
12:15 News
12:30 SportsMatinee
12:45 Man On Street
1:00 News
1:05 SportsMatinee

1:00 News
1:05 SportsMatinee
2:00 News
2:05 SportsMatinee
3:00 News
3:05 SportsMatinee
4:00 News
4:05 SportsMatinee
5:00 Local Country
Bands
6:00 News
6:15 Sports
6:20 Country Bands
7:00 Spinarama
11:00 News/Sports
11:05 Sign Off

Sunday

7:00 Protest Hr.
(ET)
7:30 News
and features
7:30 Quartet
Time
8:00 Local
Religious
Programs

12:00 Guest Star (PS)
12:15 News & Review
12:30 Lawrence Welk
1:00 Guy Lombardo
1:30 Wayne King
2:00 Sammy Kaye
2:30 Sunday
Cynthiana
(non rock pop

5:45 Here's to
Vets (PS)
6:00 News
6:05 County Hymn
Sing (Live)
7:00 Public Serv
Programs (ET)
9:00 Classical
Music

10:00 Men's   & headlines)   10:00 Music Read
   Bible Class   By
10:30 Hymns   11:00 News/Sports
   All Faith   11:05 Sign Off
11:00 Local
   Churches

WCYN carries a year-round schedule of play-by-play sports: Cincinnati Reds Baseball with Waite Hoyt, University of Kentucky Football and Basketball, Local High School Football and Basketball, "Race of the Day" Thoroughbred Racing from Keenland and the "Little League Game of the Week." On-the-spot coverage of events of major interest is carried as available.

c h a p t e r   5

"SMALL MARKET RADIO'S GOLDEN AGE"
1961/1980

*"This is the damnedest business. I've sold a lot of sta-
tions to people who actually ran them down ...
and sold out at a profit."*

*The late G. Paul Crowder, station broker based in
Nashville, Tennessee*

137

c h a p t e r   5

"Small Market Radio's
Golden Age"

KGCX — 1961/1980

Ed Krebsbach's sons, Clair and Keith, had been with him at KGCX since the 1940s. Clair was commercial manager. In the 1960s, Ed suffered a terrible loss when son Keith was fatally struck by lightning while doing yard work at his home. Clair took over as manager, while Ed kept a close eye on the business as its president.

Ed Krebsbach died in 1971, 46 years after he and his band, The Syncopators, had made their first broadcasts on what a year later would become KGCX — operating out of the back room of the bank at Vida, Montana, population 27.

Clair operated the station, then at Sidney, with branch studios at Williston, North Dakota. Two years after his father died, Clair sold the station for $380,000 — a staggering 3,040 times the $125 the Vida Bank had paid for the "broadcasting set" on which the original broadcasts had had been transmitted.

The buyers were Oscar and Faye Halverson and Olaf and Borghild Folkyard. Their primary business was farming.

Oscar had also been a radio engineer (later a television station engineer) from the time he finished college after World War II. His first radio job had been at KGCX. After 11 years there, he moved to Texas to own and operate his own station, KSTV, Stephenville.

He and Faye became homesick, sold their Texas station and returned to their farm near Williston. At that time, he hired on as an engineer at KUMV-TV, the Williston station that had gone on the air in 1957.

"When I heard that Clair wanted to sell KGCX, I asked the Folkyards to join us in buying the station. KGCX was doing a good business — over $200,000 a year (equal to three times that in 1990s dollars). It was making a good profit," Halverson says. "We paid for

139

it ahead of schedule."

In 1981, the Halversons and Folkyards added a Class C FM station at Sidney. Halverson remembers: "It cost $150,000 to put on the air. It made that back in a year."

After selling KGCX, Clair Krebsbach, who had been around his father's station since his preschool years, purchased a motor home, first touring the United States, then shipping it to Europe, where he toured the continent. When he returned, he settled in Polson, Montana — 565 miles from Vida and Sidney. He managed 50,000-watt KERR-AM there until his retirement in the early 1990s.

The Country in the '60s and '70s

Cold War tensions were growing in the early '60s. Fallout shelters were built at 300 radio stations across the country — funded by the federal government's Civil Defense program.

The most memorable page in 1960s history would be recorded when President John F. Kennedy was assassinated. The Vietnam War would escalate into the longest and most divisive war since the Civil War. Civil rights activism increased to the burning point when large sections of the nation's major cities were laid waste by riots. Civil rights leader Dr. Martin Luther King was felled by an assassin's bullet. Two months later, presidential candidate Robert Kennedy was assassinated.

Despite the turmoil, the nation's economy continued to be healthy overall, but there would be troubling signs as the decade of the '60 passed into the 1970s.

Inflation averaged 1.32 percent per year during the first half of the 1960s — it nearly doubled from '65 to '69. The Gross National Product expanded an average of 6 percent per year in the 1960s — not fast enough to keep unemployment from averaging a full percentage point more than it had been in the 1950s — five percent versus four percent.

Average wages during the '60s grew from $4,734 to $7,564 per year, but inflation caused the dollar to lose 23 percent of its purchasing power. Real wages in the 1960s grew one-third less than in the 1950s. The strain on family budgets could be clearly seen in the increase of women in the work force. Married women made up 31.9 percent of the work force in 1960. By 1970, they were 40.5 percent — and 49.5 percent in 1980.

The 1970s would be marked by America losing its first war ever. It would be marked by the first presidential resignation ever.

Even though average wages would rise during the 1970s to $15,757, the buying power of the dollar would decline by more than one-half. Rising taxes, in concert with the shrinking buying power of the dollar, marked the first time since the Depression that real wages for the average worker declined.

From 1973 through 1979, inflation roared out of control at 7.6 percent, 13.9 percent, 14.1 percent, 8.7 percent, 11 percent, 12.4 percent and 13.3 percent. (The highest post-World War II inflation was a one-year 8.4 percent spurt in 1947.)

There were also two years of record post-World War II unemployment, in 1975 at 9.1 percent and 8.3 percent in 1976. The figure was twice that in several sections of the country. By the end of the 1970s, the 10-year average unemployment was 6.25 percent — 25 percent higher than in the 1960s, one-third more than the 1950s.

In the Small Towns

In the 1960s, the population of small towns and the rural areas was down less than 1 percent. In the 1970s, that population grew 10 percent to 59 million — the first growth there since the 1940s.

The Radio Business

That the radio business was more profitable in 1961 than it had been 10 years earlier is in large part a testament to new technology and increased operating efficiency. During the 1950s, the "radio pie" (revenues) got bigger, but the number of stations competing for a piece of that pie grew so fast that industry revenues divided by the number of stations fell 21 percent. And a 1960 dollar bought only 87 cents of what it had bought in 1950.

While all advertising increased by 110 percent, radio's share declined from 11 percent in 1950 to less than 6 percent by 1960. In the 1960s, the phenomenal growth of total advertising would slow to 63 percent, but radio's would grow by 88 percent and its share would rise to 7 percent.

Small Market Radio

Good stations in good small towns were proving themselves to be rewarding investments. Owners of small market stations in the 1960s included Governors Marvin Griffin in Georgia (WMGR, Bainbridge) and Edward T. Breathitt in Kentucky (WABD, Fort Campbell), and former Gov. Alf Landon in Kansas (KSCB, Liberal, and a station at Dodge City).

The owners included country/western stars Hank Snow and Ernest Tubb (WTCW, Whitesburg, Kentucky, WHBT, Harriman, Tennessee and KGRI, Henderson, Texas), Jim Reeves (WMTS, Murfreesboro, Tennessee, and a station in Texas) and Webb Pierce. Pierce made his station, WJAT, Swainsboro, Georgia, pay off by renting a 1,300-seat auditorium from which he conducted live stage shows featuring his friends in country music.

Bob Smith, one of TV's early stars on *Howdy Doody*, in the 1960s and 1970s had small stations in Maine, including WQDY, Calais. Another early network TV star, Dean Miller, of *December Bride*, bought WMVR, Sidney, Ohio. He still owns and operates it at this writing.

Two of network radio's (then television) top announcers invested in small market radio in the '60s and '70s — Rex Marshall in New England and Olin Tice in the Carolinas.

One of the great singing stars of network radio in the 1930s and 1940s, John Charles Thomas, owned and operated KQKL, Apple Valley, California, after his singing career ended.

When George Pleasants decided to buy WBUX, Doylestown, Pennsylvania, in Bucks County, he enlisted the financial help of some of the community's leading people, including television sportscaster Don Meredith and writer James Michener. The famous author was the station's president until it was sold in the early 1990s.

The FCC

When the National Broadcasters Association met in the spring of 1961, every attendee who could get one had a seat to hear the new Kennedy FCC chairman, Newton Minow. He delivered his famous "Vast Wasteland" speech, in which he told his audience of radio and TV managers: "It is not enough to cater to the nation's whims. You must also serve the nation's needs." It was easy to understand what the new commission head had in mind: Improve your programs or get off the air.

WDKD, Kingstree, South Carolina

The FCC's newly toughened stance would become visible almost immediately. The Eisenhower-era Commission, as early as 1958, was sending out warnings that it wanted what it called "topless radio" stopped.

One person in particular disregarding the Commission warning was a disc jockey on a small town daytimer in Kingstree, South Carolina, WDKD. Charlie Walker was then a middle-aged disc jockey with several stations on his resume.

A person who heard the Walker broadcasts says: "They sound pretty mild when you hear the 'shock jocks' of the 1980s and 1990s." He remembers these Charlie Walker broadcast comments:

> "If women's skirts get any shorter, they'll need two permanents."

> "When I was young, when I went out, my pants got wrinkled. Now it's what's in them that gets wrinkled."

Walker didn't have anything against "stealing" his material. He several times addressed the following remark to the local ministerial association:

> "If you ministers don't like what I say, you can kiss my ass. He's tied up in back of the station."

That remark was lifted from W.K. Henderson, who broadcast out of Shreveport, Louisiana, in the 1920s and 1930s. Henderson had directed it to the members of the Federal Radio Commission, who were after him and his radio station, KWKH.

WDKD was a little station, not very profitable and therefore not able to put up an expensive legal defense. It went off the air when the FCC revoked its license in 1962 for lewd broadcasts.

Charlie Walker soon found another disc jockeying job at another small station. He apparently toned down his shows.

Radio Gypsies

As the 1950s saw the end of such positions as station break announcers, operating engineers and paid live radio musicians, so too the '60s and '70s made radio gypsies a rare species.

Every station with a 25- to 50-year or more history has stories about announcers or disc jockeys "who passed through here." Some random stories:

When a "floater" showed up at one small station, he visited a small loan company on his lunch break. He told the manager: "I've come in to improve the station. I want to ask you for your suggestions." The loan company manager gave him a few suggestions and thanked him for asking his advice. The "floater," then matter-of-factly said: 'My bank hasn't transferred my funds yet. I wonder if you could lend me $300?" The loan company manager said later: "I almost made him the loan, but thought I'd better check him out. I told him the girl who wrote the checks wouldn't be back for a couple of hours, and asked him to come back then."

The lender, as soon as he left, started checking him out. He found a string of unpaid bills in a dozen towns where the young man had worked in less than 10 years.

When the "floater" returned to the loan company, the manager told him what he'd found. The "floater" replied calmly: "That's true — but I'll pay you because I like you." The loan was not made.

Another manager tells the story of a short-time employee with similar problems. He jokingly advised the itinerant announcer: "You've got a lot of good answers. I'll bet you've used every 'line' in the book. You'd make a great collector; deadbeats couldn't fool you."

The young man took the advice to heart. He operated a collection business part time from his apartment. He had great results in collecting bills for merchants — "slow pays and no pays." The problems was, he wasn't remitting to his customers. As the manager said, in relating the story: "If you don't get the money because a customer isn't paying, it's a problem. But, it's a bigger problem when the customer's paying and you don't have the money."

One "floater" worked up an ingenious method of paying his travel expenses from job-to-job. Soon after he'd arrive at a new station, he'd tell his new boss that the record library needed freshening up. He'd then tell him that his new apartment was too small to house his record collection, which he claimed had been given to him by record company representatives. He'd make a low-dollar deal, offering the records at 10 cents or 20 cents on the dollar. The manager bought.

Six or so months later, when he was off to another station "where they'll appreciate me," a lot of records were missing — including some of those he'd sold to the manager.

Another manager, who did the Noon News to keep in practice,

tells of looking into the control room to signal his talented new hire to read a commercial for the newscast's sponsor. To his horror, the young man was being escorted out of the station by two MPs. He was AWOL from the service.

Some of the "floaters" were misfits who had trouble getting along with co-workers, were not dependable and/or couldn't follow direction. Many were dreamers looking for a perfect job in an imperfect business in an imperfect world. A lot of them were talented people who couldn't put it all together. Some had fabulous senses of humor, such as the young floater who ran ads in *Broadcasting* that included a great line: "Would like living wage, but will work for the usual."

The "floaters" were largely put out of business by managers who rightly believed that a radio personality, no matter how talented, was a detriment to the station when his bad credit caused bad feeling in the business community. More station managements invested time and effort into training local people instead of shopping for an out-of-towner with a resume that would prove to include a lot of bad entries.

A growing number of radio stations were operating with directional arrays, requiring a first-class license on duty at all times the station was on the air. Many of the combo announcer/engineer "gypsies" were not good at either. They got jobs simply because they had that piece of paper. The FCC relieved the operators of that burden in the early 1970s, when they relaxed the rules to allow use of operators with restricted licenses to operate directional stations.

Another thing that put the gypsies out of business was the change in the type of people managing most small stations. As the years passed, there were more people who had their own money invested (or wanted to).

Bill Taylor, now owner of KQSS, Miami, Arizona, tells about his first radio boss. "He had his shortcomings, but he gave me my first chance.

"John Cashion, then at WGCD, Chester, South Carolina, hired me over the phone. I was working at WLBC-TV, Muncie, Indiana, as an engineer. I wanted to be a disc jockey.

"I pulled up to the radio station. There was John with a paper bag next to his chair at the control board. He was on the air. He was talking (on the air) about the 'most pregnant woman I've ever seen.' He broadcast her name. He then announced: 'Here's one of those gut bucket songs the kids all like.' He then played Pat Boone's record of

Ain't That A Shame.

"When he saw me, he called in somebody to finish his show. He took me to the Moose Lodge and got me drunk. He took me home, saying: 'I'll see you in the morning.'

"John had been 'sent down' by the station's new owners in North Carolina. John's drinking and lack of management ability soon lost him his job at WGCD. His air talent got him a job doing a daily record show on WORD, Spartanburg. When he died in the '60s, it was the biggest funeral Spartanburg had ever seen."

FM

The first FM stations had gone on the air 21 years earlier, when, in 1961, the FCC approved FM stereo transmission. First high fidelity, then stereo records had come out in the 1950s, building a market for the former languishing FM medium.

Soon after making the stereophonic FM ruling, the FCC issued a Table of Assignments with new spacing rules. The first AM-FM radios appeared in 1963 model cars.

With the new enthusiasm for the attention at the Commission and the growing interest in hi-fi and stereo music by the public, FM radio finally looked like a "real business." Within five years of the stereo ruling, 631 new stations were built. In 10 years, the total of new stations was 1,968.

Most of the FM station builders were AM station owners who wanted to hedge their bets just in case, as some people were predicting, FM might replace AM radio. The thing that made building an FM station to combo with an AM station the way to go was a late 1950s invention of a longtime West Coast broadcaster, Rogan Jones. He had owned KPQ in Wenatchee, Washington, since 1932. He also owned a station in Bellingham, Washington, KGMI.

Jon Holiday, now a syndicated music producer, was a young owner-manager in the South when he was invited to visit an Atlanta hotel to witness a demonstration of Jones' I.G.M. system. He recalls: "The salesman, as part of his pitch, said that Jones had invented the 'automated station' because he was tired of announcers leaving without notice and tuning in to announcers playing music outside the format. The salesman said: 'Mr. Jones is using the system on his own stations.' "

The tapes on the reel-to-reel machines were made at I.G.M.

mainly from records from Rogan Jones' own collection, said to be at the time worth a million dollars. An AM station could separately program its FM station, using I.G.M. equipment and tapes, monitored by its AM announcer.

The new FM stations, coming on the air with music different from what was being played on AM and a lot fewer commercials, sparked a dramatic increase in sales of radio sets. From 1961 to 1965, radio set sales averaged about 20 million a year. In 1966, they jumped dramatically to 32 million (60 percent) and averaged 34 million the remainder of the decade.

In 1965, the FCC further spurred FM growth by mandating that stations in communities of 100,000 or more could only simulcast 50 percent of the time. New FM programming followed: CBS, for its own FM stations, came forth with the "Young Sound," programming designed to reach a younger audience than that enjoyed by the typical FM station then and its AM radio stations. Others followed, like Burkhardt-Abrams with an "album rock" format hosted by local disc jockeys, and Bill Drake with a "soft rock" format called "Hit Parade."

The biggest winner in the FM programming derby was Jim Schulke. He was contracted by the FM association to find a winning format for an FM station. After the research was completed and paid for, he launched his production company. His product, which radio industry critics called "elevator music," was an almost-instant success. His client station in Phoenix, Arizona, was the first FM station to be Arbitron ranked No. 1 (1969). His client in Grand Rapids did the same a year later (1970).

Nationwide, FM radio listening surpassed AM in 1978. In the mid-1990s, FM accounts for roughly 75 percent of radio listening, AM 25 percent nationwide.

FM in the Small Markets

When the FM Table of Assignments came out in 1962, AM station owners anxiously looked for their town on the list. Often, they were relieved when it was not on the list. FM, while showing promise in the cities, was impacting negatively on the operating statements of small AM stations built in the 1940s and 1950s. These were mainly full-time AM stations.

Daytime stations felt a little differently. Their customers and listeners often expressed disappointment that their local station wasn't carrying the high school games like the station in "the next town did."

However, a good, well-managed daytimer generally enjoyed a wider profit margin because it didn't have to cover unprofitable nighttime. Even local sports was generally a 50 cents on the dollar proposition after all the direct expenses were figured against the advertising sold on the game.

As the late Elmo Mills, owner of several small town AM stations (some full time, others daytime), said: "I'm going to file in all of my towns. It's going to cost me money — but, I think not doing it will cost me more in the long run."

Where the assignments were not applied for, outsiders did file. Initially, these "second stations" in small towns had an uphill battle. As Billy Evans, who built stand alone WQXE at Elizabethtown, Kentucky, in 1969 says, only slightly humorously now: "During the first 10 years, we went broke 100 times."

His FM was competing with a 20-year-old Class IV AM, WIEL, well-managed for years by Walter "Dee" Huddleston, later to become a U.S. senator. Ultimately, WIEL bought a nearby Class A FM. "The town grew," he says. "I think we're both doing well now."

Joe Young built WYTM at Fayetteville, Tennessee (population 7,500), which had two AM stations: a Class IV (WEKR) and a regional daytimer that went off the air in the 1980s. Twenty years after going on the air, Young recalls: "The first 10 years we barely stayed in business by being an alternative to real radio. By 1980, we decided our station could be a real radio station. We started carrying high school sports with great success. Our FM signal was far superior at night to WEKR's."

In the early 1990s, the owner of WEKR was afflicted with a terminal disease. Young bought WEKR, and the town is once again a one-operator radio town, with what Young calls "real radio on both stations."

Stand Alone Builders

In 40 years, Mike Freeland would own 22 radio stations. In the 1950s, he had built AM-daytimer WHDM, McKenzie, Tennessee (population 4,200). When he moved to town, "on the longest, easiest terms you could imagine," he says, he acquired a mansion, complete with its own tennis courts. In 1965, he approached the late Earl Nolting, to whom he'd sold WHDM eight years before, about buying it back. Nolting later said: "He didn't want to pay me any more than I'd paid him. I'd improved the station and thought I deserved a profit."

Freeland decided he wanted to move back into his mansion, so he filed for an FM station at McKenzie. After he'd been on the air a couple of years, with the FM station, WWYN, located by his living quarters in the mansion, Nolting would say: "I think he's making money — and I'm surprised that he hasn't hurt my business. My customers are almost all spending money with him. It's a shame I didn't know they had that much to spend."

Obviously, Freeland's audacious McKenzie investment was doing well enough that he went into towns without radio stations with new FMs.

Tennessee, with its low AM radio ground conductivity, was saturated with radio stations. Freeland says: "All the good towns, and most of the bad towns, were taken." Freeland looked north to Indiana and Illinois. There, he found towns of 4,000, 5,000, 6,000 — even 10,000 population with "good-looking Main Streets." Unlike Tennessee, Indiana and Illinois had high ground conductivity and fewer AM stations could be wedged in than in the South.

A year after he'd started his McKenzie venture, he put what is now WJNZ on the air at Greencastle, Indiana, a university town of 6,500.

Freeland didn't program the station as an "alternative to real radio." He would say: "I couldn't do that, even if it had been the right thing to do. All I knew was 'real radio.' "

The approach at Greencastle was the same as he'd done in every one of his stations, before and after — "good small town programming." This was coupled with what a longtime Freeland watcher called "a very superior selling effort."

Freeland critics claimed that he'd taken a course in hypnosis and used "hypnotic spells" to sell advertising. That was never proven. What is known is that he had acquired, over the years, an advanced degree in physiology and probably, as he claimed, "had read every book ever written on selling."

As was his pattern, other stand alone FM stations went on the air in the black, were operated profitably for a couple of years, then sold at a profit.

In the 1980s, Freeland would venture outside the radio business into farming, land speculation and banking investment. The domino effect set in and he lost all his business investments, including his last radio station.

The day after the radio station was sold in bankruptcy proceedings, Freeland, then 67, said: "There's always another mountain to climb. I will probably do full time now what I've been doing part time for years — college teaching. I have a lot of experience to contribute — a lot good, some bad."

Until 1970, building a stand alone FM station, even in a town with an AM competitor, was seen by most as a very risky venture. Stations that had tried it and failed little more than 10 years before were vivid memories. Even so, a dozen were built in Indiana, half that many in Ohio and Illinois. The numbers were small in other states. Although some were not great financial successes initially, they all survived.

The Kennedy FCC

Newton Minow quickly proved that his strident talk at the 1961 NAB Convention was more than just words. Stations would be fined for the first time. The first fine, $10,000, was issued to KDWB, Minneapolis, for "repeated technical violations."

Stations were told to ascertain the needs of their communities. When license renewal time came, they were told, a station's license renewal would be based on how well its performance measured up to the promises it had made when its license has been renewed previously. In 1962, the Commission renewed the license of KORD, Pasco, Washington, for only one year, on that issue.

In a speech, Minow had compared listening to many radio stations with being assaulted by a "barker in a bazaar." Broadcasters were told to reduce the amount of time they were devoting to commercials.

The Torch Passes

When John F. Kennedy was assassinated, his vice president, Lyndon Baines Johnson, succeeded him. Johnson was the richest man ever to occupy the White House. That wealth came mainly from his wife's investment in Texas radio and television stations. Johnson also carried the stigma of being thought of widely as a "typical Texas wheeler-dealer." Would the tough regulatory stance of the Kennedy Commission be eased by a man who "knew our business?"

It wasn't!

After Johnson won a term in his own right, "his" FCC put teeth into some of the warnings issued by the previous FCC It adopted "acceptable" commercial limits, 18 minutes per hour set forth in the industry's own code of good practices (the NAB Code). Small market broadcasters quickly turned that into a benefit to their operations.

For the first time, commercial time was not an unlimited commodity — it had real value. Stations responded to the FCC rule by shortening their average ads from one minute to one-half minute. They told their customers rightly that frequency was the important thing and that you could usually say as much in 30 seconds as you'd been saying in a minute. (If a customer insisted on a minute, he was generally charged one-third to one-half extra. Most ran 30-second ads.)

The "dollar a hollar shotgun stations" that were found widely in poor but overcrowded markets in wide areas of the South became relics. (Those featured $1 spots "fired" in rapid succession in clusters between records.)

The Commission had, for several years, believed that "double billing" was widespread and dishonest. In 1965, it outlawed the practice, threatening stations found guilty with revocation of their licenses. That practice quickly disappeared, except in one notable instance.

The Berlin, New Hampshire, Case

Bob Powell had gotten into radio after World War II. After working at small market stations, he moved up to stations in Pittsburgh and Philadelphia, and finally to WNEW, New York City. In 1957, he says: "I was doing the all-night show, wondering, as you do in your mid-30s, is this really what I want to do the rest of my life?" Powell decided it was time for a change. That change came quickly when he found a small town printing and newspaper business in Vermont. By the late '60s, that business was doing so well that he contacted Blackburn Company, media brokers, to tell them that he'd like to buy a radio station. In 1969, he bought WMOU, Berlin, New Hampshire. The station had been on the air since 1938. "The station was solid, the management seemed to be very good, so I decided to be an absentee owner."

It was 13 years after the FCC passed its rule against "double billing" when the Commission refused to renew the licenses of WMOU-AM/FM and competing AM station WBRL.

In the hearings that preceded the action, WMOU pleaded

"business necessity." Its lawyers summoned the management of the other radio station and the local newspaper, who both, under oath, admitted to sometimes issuing fraudulent billings to advertisers.

A local appliance dealer said he often submitted fraudulent bills to collect excessive co-op reimbursement. One of the factory representatives who called on him said that he knew of the practice, but didn't see anything wrong with it.

Nevertheless, the $22,000 in inflated bills the station was found to have issued was sufficient grounds to take the licenses away. The station appealed to an appeals court which, in addition to upholding the FCC, said that fraudulent billing also violated mail fraud statutes.

Bob Powell spent $150,000 in legal fees in his unsuccessful fight. He says, 20 years after the incident: "I didn't know the people at the station were doing it, but I should have made it my business to know."

When the Commission opened the AM and FM to new applicants, one of them was Stephen Powell, just out of Harvard Business School. His challengers charged that he was just a "front for his father." But Stephen was a qualified applicant, and they saw no reason not to believe that Bob would have nothing to do with the new operation, even though he had agreed to lend Stephen money. That, said the Commission, "was nothing more than any parent who could, would do for a son."

There were three applicants. One withdrew for his expenses in seeking the licenses. Another settled for the AM facility. The third, Stephen, was awarded the FM license.

He decided to upgrade the FM license to full power with an antenna 3,870 feet above average terrain. The station, WZPK, programming a CHR format, became a regional success story.

WMOU did not fare well under its new owner. It left the air in the late 1980s. When WBRL became available to applicants, there were no takers. It, too, went off the air.

Stephen thought Berlin should have a local AM station. He applied for and was granted the Class IV facility. He says: "Candidly, it doesn't make a lot of money, but it's good for the town."

Ironically, in 1986, the FCC deleted the fraudulent billing rules, leaving it to other government agencies and competition in the marketplace to "keep the bills honest."

The Networks Return to Profitability

In the 1960s, network programming was distributed to stations over expensive leased telephone lines. Fewer than 1,000 of the nation's 5,000 radio stations were on national networks.

It was ABC, which had nearly decided to close down its radio network in 1957, that came up with a unique idea that would be copied by the three other national networks of the time.

By 1967, ABC was programming mostly newscasts on the hour and some sportscasts. The management decided the answer to making the network profitable was using the telephone lines more and increasing the amount of time it could sell.

It submitted a plan to the FCC that called for the broadcast of four separate newscasts and feature programs aimed at stations with different formats. At five minutes before the hour, there would be a fast-paced five-minute newscast favored by Top 40 stations like ABC's O-and-O highly successful WABC, New York, and WLS, Chicago.

On the hour, there would be a 10-minute newscast for talk and news stations like ABC-owned KABC, Los Angeles, and KGO, San Francisco; at 15 past the hour, a "laid back" five-minute newscast for FM stations. On the half hour was a five-minute newscast designed for middle-of-the road stations.

The network asked that the prohibition against a network having more than one affiliate in a market be ended so that ABC could have one station per market for each of its services. The Commission approved, and the service became an instant success.

The other networks followed, Mutual adding a network targeted to black stations and several feeds of its main service, so a station could run its network news at its discretion. NBC added *The Source* for rock FM stations, CBS *Radio Radio* for other rock FM stations.

Mutual pioneered distributing its programs by satellite, enjoying better quality and considerably lower distribution costs than by telephone lines. Mutual went on the "bird" in 1975. The other networks followed.

The networks also ventured into long-form programming. An NBC attempt at a 'round-the-clock constant news and information service was a costly and short-lived effort. ABC had a big failure in the 1980s with a 24-hour talk network. In the early 1990s, there would be a consolidation in the radio network business. At this writing, there are three major companies in the business: CBS, ABC and Infinity. Virtually every station carries some network programming. Unbelievably, the long-suffering Mutual Network shares at least equal status with the oldest network, NBC, in the far-flung Infinity portfolio.

Thanks to the innovation and the technological advances of the '60s and '70s, network radio programming would become available to even the smallest, most remote radio stations. Although the programming is available almost universally, the network share of radio revenues remains less than 4 percent of the total vs. 43 percent at the end of World War II. But, the radio network business in the mid-1990s is solidly profitable.

1970 FCC Radio Financial Report

Radio had had its third billion-dollar year, with total industry sales coming in at $1.257 billion. The national networks got only $50.9 million (3.9 percent of the total), but that was better than earlier in the decade.

Their 20 owned-and-operated stations were doing better, too, making a combined profit of $1.7 million after losing a combined $9.7 million between 1967 and 1969.

Radio's good news was apparently being enjoyed throughout the industry — particularly in the small markets:

Community size	01 to 2,499	2,500 to 4,999	5,000 to 9,999	10,000 to 25,000
1970 Avg.	$80,060	$86,000	$108,000	$155,000
1960 Avg.	$52,899	$51,357	$67,415	$92,308
	+$27,161	+$34,643	+$40,585	+$62,692

Inflation was up 31 percent for the decade. Station revenues had grown by an average of 57 percent.

There were 2,872 AM stations on the air and 2,061 FM stations, of which 506 were FM stand alones, 208 of them in non-metropolitan communities. The average gross of non-metro FM stand alones was $40,532.

Three radio stations went silent in 1970.

1970 was the first year of the ban on cigarette advertising.

Television advertising was down 0.4 percent. Radio was up 4.7 percent.

Goodbye to an Old Customer

In the glory days of network radio, their No. 1 customers were the tobacco companies. In 1969, they lost a combined $6.9 million. At their lowest ebb, they scored one of network radio's greatest successes.

One of the tobacco companies had developed what they called a "safer cigarette." They were in a hurry to get it to market. There wasn't time to create, execute and schedule a big TV campaign, so they turned to network radio.

The commercials began on the networks on a weekend. There wasn't time for anything fancy — just cold copy, without sound effects, music or actors. The copy simply told customers about the product and asked listeners to try it. The cigarettes started moving off the shelves in large volume immediately. Listeners wanted to find out if, as the one of the most memorable ad closings ever asked: "Shouldn't Your Cigarette Be TRUE?"

Thinking Big in Little Places

The average station in a town of 13,000 was doing about $125,000 a year. A man in Missouri was doing more than $300,000, and he was going to tell how he was doing it.

Jerrell Shepherd had spent World War II in the Air Force. He would say later of that experience: "There is no room for creativity in that kind of thing. There's only one way to do it — the right way."

To the amazement of his friends, when he returned from the service he got into the radio business, a business made up of individuals and creative types, so unlike the Air Force. Jerrell and his brother-in-law, C.R. Horne, formed a partnership to build KARV, Russellville, Arkansas.

Of his year at Russellville, Shepherd would recall: "We did things a lot of other stations did — maybe a little better. I wrote most of the copy and, modestly, I'll say it was pretty good. We carried primarily institutional ads, like most stations.

"I remember our first business slowdown. Those things happen every so often in little towns. We had a lot of cancellations. The businesses said there was nothing wrong with their radio advertising. They assured us they'd be back on when business picked up.

"One of our customers was a small grocery store. He didn't cancel. Actually, he doubled his schedule. 'Things are tough,' he said.

'We've got to get more people in here.'

"That customer taught me something. He never ran institutional ads. They always featured a lot of prices and items. When I sold him originally, I didn't suggest that. That's what he wanted," Shepherd says. "I never admitted it, but I was subconsciously afraid that if nobody went in to buy those advertised items, a customer would cancel. The listeners went in and bought what they'd heard on the radio. He never canceled. He kept buying more."

By the time Shepherd got to Moberly, where he built KWIX in 1950, he encouraged, but never insisted, that specific items and prices be featured in radio ads. KWIX did well enough for Shepherd to buy, then sell at good profits, stations in Hannibal (KHMO) and Jefferson City (KLIK).

In the mid-60s, KWIX was grossing $150,000 a year — a good figure. "But," he recalled, "my Air Force experience made me a strong believer in a chain of command with good people in key positions. Those key people often told me: 'If we were doing more business, we could hire more people, better people, and keep them longer. We could buy more equipment.' " Shepherd decided to do something about it.

At the NAB convention in the spring of 1967, the printed program carried, among dozens of other itinerary items: "How I Do $300,000 a Year in a Town of 13,000."

The room was packed with small town operators, and a lot of operators from cities who weren't doing $300,000 a year. (In 1970, the 12 stations in Phoenix were averaging only $306,000 each.) The attendees had, no doubt, expected to hear a high-powered recitation of glitzy programming and promotion ideas. Instead, they got a low-key, down-to-earth talk about "how it's done in Moberly."

He told, first, why he decided to make his a high-gross radio station, telling of his trips several hundreds of miles from his station to KICD, Spencer, Iowa, and KOEL, Oelwein, Iowa — two stations that had for years achieved high grosses thanks to the determination of their operators — Ben Sanders at Spencer and Walt Teich, later Paul Ruse and Ray Leafstedt, at Oelwein. Shepherd said: "I picked up a lot of good ideas from both of them." He did not clone them.

At KWIX, the music, he said, was non-controversial, right down the middle of the road. There were no station jingles and no disc jockeys. Instead, the steady stream of local news, sports, farm and business information was delivered by what Shepherd described as communicators. Each one took turns hosting a segment of the programming, then gathering the information from the station's area or doing a segment of listener want ads, conducting phone-in shows, interviewing area coaches and players, doing play-by-play and doing on-the-spot coverage of area events.

Early on, Shepherd was a syndicated music client. He says: "By getting the music out of the station, we get people interested in the community. They're a lot easier to get along with than people who are into music."

Shepherd told his listeners: "You probably won't like the way our station sounds, but you don't live in the nine counties we call 'Kwix-land.'"

Shepherd then described his commercial policies at KWIX. The most shocking aspect was the fact that there were no public service spots on the station. He asked: "If ads are the only thing you have to sell, how can you afford to give them away?"

(Over the years, Shepherd's policy on public service spots set up an uneasy relationship with the FCC. The renewal forms at that time asked how many public service spots the station had carried in its sample week and how many it intended to carry during the following license period. When the Shepherd renewal applications showed up at the Commission saying that no public spots had been carried or would be carried, a flurry of letter-writing began. Shepherd would explain in great detail that his station had carried so many news reports, interviews and other programming on behalf of public service organizations — but no free spots. Although the Commission did not approve of the Shepherd policy, the licenses were always renewed. "We felt that we were on solid enough legal ground that they weren't going to actually challenge us," Shepherd would say years later.)

In addition to the no free public service spots, another Shepherd commercial policy seemed radical to many attending. The station sold only 30-second ads. A customer could buy, but was never sold, a 60-second ad — at twice the 30-second rate.

The station by then not only recommended, but insisted that every ad on the station include items and prices. No institutional copy was accepted. Shepherd said he firmly believed that stating a price was absolutely necessary to a listener in making a decision to investigate an offer being made in a radio ad. Shepherd asked his audience to "look at the newspaper — 85 percent of the ads are price and item."

The 30-second ads on KWIX did not utilize sound effects,

music backgrounds, multiple voices, etc. They were 30-second ads, delivered in a friendly, conversational tone.

The rates were "flat." The largest customers paid about the same as the smallest. "If you don't do that, a few big customers will dominate your station. The medium-size and small businesses will shy away from you, feeling that they won't be heard, but drowned out by the big ones," Shepherd theorized. His station was sold as "basic advertising," not as a supplement to other media. He was opposed to "media mix." He said firmly: "We believe KWIX can do it all."

Exchanging ideas on the Shepherd "basic medium" stance was the operator of KIMB, Kimball, Nebraska, now a group operator in Nebraska and Colorado. Norton Warner, first of all, believed that a radio station "was not in the music business, or the news business, or the sports business, or even the public service business. We do all of those things well to make the business better — the advertising business."

Warner, like Shepherd, believed a station had to earn big investments from advertisers. In both their stations, a fact-finding call was the first step in the selling process. The centerpiece of that call was "The Marketing Bridge," which Warner said he devised in the college marketing class he had taken. (See illustration next page). After the fact-finding call, the radio salesperson returned with a plan designed to help the client reach specific goals he'd mentioned during the fact-finding call. (Warner in the '80s developed a videotape series called *The Concept* in which his sales theories are demonstrated to station managers and salespeople.)

Few in the audience were willing to embrace the Shepherd "Moberly Story" completely. Most came away with a new idea about the potential of their radio stations. Almost universally, elements of the Shepherd way of doing business showed up in the operation of their stations.

KWIX (and later KRES-FM) were visited by scores of broadcasters from all over the country. Still more broadcasters heard the "Moberly Story" at state broadcasters' conventions nationwide.

Some myths grew about Shepherd over the years that should be dispelled. He did not, as was often told, build his sales by hiring big-time salesmen from stations in St. Louis and Kansas City. For most of his salespeople, he went outside the radio business. He was not generally interested in the typical Package of the Week or Promotion of the Month time salesman, no matter how skilled. Instead, he hired salespeople from other fields like home improvements, automobiles,

ADVERTISING:
Proper Media
Quantity
Consistency
Planning
Timeliness

PRICE: Value

PRICE: Competition

MERCHANDISE:
Clean
Attractive Display
Lighting
Properly Marked
Orderly
Timely

THE BUSINESS:
Quality Product
Location
Reputation
Service
Delivery
Financing
Parking
Business Vitality

PERSONAL SELLING:
Product Knowledge
Suggestion Selling
Product Benefits
Sincere
Helpful
Cheerful
Smiling
Well-Groomed

THE COMMUNICATIONS PROCESS:
Unawareness — to — Awareness — to — Comprehension — to — Conviction — to — ACTION!

— Norton Warner,
"The Concept"
4343 O Street
Omaha, NE 68510

real estate, insurance. He would say: "We were selling radio differently. I didn't want to have to take a lot of time to break what I thought were bad habits." He also went outside the industry for his training materials, feeling that companies like IBM, Xerox and the major insurance companies were light years ahead of radio in their sales training.

Myth No. 2: Shepherd was very hard to work for. On the contrary, several of his former employees say that perhaps his greatest ability is keeping the level of enthusiasm high. For years, visitors to the Moberly station were astonished to find, posted on a blackboard for everyone to see, the station's gross, percent attained of the monthly goal and comparison with the year before. Shepherd always said: "We do that to keep everyone, not just the salespeople, focused on the business — the advertising business. (Shepherd has long had a monthly rewards system for his non-salespeople.)

Myth No. 3: Moberly is a unique place, and radio business could not be done that way anyplace else. In the '80s, Shepherd built KAAN-AM/FM, Bethany, and bought KREI/KTJJ, Farmington, and KJEL/KIRK, Lebanon, all Missouri. Although the scale is different and sometimes acquisitions have taken patience, the "Moberly Story" has been duplicated in each of those operations.

Myth No. 4: Shepherd is a one-dimensional man who knows little about anything but radio. The truth is, for years he has had an extensive farming operation, best known for its production of pecans, and a prize herd of buffalo. In the early years, when the high-gross radio operation was in its beginnings, he told friends over dinner, matter of factly: "I'm pretty sure the buffalo herd is worth more than the radio station."

Myth No. 5: Shepherd is an intense, hard-driving, humorless man. Tom Donnelly and most of his present and former employees see him quite differently. Donnelly was a young salesman at one of the stations owned by Jerrell's in-laws. Tom, longtime owner of KRJH, Hallettsville, Texas, remembers attending sales meetings where the two families' stations' salespeople would meet together. Jerrell conducted the meetings.

Jerrell, he says, was a great storyteller. "When he'd start telling one that he'd told before, he'd look at the crowd and would realize what he was about to do. He'd quickly say: 'Oh, your remember that. It's Number 16.' The salespeople would howl. More important, I remember some of the illustrations he'd use," Donnelly says.

"The salespeople," Donnelly remembers, "were all straight commission. Shepherd was lecturing the discipline a salesperson was supposed to follow.

"One of the salespeople," Donnelly recalls, "got up and said: 'Look, we're on straight commission. We work for ourselves. We should be allowed, if we want, to take an afternoon off, set our own hours.'"

Shepherd walked over to a blackboard that he used in conducting the meetings. In very small print, he wrote: "15 percent." In much larger print he wrote: "85 percent." He then said, pointing at the 15 percent: "That's you." Then, pointing to the 85 percent, he said: "That's me." He paused, then said: "If you don't remember anything else, remember that 85 percent is always bigger than 15 percent." Donnelly says: "I've used that 100 times."

Dealing With the Traumas of the '60s and '80s

When racial unrest laid waste to large parts of the major cities in the 1960s, most small towns suffered little. As the mayor of one small town said: "We don't have enough people here to have much of a riot."

Not all small towns were so lucky, though. Cairo, on the banks of the Ohio River in southern Illinois, still shows the scars of racial violence that occurred there more than 30 years ago.

In another small town, the theater owner angrily called the manager of the local radio station, complaining: "One of your announcers is carrying a sign out in front of my show, demanding that I let 'coloreds' sit on the first floor." The station manager replied calmly: "He won't be there much longer. His shift starts in 10 minutes." The theater manager replied: "That's good."

Soon, like the story line in the motion picture *The Last Picture Show*, movie business got so bad, he was glad to have patrons of any color sitting anyplace in his theater.

When the Vietnam conflict broke out, community tributes to the first fallen local man were often held and broadcast live on the local radio station.

Station managers, like their fellow small town businessmen and women, generally held views close to the center in the emotional issues that dominated the 1960s and 1970s. Business conditions aside, the 1959 Fairness Doctrine made expressing strong opinion on the air inadvisable.

Two small stations ran into Fairness Doctrine trouble. The most famous was in the small town of Red Lion, Pennsylvania, where local station WGCB-AM/FM carried the daily paid broadcast of conservative preacher Billy Joe Hargis.

Hargis, on a taped broadcast carried by the Red Lion station and other stations nationwide, attacked Fred Cook, who had been critical of the GOP 1964 presidential candidate, Barry Goldwater. Cook wrote to WGCB and other stations carrying the Hargis broadcast, demanding time to reply to Hargis' "attack." The station sent him a letter saying he could buy time, as Hargis had (enclosing a rate card).

Cook, who, it turned out, was in the employ of the Democratic Party, went first to the FCC, then through the courts, ultimately to the Supreme Court. In an opinion, the high court said, in effect, that the Red Lion station and others had an obligation to make free time available for contrasting views.

In another case, a station got a strong reprimand for "doing nothing." The United States Chamber of Commerce mailed tapes to stations in West Virginia arguing against a proposed strip mining bill. A congresswoman from the area sent a tape out in favor of the bill.

WHAR, Clarksburg, West Virginia, which had not run the Chamber tape, refused the congresswoman. She and others complained to the FCC, which ruled that the station's failure to air either side of the issue was a violation of the Fairness Doctrine, for "failure to bring up an issue of great local importance."

The Fairness Doctrine was eliminated in 1987 by the FCC Efforts to revive it, at this writing, have been unsuccessful.

Taking a Stand — Loud and Clear

Even with the Fairness Doctrine constraints, some small stations did speak out, taking a high-profile activist stance. One was a feisty lady in the small town of Fredericksburg, Texas, named Alene Wendel Fritz.

From the time she and her engineer husband, Norbert, bought KNAF in the late 1940s, she took a central role in the operation. She conducted the small town staple women's program and served as a disc jockey, quickly becoming known as the "Polka Queen of the Hills." Fredericksburg is in Texas' rolling Hill Country.

She used her microphone in the 1970s to stop a U.S. Navy proposal endorsed by no less than the powerful U.S. Sen. John Tower. The proposal was to bury low-frequency transmission lines through the Hill Country. The lines, even the Navy and senator agreed, would have destroyed many trees and gutted much of the countryside. It would have crisscrossed the entire area.

The San Antonio newspaper, 60 miles away, wrote at the time of Mrs. Fritz's death in 1993: "Her broadcasts stirred up so much public sentiment against it, that despite the Navy brass and senator's pressure, when she didn't back off, the project was dropped."

A New Industry

Ed Livermore was the owner of a very profitable group of small town Oklahoma newspapers. Over the years, he had bought several failing small radio stations in some of his newspaper towns.

By 1970, after years of pressure, the FCC was considering a rule for newspaper owners to sell either their co-located papers or radio stations. Livermore decided that when the edict finally came, there would be so many stations on the market that the sale prices would drop appreciably. Like most of his fellow newspaper-radio owners, he was primarily a newspaper man. It would have been out of the question for him to stay in the radio business and leave the newspaper business.

One of the casualties of the Livermore decision was 33-year-old Jim Williams. He had spent all of his working life in radio, first as a "not very good radio announcer," then a dozen years with Livermore as a salesman, then manager. At the time of Livermore's decision to sell his stations, Williams was manager of what is now KCOJ, Sapulpa, Oklahoma, "a high-dial daytimer" not far from Tulsa.

"Mr. Livermore offered me a job as editor of one of his newspapers, but I knew I didn't have much talent for that sort of thing." Williams says, only half-jokingly: "I didn't have that first prerequisite for that job. I'm not a very good speller."

Williams says: "I wanted to go into business for myself, but I didn't have the money to buy a radio station. I was amazed to find that of the about 600 colleges and universities offering courses in radio, only a handful offered a course in selling radio advertising, and those were only a couple of credit hours. I decided to set up a school to train beginning radio salespeople." And so, the Welsh Company was born. The name refers to Williams' ancestry.

Prior to the 1970 birth of the Welsh Company, there was little training for radio salespeople. Fred Palmer is generally acknowledged as radio's first radio sales trainer. (In the 1940s, Palmer got fired from his job as manager of WCKY, Cincinnati, by the station owner, the late L.B. Wilson. Palmer had made friends with the manager of the hotel where the station's studios were located. "After Wilson fired me, I walked downstairs and rented a meeting room. I wrote letters to 50 radio managers around the country, asking them to come to Cincinnati for a one-day radio sales seminar. They came and brought their sales managers and some of their salespeople." Palmer conducted his little business on a part-time basis, between management jobs and operating his radio stations, WATH-AM/FM, Athens, Ohio. He also did a lot of business outside radio.)

Williams says: "When I started my school, there was little material available on which to build a sales study plan. I built mine on what Ed Livermore, a newspaperman, had taught me about selling advertising. I thought that was a good place to start. In an average small town, the daily newspaper was doing five or six times the business of the local radio station."

Williams, a voracious reader all his life, had read and taken to heart the information he had gleaned on selling from writings by successful salespeople in many lines outside the broadcasting business.

"The tacky mailings" (a Williams' trademark) brought more than a thousand owners, managers, new and old salespeople to Tulsa every year for 10 years. The courses, which attendees nicknamed "boot camp," lasted four days, from 8 a.m. to 10 p.m. Williams explains the long hours by recalling that before the Welsh Company, radio sales presentations were customarily conducted during state and national conventions, where they were overshadowed by the social events on the programs. "I wanted to get away from that. Our sessions were all work — no play."

Williams points with some pride to the successes enjoyed by many of the graduates of his boot camp in Tulsa. "We dealt with direct selling, not agency selling. We did not teach rating points. We taught how to sell to the decision makers."

A mid-'70s boot camp alumnus is the CEO of Clear Channel Communications. "He went though the course, as he should have, to find out what I was telling his salespeople," says Williams.

In 1994, the trade and financial press would quote Lowry Mays as saying: "We believe business should be conducted in stores and offices — not over lunch, golf or cocktails. We sell direct to the customer. We don't believe our prices should be dictated by a rating book. That's a decision that should be made by the 'partners.' " Mays' objective in his far-flung radio-TV group is for his salespeople to forge strong partnerships with advertisers.

The results are best evidenced in San Antonio, where Clear Channel has operated WOAI for almost 20 years. The station is usually ninth or 10th in the ratings, and is consistently the town's highest-grossing station.

It has been several years since Williams has worked with Clear Channel. They have developed a strong, in-house sales training program. In Williams' words: "A company that big should do that, but I think we made a contribution to them in their early days."

Sales training and consulting have grown tremendously since the 1970 start of Williams' boot camp. There are probably more than 500 sales trainers and/or consultants operating nationwide now. Two of the most prominent, Chris Lytle and Darrell Solberg, are both alumni of the boot camp. Without the slightest trace of rancor, Williams says: "They're doing very good work."

In 1981, the Welsh Company went broke. In Williams' words: "It was a combination of things. Speaking 14 hours a day took a toll on my voice. My doctor said: 'Give it a rest — or else.' Airline fares and hotel room rates had skyrocketed. If you'll recall, 1981 was a recession year. Unfortunately, when dollars were short, many station managers decided to cut back on sales training. That doesn't make sense, but it usually happens."

Since 1981, Williams has operated on a more limited scale — without support personnel. At the height of the Welsh Company, he had four support people. "I have also evolved into a continuing relationship business, instead of the old four-day boot camps. Training is really an ongoing process. Salespeople are like athletes — they have to train on a regular schedule during their entire career, and management has to do the same."

Williams' teaching style is called by many "heavy-handed, intimidating and even sadistic." He calls the term sadistic "very unfair," saying: "Sadistic is defined as 'inflicting pain.' I do not do that. If I sometimes come across as heavy-handed or intimidating, please chalk that up to 'excessive zeal.' "

He continues: "I do not suffer fools — even though they're paying me. I am tough because I believe radio is capable of a lot more success than most people in it believe. It is the easiest way I know to make money that's legal."

Williams says he's appalled by the high failure rate of salespeople and the poor financial showing of many radio stations. "Traditionally, one-third of stations make a useable profit, one-third barely get by, one-third lose money. That's inexcusable, and we should all be embarrassed."

Williams believes that the single problem holding stations and salespeople back is a lack of "station belief." The owners, the managers, the salespeople don't believe in their station. Williams' antidote: "Sell big schedules. Get enough to be important. If he spends a lot of money, he'll do his part to make the advertising work. Advertising works when it causes a profit.

"When advertising works," Williams continues, "everybody gets station belief — the owner, the manager, the salesperson and the customer."

For Williams, "station belief precludes a salesperson from recommending other stations or media. Recommending a media mix means you don't have station belief. You have to believe 100 percent that your station, used heavily enough, can do the whole job. If he wants to buy something else in addition to running heavily on your station, that's his business — not yours.

"Big schedules keep a station growing," he says. "If there's business turndown, big expenditures *may* be cut — little ones *always* get cut out."

Changes

With few exceptions, most small market operators did well. Thanks to inflation and generally good business conditions, radio had grown a little faster than total advertising from 1961 through 1980, increasing its share from 6.7 percent in 1970 to 6.9 percent in 1980. The number of stations had grown an average of 142 per year in the 1970s. Many of the new stations built in the small towns were FMs, built by existing AM operators. Most were simulcast. The ones that weren't were often on automation system, operating out of the back room with few commercials.

Even factoring in the inflation of the 1970s and the new stations, revenues per station were up $2\frac{1}{2}$ times equal to 20 percent more than inflation. It's no wonder that radio station sellers found that instead of the 1- to 1.5-times gross that they could expect in the early 1960s, they now could expect 2- to 2.5-times gross. Some stations were even selling at 3-times gross. There wasn't much talk about cash flows. As brokers frequently advised: "Put the gross on and collect it. The buyer is always smarter than the seller."

The mid to late '70s showed some disturbing signs that few operators took the time to study. Small town stations started filling up with a lot of "over the transom business." Among these were gold buyers; banks and savings and loans that advertised high interest rates on certificates of deposit; new shopping centers and chain stores that were "discovering the small towns" and long-established retailers that were holding cash-raising sales or going out of business sales because they couldn't cope with higher borrowing costs at the bank and tougher terms from their suppliers.

By 1980, the combination of stagnant growth and high inflation, nicknamed "stagflation" by the politicians, was clearly taking hold in small town radio stations. For the first time in 20 years, many owners found that their radio stations could actually have ups and downs like the businesses of their friends around town.

The 1980 FCC Radio Financial Report

Radio had a $3.547 billion year — $2.29 billion better than 10 years before — +282 percent. The radio networks did $157 million — more than three times better than 10 years earlier. They accounted for 4.5 percent of radio industry totals vs. 3.9 percent in 1970. National spot had shrunk from 28.3 percent of the industry total to 21.2 percent (1970 vs. 1980), coming in at $746.2 million. Local business had grown fastest of all, to 74.5 percent of the industry total — growing three times in the decade.

The 35 (up from 20 in 1970) network owned-and-operated stations were doing brisk business and showing handsome profits vs. a paper-thin margin in 1970.

There were a total of 6,391 AM and AM-FM combos, plus 1,039 stand alone FM stations. Some 59 percent of the AM and AM-FMs showed a profit. Of the stand alone FMs, 50 percent were profitable. No stations had gone silent in 1980.

While the industry as a whole was profitable, the reports of pretax profits were troubling: Industry profits had set records in 1978, then declined by 25.6 percent in 1979, then by another 31.2 percent in 1980.

The 1980 report contained the following information about radio stations in non-metropolitan areas. The small markets had become increasingly more competitive during the 1970s. They totaled 4,069, 56 percent of all stations on the air.

	Avg. Rev.
1,50l such stations were in 3-station markets	$225,535
1,760 such stations were in 2-station markets	$159,790
803 such stations were in 1-station markets	$154,997

The non-metropolitan stations reported an average pretax profit of less than $2,500.

The report included breakdowns of non-metropolitan markets with three or more stations. There are some interesting small market figures.

At Thomasville, Georgia, where Hoyt Wimpy had moonlighted with his PA system to augment his small earnings from WPAX, there were, by 1980, three radio stations, averaging $152,974 billings and an average profit of $16,804. There had been just two radio stations in Thomasville 10 years before.

Valdosta, Georgia, where the original Rivers family station had gone on the air in 1939, was, by 1980, home to seven radio stations, averaging $164,664 gross and $10,664 profit. Ten years earlier, there were four stations there averaging $117,000 with profits of $17,003.

At Paducah, Kentucky, where Pierce Lackey and his station became local heroes during the 1937 flood, there were five stations averaging $297,400. In 1970, three stations had done an average of $157,196.

At Greenwood, Mississippi, where WGRM finally found a home after two other stops in its early life in the 1930s, there were four radio stations averaging $104,325 with average profit of $3,002. In 1970, three stations there had averaged $113,549 with profits of $13,842.

Kalispell, Montana, where Don Trolard had moonlighted from his schoolteaching job as manager of KGEZ and the chamber of commerce in the 1920s, had, by 1980, three radio stations averaging $282,211, with profit averaging $48,198.

At Wenatchee, Washington, where KPQ was moved from Seattle in the early 1930s, there were four stations, averaging $377,256. Ten years earlier, three stations averaged $138,024.

Finally, at Cleveland, Tennessee, where Bob Rounsaville had made so many 1940s and 1950s dollars with WBAC, there were, by 1980, four radio stations averaging $161,171 and losing an average of $16,866. Rome, Georgia, which his partner in the Cedartown,

Georgia, station thought was too small for a second station, by 1980 had six, averaging $232,622 — up from the four there in 1970 averaging $183,327.

During the 1960s and 1970s, the block programming and program titles that were commonplace in the 1950s had largely disappeared from small town radio stations. Few were any longer trying to "be all things to all people," but had, instead, settled on a steady format of the music they believed would satisfy the greatest number of their market and offend the fewest.

Program Schedule: WAOP, Otsego, Michigan

MUSIC: Modern Country. All segments hosted by personalities. Programming features a steady stream of information about area events and causes.

   A "Citizen of the Day" is saluted daily. There is also a salute to an area high school student who has excelled in scholarship, sports or school activities. An area retail, service or manufacturing business is saluted on the "Business Salute."

NEWS: Local news is broadcast at 6:30 a.m., 7:55 a.m., 9:30 a.m., 12:30 p.m. and 5:10 p.m.

   ABC Information Network News is carried on the hour, followed by a 1½-minute broadcast of state news from the Michigan News Network.

SPORTS: 7:05 a.m. and 5:05 p.m.

FARM: 2 farm programs daily, at 6:45 a.m. and 12:15 p.m., and market summaries at 10:45 a.m. and 2:45 p.m.

PUBLIC AFFAIRS: *WAOP Calling*, a five-minute interview with a civic or government leader — Monday through Friday at 8:30 a.m.

   Allegan County Roundtable, a 30-minute, in-depth panel discussion on a topic of local interest — 4:30 p.m. to 5 p.m. Sundays.

SPECIAL EVENTS: The station provides live coverage of fairs and festivals and other events in Wayland, Allegan, Otsego, Plainwell and 18 smaller communities in the WAOP listening area, reaching into four counties.

RELIGIOUS: Paid religious programs accepted Sundays until noon, and five-minutes or less at other times.

chapter 6

"THE CHALLENGING
YEARS"

1981/1995

"This still pays pretty good for having fun."

Bill Buchanan, KSHN,
Liberty, Texas
(during the "bottom" of the mid-'80s Texas "bust"
economy)

chapter 6

"THE CHALLENGING YEARS"
1981/1995
KGCX — 1981/1995

"We ran out of money!" That's what partner Oscar Halverson told a daily newspaper when he was called to comment on KGCX (and KGCX-FM) going silent in August 1993. The station had gone on the air, first without a license, 68 years before, in 1925.

Of KGCX's leaving the air after so many years, Halverson says: "There were a lot of contributing factors. The six counties in Montana and North Dakota which make up the KGCX listening and selling area lost population steadily from the 1970s into the 1990s.

"Dry-land farming suffered several major droughts during the period. There was a consolidation of small farmers into larger operations. Mechanization required less farm labor. A farmer who operates twice as many acres doesn't buy twice as many groceries or twice as many pairs of overalls."

There was a boom in the area in the late 1970s and early 1980s, thanks to oil. Then, Halverson recalls: "That 'boom' went 'bust' when oil imports started running freely again. Prices plummeted. It seemed like, almost overnight, our business at KGCX nearly disappeared."

Population in the six-county area, according to Halverson, dropped from more than 70,000 to 54,000. At the same time, a host of new radio completion had came on the scene:

A second 100,000-watt FM station came on the air in Sidney. (It since has left the air, lasting only a year and a half.)

In Williston, where KGCX still maintained branch studios and offices, Charles Scofield built a Class C FM, KYYZ, to pair with his AM station. He improved his AM station, moving it to one of the now-available clear channels, 660 kHZ, from 1460 kHZ.

173

KDSR, a second 100-kW FM station, came on the air in 1985. It was bought in a distress sale by longtime Scofield employee Bob Miller.

Also in Williams County, of which Williston is the county seat, there's a 1-kW daytimer on 1090 kHZ at Tioga.

At Glendive, Montana, where there had been just one station, KXGN, a Class IV built in 1948, there were two other separately owned stations — KGLE, a 1-kw daytimer on 590 kHZ, and a 100,000-watt FM station, KDZN.

Additionally, there was a commonly owned, though separately programmed, Class IV AM and Class A FM combo — KVCK/KYTC(FM). KGCX had been at Wolf Point in the late 1920s and 1930s.

A 5-kW AM daytimer on 1070 (and companion Class A FM) was on the air at Plentywood, Montana, (whose home county in 1990 had a population of just 4,500). KATQ-AM/FM was saved from going off the air in 1991 when local residents chipped in to alleviate its money problems and save it.

In 1993, there were 12 separately programmed radio stations in the area where Ed Krebsbach had struggled until the end of World War II to keep KGCX on the air. That's one station for each 4,500 people, one station for each $29 million in retail sales.

In addition to the area's economic problems, population loss and the proliferation of radio stations, the Halversons and their partners experienced a problem faced by most inactive owners: high manager turnover. "It's very hard to find, then keep, a good, strong manager in a small station. They either go to a bigger station or go into business for themselves," Halverson says.

Shortly before going silent, the Halverson partners, Mr. and Mrs. Olaf Folkvold, turned over their interest in the stations to daughter and son-in-law Kay and Ted Tescher. The value of the 50 percent, according to FCC filings, was $1,708 for the same station (plus a Class C FM) that had, in Halverson's words, "been a good deal at $380,000 in 1972."

The Country

When Ronald Reagan came into office in January 1981, the country was getting a dose of strong medicine designed to cure a horrible disease that had persisted since the late 1960s — inflation.

Richard Nixon had installed wage and price controls for a brief time in 1970. When Gerald Ford assumed the presidency, inflation was still a problem. Americans still remember the lapel buttons he sponsored — "WIN" (Whip Inflation Now). When Democrat Jimmy Carter came into office, his advisers told him that only a dose of "very bitter medicine" would reign in inflation. He appointed Paul Volker to head the Federal Reserve Board. Interest rates skyrocketed all the way to 18.9 percent. The inflation rate was 13 percent.

Reagan and his advisers couldn't, and most probably wouldn't have wanted to, interfere with Volker, an appointee who operates, by law, outside politics.

The Reagan program, despite all the campaign rhetoric about school prayer, abortion, home and family values, centered on two things: a massive buildup of the nation's defenses and a big tax cut. Reagan promised that the tax cut would actually increase government receipts, as a tax cut had done during John Kennedy's presidency. Reagan critics would call his two part program "Get elected now and put it on Master Charge."

Incredibly, the massive defense buildup bankrupted the nation's longtime Cold War adversaries and, many would say, almost bankrupted the United States in the process. The predicted improvement in government finances did not come about. Reagan and Congress built up annual deficits three times the size of the 1980 deficit.

There had been a brief recession in 1980. There was another one later in 1981 into 1982. Then, in 1983, inflation was dropping, interest rates were coming down and the massive defense buildup and the tax cuts were showing up in rising retail sales, particularly on the East and West Coasts, where much of the defense industry and emerging high-tech industries were located.

As in the '20s, there would be a lot of pain in much of the country that lies between the two coasts. First, there were terrible farm problems in the Midwest, then problems in the mining and oil producing states and trouble in the "old" industries of the Rust Belt, which weren't competing in the new world economy. From 1982 to 1987, farm assets would drop from $843 billion to $579 billion. Farm income would drop from $37.6 billion to $26 billion — by almost one-third. During the 1980s, employment in coal mines would drop by 409 percent. Oil and gas employment would drop by 30 percent. The country would lose a million high-paying jobs in durable goods industries.

It was a new world. Employment in service industries increased by 58 percent, in eating and drinking places by 42 percent, retailing

42 percent and government 13 percent. As the heavy industries declined, many a thoughtful person was asking: "Can we really have an economy selling each other life insurance?"

Through all the change and widespread turmoil, Ronald Reagan stayed popular with most Americans. He was re-elected in 1984 by a landslide and was succeeded by his vice president, George Bush, by another landslide in 1988. Reagan was called by friends and adversaries alike "the Teflon president." In retrospect, his rare talent may well have had its roots in his radio career.

When Reagan came to office, millions of people, many of them in small towns, felt they really knew him. Between the time he served as California governor and president, he had conducted a daily five-minute (with a minute "hole" for the local sponsor) news commentary on almost 500 radio stations.

Jon Holiday, whose duties with Reagan's radio program syndicator, Harry O'Conner, included producing the Reagan radio programs, has several times told of his amazement. Reagan — who had been governor of the nation's largest state for eight years, had run for president in 1976 and was sure to do it again in 1980 — "drove himself to the studio in a nondescript convertible. He had no assistants with him. He would sit down at the mic and ask: 'Are you ready?' Then he'd read 10 scripts, nonstop. The scripts were written in his own handwriting on the pages of a legal pad."

Holiday, who'd been in radio for 35 years at the time, says: "He never fluffed. I've never seen anybody who could do that."

After Reagan finished his 10 commentaries, he'd generally stay around to trade jokes with Jon and the engineer, Holidays says. "He knew more jokes than anybody I've ever known — and no, I'm not going to repeat any of them."

The Reagan commentaries would serve as a model for the weekly five-minute Saturday radio talks he delivered almost every week of his presidency. In his mostly unflattering book about the president, *Reagan's America*, Gary Wills claims that Reagan used radio more often and more skillfully than any chief executive since Franklin Roosevelt. On the other hand, he says, Reagan appeared on television press conferences less than any president since Dwight Eisenhower.

The Small Towns

In the 1970s, the non-metropolitan areas had increased their population overall. But that was not to be the case in the 1980s. First, there were the farm crises, then the "oil bust" and then the manufacturing plants were either cutting back or leaving altogether. There was considerable movement out of the high-tax, high-wage states in New England and the Midwest to the lower taxes, lower wages, better weather in the Sun Belt. It seemed, during the 1980s, that every small town would have at least one, if not many more, sad stories to tell.

Wallace, Idaho

In 1980, the Bunker Hill Company, the Osburn area's largest employer, spent $8 million to upgrade its facility. It employed 2,500 people (equal to more than 14 percent of the about 18,000 county residents.) In 1981, the plant's absentee owner closed it.

As the price of silver plummeted, other mines closed as well. By the mid-'80s, the area's 4,000 high-paying mining jobs had shrunk to a few hundred. By the 1990 census, the population of Shoshone County, the richest silver mining area in the nation, had shrunk to 13,800 — 4,200 people had left. Household incomes, formerly among the highest in the nation, were just $22,000 (vs. the national average of $36,000).

The county's radio station, KWAL, had been on the air since 1938. Paul Robinson, who came to KWAL as sales manager in 1969, bought it in 1971. During the good years in the 1970s, when silver prices and production were high, there were 11 employees at the station and, Robinson says: "I turned down three quarters of a million dollars for it."

Robinson believes that the price of silver would have to double or even triple its current price to bring the glory days back to the Silver Valley. "That's not going to happen unless we have a big war. Nobody wants that."

When the silver business collapsed, Shoshone County lost one-fifth of its retail stores. In the mid-'80s, Robinson was saying: "There are seven of us still here at the radio station. Like the businesses still open, we're working a lot harder for a lot less money. But, like those other businesses still open, there's a need for us. If there is a need, you'll survive." As this is written, he and KWAL have survived.

The Silver Valley began remaking itself during the '80s. Its real opportunity, those who chose to remain there felt, was to develop tourism. The business districts in Wallace and Kellogg refurbished themselves by establishing Local Development Districts.

"I decided quickly," Robinson says, "that my station would not survive unless the area did. My priority had to be to get in and do as much as I could for the area." That meant, many days, attending as many as five meetings a day in the little towns. The largest is Kellogg, population just over 2,500. "I could not have been away from the station that much if it were not for my sales manager, George White, and my wife, Marge. They not only worked very hard, but they stayed optimistic."

Robinson and his fellow Silver Valley businessmen and businesswomen decided early on that they'd have to rebuild the valley by taking advantage of its natural resources: its mountains, lakes and location on busy I-90. They needed to develop its tourism potential and perhaps attract some light industry.

The most dramatic tourism attraction built to date is a 3.1-mile gondola that transports tourists to the top of Silver Mountain for skiing in the wintertime and for bicycling on the breathtakingly beautiful bike trails. There is also a 2,500-seat natural amphitheater where nationally famous entertainers perform each weekend during the summer.

Some light industries are in their early stages of development. "Another thing that's helping us is a steady influx of people moving in from cities, particularly from California," Robinson says. "They're selling their houses and re-investing in houses here. They can buy so much more house for the money here, they can bank the difference."

Not all of the displaced high-paid mining workers left. One who didn't is John Davis. When Bunker Hill terminated him, he took advantage of a re-training program the parent company offered. He spent nine months in Spokane, where he took a course in radio announcing at a trade school. When he finished the course, he looked up Robinson.

"He had an opening," recalls Davis. "That was 11 years ago. I make about one-third what I did at Bunker Hill. But, that's not as bad as it might seem. When the high-paying mining jobs left, the cost of living dropped dramatically."

John continues: "Every day when I went to work at the mine, I couldn't wait for my shift to end. Being in radio isn't like that. It's satisfying and fun. That's worth a lot."

Canton, Illinois

In 1982, not only did the farm crisis strike hard in Canton, in southern Illinois, but the town experienced a near-fatal blow when the largest employer, International Harvester, with nearly 2,000 high-paying jobs, closed. Canton's population was about 13,000.

Within a year, 27 merchants were gone and, with them, says Charlie Wright, owner of WBYS-AM/FM, went "25 percent of our gross."

Charlie had bought a 49 percent interest in the station for $2,500 in 1954. The majority owner was the town's daily newspaper owner. "It wasn't a bargain," Charlie remembers. "The stock had a negative value on the books after seven managers in seven years had piled up debts."

When he went to Canton, the station's three salespeople walked out. In Charlie's words: "They didn't like the accountability I demanded. For three years, my wife, Ruth, and I handled the sales, so it got done the way I knew it had to be done.

"Ultimately, we found the right people. The business grew." In 1971, facing government pressure to either leave the radio business or the newspaper business, the newspaper owners sold Charlie their 51 percent interest in the station. WBYS and the FM station, built in 1968, continued to grow until 1982.

When the 25 percent drop in business hit WBYS, Charlie quickly went to work streamlining his operation. He insisted that the changes made could not compromise the station's programming or the service it provided to the community. By putting computers to work, he accomplished that, with a net savings of three full-time jobs. "We had been automated on a part-time basis all the way back to 1968. We knew from experience that by careful planning and attention to details, you could be just as local and relevant as you could be by doing things the expensive, old-fashioned way."

One problem that showed up quickly as things tightened up financially in Canton was an abnormal number of past-due radio advertising bills. Like cutting his overhead, Charlie gave his collection problems immediate attention. Among the steps taken was this classic Charlie letter to 90 days past-due accounts:

URGENT! URGENT! URGENT! URGENT!

WBYS is many things to many people. One thing it is NOT is a philanthropy. We are like all of you. In our case, we sell a service and send out the bill. About 80 percent of the costs of providing our service are paid for before the advertiser receives the bill.

We have accounts of all sizes, from $25 to $1,500 per month. When more *than 40 accounts do not pay their bills for three or more months, it adds up to a sizable sum.*

If we could, we would not charge anything for our advertising and live in a "never-never land" where the fairy godmother waves the magic wand and everything is hunky-dory. But that is not the way it is.

So — will you please send us a check?

If you can't pay the entire amount — send a partial payment. If you can't send a partial payment, call or write us to tell us when we can expect payment. If we don't hear from you by February 10, someone will call on you to collect.

We appreciate your business and your cooperation in this matter.

Thank You,

Charlie Wright

By February 10, 60 percent of the accounts who were sent the letter paid. Another 20 percent made partial payments. The other 20 percent were called on and made at least partial payment and arrangements to pay the balance. Several of the accounts called to compliment Charlie on the letter.

At this writing, farm prices are a lot better than they were in the early 1980s. The town has gotten several good, small industries — including one Charlie calls "recession-proof — a state prison."

Charlie's good sense and good humor kept him in business during his town's tough times. His appraisal at this time: "The town's doing pretty good, the station is doing pretty good and I'm doing real good."

Liberty, Texas

The business community in Liberty, Texas, took a four-way hit in the mid-'80s: Oil prices fell dramatically; the price of rice, the area's main agricultural cash crop, sustained a heavy price drop; the town's largest industry, employing 800 — 10 percent of Liberty's population — closed; and Wal-Mart and other discounters, which had overlooked the town previously, set up shop.

In three years, 200 of the area's retailers closed their doors forever, and 40 new ones, many without business expertise or capital, took their place. Net loss: 160 retailers. The Liberty radio station's fortunes mirrored the hard times in the market. Billing dropped by 25 percent — and collections became a major problem.

Bill Buchanan, owner/operator, bought what was then KPXE, a 250-watt daytimer located less than 30 miles from Houston, in 1977. He recalls: "I became a better manager, because I had to. Through attrition, the payroll was cut by three full-time people: an announcer, a second newsperson and, hardest of all, one of our two salespeople. We also cut two part-timers."

The newswire was replaced by a national network and a state network (both on trade). Some other things that were nice to have, but really not necessary, were eliminated. By taking those steps, while the gross was off 25 percent, the cash flow remained strong enough to make the station's payments, pay its bills and make Buchanan and his slimmed-down staff a fair living.

At the time, Buchanan said: "Of all the cuts I made, cutting the salesperson was the hardest decision. Logic tells you that when business is bad, more calls need to be made. But in our case, with one-third fewer people to call on, I felt we didn't need as many salespeople.

"When you do 25 percent less business, the work load doesn't drop 25 percent. The people who are left have to work longer and harder. There was no griping. It isn't that the people who are left are happy to keep their jobs — maybe a little. It has worked because I've worked harder alongside them." He took over 60 percent of the station's sales, along with many of the duties that had been covered by the second newsperson, and "whatever else needed doing." Even in the boom times, KPXE was severely limited by its low-power, daytime-only status. When a 50,000-watt FM channel became available at Liberty, Buchanan saw the chance to have the "kind of station I'd always wanted — a full-time facility with good coverage." When the window for applications opened, there were three other applicants — all much better-financed than Buchanan.

"I had the daytimer preference, but I knew there was the real possibility of long, expensive hearings. All of them could have broken me during the proceedings." He realized that his little daytimer operating beside the 50-kW FM station had, realistically, no chance of surviving — particularly in that bad economy. He discussed exit strategies with friends during the months that followed the window opening, a painful prospect for a man who had spent more than 10 years in the community.

When the FM license was about to be set for a hearing, remarkably, all three competing applications had flaws that, under the FCC's "hard look policy," could not be cured. Buchanan got his license, telling friends: "You have to work hard, and I guess you've got to be fairly smart to make it in this small town radio business, but I guess somebody up there has to be looking out for you, too."

When he went out to finance his FM station, the well-publicized Texas banking crisis was in full swing. Three of his town's four banks were being operated under RTC supervision. The one bank that wasn't had a lending limit too small to fund the project. After lengthy negotiation, that bank acted as lead bank, cooperating with the other three to fund the project.

The oil boom years in Liberty are history and, in the view of most of the locals, will never return. But Liberty, like many other small towns, has started to grow again: Small industries have come to the area, and there has been a residential building boom as increasing numbers of people from Houston trade the rigors of big-city living for the more comfortable attributes of small towns like Liberty and nearby Dayton, the Liberty station's second market, five miles away. The biggest industry to locate at Liberty is a prison, which has expanded twice since it was built there.

"When talk of building the prison here first circulated, there was a lot of noisy opposition. But it came, and its big payroll was the shot in the arm we needed. Nobody talks about it now. I'm sure it's one industry that will not close and, I hate to say it, its business will probably get better and better," Buchanan says, only half-jokingly.

After the FM station, KSHN "Shine," went on the air, Bill decided to surrender the AM license. "It was a hard decision, but we were going to have to spend a lot of money on it. We no longer needed it here. My thought was to help clean up the terrible overcrowding of the AM band."

Thanks to going full time on FM and the improving economic climate of the community, the Liberty station is doing twice its recession business and a third more than it had in boom times. Of the very hard times, Buchanan says: "They're hard when you're going through them, but afterward you're a lot smarter. There was a time, the boom time, when a dozen customers made up 70 percent of our income. Now, the top dozen accounts make up 30 percent of our income. That's a lot healthier. If bad times ever return, and they might, we'll be better prepared."

Deregulation

When Jimmy Carter came to the presidency in 1977, the problem of inflation that had troubled both Presidents Nixon and Ford was accelerating. Carter appointed Ivy League economist Charles Schultz as his economic czar to get inflation under control. Schultz believed that government regulation was a big part of the inflation problem, by increasing the cost of doing business. Schultz also believed that increased competition would keep price increases in check. Deregulation got under way in airlines, banking, trucking ... and broadcasting.

Carter appointed Charles Ferris as his FCC chief. Ferris, a lawyer, came to the post with no background in broadcasting. He had been Democratic Sen. Mike Mansfield's senior aide for 12 years, then a committee counsel for a short time. Upon taking office, he admitted he did not own a CB radio and only watched television infrequently. His major concern seemed to be curing the Commission's reputation for falling short in efficiency and general housekeeping.

He let it be known early on that he felt the Commission should not intrude in program decisions, saying he thought that should be left up to broadcasters and the public. "People can write in, picket and let advertisers know how they feel, but I'm not sure we on the Commission have a role to play in that area."

During his tenure, Ferris and the Commission set into motion the possibility of hundreds of low-power television stations, more VHF stations, as many as 125 new AM stations by breaking down the remaining 25 clear channels and hundreds of FM stations ("80/90" initiated in 1980). His Commission also favored reduction of channel spacing from 10 kHZ to 9 kHZ. That was derailed shortly after he left.

He set into motion a long list of deregulation in radio and greatly reduced the time and paperwork necessary for radio stations to renew their licenses. The percentages of news programming and public affairs programming that were thought to be necessary to keep a license no longer were scrutinized by the FCC.

Inside and outside the industry, Ferris' actions were widely criticized. Of his creating less regulation and more competition in the broadcasting business, he would say: "We (at the FCC) have become regulatory Darwinists. We now ensure the survival of the fittest — not the fattest."

Unlike Ferris, his successor, Mark Fowler, appointed by President Reagan, came to the chairmanship with a broadcasting background. He started as a part-time disc jockey in high school at WABR (now WWZN, Winter Park, Florida). After high school, he worked on the air at WHOO, Orlando, Florida; WDVH, Gainesville, Florida; WKEE-AM/FM, Huntington, West Virginia, and finally as an announcer, program director and sales representative at WDVH while completing his degree at the University of Florida. He got his law degree in 1969.

With his law degree in hand, he moved to Washington, D.C., joining the communications law firm in which Vince Pepper was senior partner. He formed his own communications law firm in 1975 at age 34.

Before coming to the commission, he held the top legal spot for communications in the Reagan campaigns of 1976 and 1980. He headed the transition team that studied FCC operations after Reagan was elected.

Fowler accelerated the deregulation and the station creation that started in the Ferris years. Shortly after taking over his new post, Fowler called the FCC "the remaining dinosaur of the New Deal."

During his tenure, he repeatedly said that commercial broadcasters should be governed by "market forces rather than trustee duties, where stations act under close government supervision." Broadcast historians Sydney Head and Christopher Sterling say that "Fowler transformed the FCC into a more efficient processor of applications, a sympathetic patron of new services and an active deregulator of existing media." They theorize that "the move to deregulation can be seen as a huge, risky experiment. Only time will tell whether the FCC's lower regulator profile will have a positive or a negative effect — or any effect at all on the electronic media's service to the public."

A Leader out of the Plowed Ground

No single national trade association represents as diverse a membership as the National Association of Broadcasters. Its members range from low-power AM stations in small towns all the way up to the huge television networks. The leading TV network is, by itself, the largest single advertising medium in the world.

NAB, by virtue of its size and diversity, cannot represent the unique interests of all of its members. Over the years, small groups of stations have organized to further their unique interests: regional AM stations, clear channel AM stations, newspaper-owned stations, Class IV AM stations, daytime AM stations, FM stations. Of necessity, generally, NAB has stood aside in these intramural disputes within the organization. Historically, these organizations have started up, seen their mission to a successful or unsuccessful conclusion, then gone out of existence.

The primary purpose of NAB is lobbying Congress and the regulators, primarily the FCC, on issues that affect the entire industry. The singular interests of small segments of the industry have to be relegated to those small segments.

For the first 15 years of its existence, NAB's presidency was a part-time, largely ceremonial job. Since 1938, the job has been a full-time one. The first full-time NAB president was Neville Miller, a former Louisville, Kentucky, mayor. He was succeeded by a former judge, Justin Miller. During the 1950s, the NAB president was Harold Fellows, who came to the post from WEEI-AM, Boston, where he had been general manager. Fellows suffered a fatal heart attack in 1960.

To fill the Fellows vacancy, the NAB board went outside the industry, hiring former Florida Gov. LeRoy Collins. Of Collins, said an NAB director during his tenure: "We never really knew whether he was running NAB or running for senator or maybe president." Collins left NAB in 1964 to take an appointed government post.

To succeed Collins, the NAB board selected a career NAB staff member, Vincent Wasalewski.

Wasalewski had, in turn, served as NAB legal council, then as executive vice president. His 17-year tenure was the longest of any NAB president to this writing.

By the late 1970s, Wasalewski was faced with an increasing number of contentious board members, some of whom were publicly asking for his removal. A majority of the board quieted his critics, but, by the early 1980s, it was obvious to most that a new leader was needed. After an exit plan was negotiated, the presidency became open. A close friend and board member would say at the time: "Vince is a manager, by experience and temperament — not a politician. He's had a problem balancing the TV and radio people. The television people think too much attention is being given to radio. The radio people think too much attention is being given to television. It's a tough job."

At the time of Wasalewski's departure, the chairman of the NAB Joint Board was Edward O. Fritts, the head of a group of small radio stations in Mississippi, Louisiana and Arkansas. It was his responsibility to form and head a committee to search for a new NAB president.

One of his appointments, who had served on the NAB board in the 1970s, was Stan Mackenzie, long-time co-owner-operator of KWED, Seguin, Texas. He remembers vividly the first meeting of the search committee: "We were unanimous on one point, that the new president had to be someone who knew our business. There was no discussion about whether the new president would come from television or radio, a big market or a small market. But he (or she) would have to come out of broadcasting."

Ultimately, three of the top contenders would come out of small market radio: Bob Wells, who ran the Garden City, Kansas, Harris Newspaper group of small town radio stations, who had served a term on the FCC in the late '60s and early '70s; Donald Thurston, a recent Joint Chairman of the NAB Board and recipient of its Distinguished Service Award, and Edward O. Fritts. Fritts as Joint Board Chairman had appointed the committee charged with searching for the Wasalewski replacement. During the selection process, he had resigned the Joint Board Chairmanship and his spot on the search committee.

Fritts' entry into consideration for NAB president signaled the first spirited contest for the post in the association's history. In Chicago, at a specially called meeting of the NAB Board, neither Thurston nor Fritts, the two finalists, was present. Lively campaigning was carried on by their supporters, with neither candidate taking part. When the ballot was taken, Fritts won by four votes. Fritts' political skills were in evidence immediately as the board put the election behind it and, behind their new leader, set about tackling the longest and by far the most complicated issues in the history of broadcasting. For Eddie Fritts, it was a midlife career change that his family and close friends say was not even in his thoughts only a few months earlier.

Eddie Fritts' father, Edward M. Fritts, had gotten into radio by accident. He owned and operated a small, regional bus line in the 1940s and early 1950s. He then opened the second theater in his hometown, Union City, Tennessee, and a drive-in theater at nearby Fulton, Kentucky.

"The prospects for small town theaters were not very bright back then. I had never given any thought about getting into the radio business until the manager of the local station, WENK, told me he was leaving for a better job. His boss, the late Aaron Robinson, a west Tennessee small market radio group operator, told him he could leave as soon as he found a replacement."

Fritts traveled to Robinson's office in Jackson, Tennessee. Robinson told Fritts: "WENK is a good station. We don't need any changes. Just run it like it's been. You'll do all right."

Years later, Fritts is amazed that more stations haven't copied one of the ideas in force at WENK and other Robinson group stations. "The bookkeeper gave you the bills on the first of the month. You checked them, then carried them to each local customer. Most said: 'Let me write you a check. You can take it back with you.' Robinson paid his managers a bonus based on collection by the 10th of the month. After you collected the money, you could spend the rest of the month selling business for the following month.

"I was about 40 when I got the WENK job. The only real regret in my life is that I didn't get into radio earlier," Fritts said recently.

Eddie Fritts went to work for his father during his high school years when a part-time announcer quit. The senior Fritts recalls proudly: "Eddie did a good job, and there were never any rumblings about him being the boss' son." When he went off to college at Mississippi ("Ole Miss"), he continued to work summers and pitched in during holiday breaks "so that our full-time help could spend time with their families."

When Eddie came home from college, telling his father he planned to get married: "I told him, you can't support a wife and family on what you can make in a small station — unless you own it." The Frittses found three small stations for sale: one in central Kentucky, another in west Tennessee and WNLA, Indianola, Mississippi.

During his college years, Eddie had become familiar with the Mississippi Delta area and believed it had good prospects. Eddie was 22 when he bought WNLA.

"I didn't buy WNLA for Eddie," the elder Fritts says. "His mother and I guaranteed a loan to get him started. The money was paid back ahead of schedule. That was our last financial involvement with Eddie. He never asked us."

Fritts continues: "By the time Eddie bought WNLA, he'd been around the radio business as long as I had. I didn't feel qualified to tell him how to run a station 250 miles from Union City."

Eddie and his bride, Martha Dale, settled into community life at Indianola and started raising a family. WNLA, thanks to the tender loving care given it by its youthful owner, prospered.

The senior Fritts enjoys telling a story of the trip he made with Eddie to close the purchase. "The previous out-of-town owner had a note at a little bank in town. We went in to make sure he paid it off. Eddie asked for the president. A little old lady behind the old-fashioned banking cage announced that she was the president. When he told her he was buying the station, she quickly said she didn't think she'd want to make another loan to the station. I assured her we'd brought our money with us." When WNLA-FM went on the air in 1969, it was financed by that bank, which solicited the loan. In 1970, an auto accident nearly cost Eddie his life. He was hospitalized for six weeks, followed by three months of intense therapy. The senior Fritts stepped in to make sure WNLA didn't miss a beat during Eddie's absence.

The success of Eddie's station prompted Ed to buy a station of his own, WPAD-AM/FM, Paducah, Kentucky. During Eddie's hospital stay, Ed divided his time between Paducah and Indianola, 250 miles apart, in effect managing both stations.

Years later, Eddie would say: "It was during those months away from my station that I decided on the course for the rest of my life."

He was elected to the board of directors of the Mississippi Broadcasters Association and "went through the chairs," ultimately serving as its president. He then was elected to the board of the National Association of Broadcasters, serving in turn as chairman of the small market radio committee, Radio Board Chairman, then Joint Board Chairman.

By 1974, 10 years after he'd bought WNLA, he began to branch out, first buying underperforming KMAR-AM/FM, Winnsboro, Louisiana, then stand-alone FM KCRI, Helena, Arkansas, then short hours daytimer WCFB, Tupelo, Mississippi. That station was sold to make way for the purchase of the town's premier radio facility, WELO/WZLQ.

Eddie was a hands-on group owner. He traveled from station to station in a motor home that served a dual purpose as his office on wheels and a radio station remote unit. Lon Sosh, who worked at a couple of his stations as a salesman-air personality, recalled his visits as "very organized. He got good performance out of people. Conversations always started with: 'What do you need to get more done?' " As Eddie's group expanded and his industry activities increased, the motor home would be replaced by an airplane he personally piloted.

A Radio-Only Organization

The FM Association had existed on and off, inside and outside the NAB, since the 1940s. It had had its ups and downs with the medium it undertook to serve. By 1977, FM was doing so well that the FM Association decided to stage its first stand-alone convention. The Reno, Nevada, Convention was so successful that the association's leaders decided to change the name of the organization to National Radio Broadcasters Association and open membership to both FM and AM radio stations.

Steve Trivers, then operator of a stand-alone FM station, WQLR, Kalamazoo, Michigan, was first a director of the FM Association, then a director-Midwest Vice President of NRBA. He recalls: "There was a widespread feeling that NAB was a television association first, a radio association second. We felt, at that time, that radio needed its own association, devoted exclusively to representing the issue of radio."

Bev Brown, then owner-operator of KGAS, Carthage, Texas, was part of the industry that felt that the vast majority of issues were in fact not radio-only issues, but radio-television issues. "We felt," he says, "that the industry would not be well-served by two voices. It's true that the radio people, particularly the small town radio people who did not have television interests, felt that their needs were not given a full hearing at NAB but, in truth, a lot of my friends and I thought that radio was being adequately served by NAB, and if it wasn't, that could be corrected within NAB."

NRBA, despite operating with a very small budget, quickly started lobbying radio-only issues. Its board, unlike the NAB's, paid its own expenses to attend board meetings and make lobbying trips to Washington. NRBA's business was conducted from a small, upstairs office by seven paid staff members (vs. more than 100 at NAB, housed in its own buildings — one of the city's most imposing association headquarters).

Not accidentally, the NRBA board staged a Congressional visit in the deep snow of Washington in February. *Broadcasting* magazine carried a picture of them trudging though the snow en route to the Capitol, while their contemporaries on the NAB board were conducting business in a balmy "vacation paradise."

NRBA's first president was Jim Gabbard, then owner of FM stand alone KIOI, San Francisco. He was succeeded by Sis Kaplan, who, with her husband, Stan, owned and operated what are now WAOS and WAQQ, Charlotte, North Carolina. When Ms. Kaplan left the presidency, the reins were turned over to a fellow North Carolina broadcaster, Bernie Mann, the owner of WGLD, Greensboro/WWWB, High Point.

Mann gave the organization high-profile leadership like it had not had before. He first negotiated a merger of NRBA's "Radio Show" with the competing NAB "Program Conference." He then proposed the creation of a "Super" radio association, composed of the radio members of NAB, RAB and NRBA. The proposal for a summit meeting of the executive committees of the three organizations during the NAB-NRBA fall convention was sent to the other organization's heads.

Walter May of WPKE/WDHR, Pikeville, Kentucky, the unofficial campaign manager for Eddie Fritts' election as president of NAB, said at the time and has repeated since: "I was for Eddie because of his great political skills — a necessity for the head of a lobbying organization." When the "Super" radio idea surfaced, Fritts quickly put those skills to work.

Instead of a meeting during the convention, a meeting was called shortly after the "Super" radio idea first circulated. In addition to the RAB and NRBA leadership, the leaders of six other organizations were also summoned to the NAB Building in Washington: Radio-Television News Directors Association, American Women in Radio and Television, Broadcast Financial Management, Broadcast Promotion Managers Association, Radio Network Association and Station Representatives Association. Also summoned were the executive directors of three state broadcasters associations.

The idea was voted down by all but the NRBA. Jim Wychor, then manager of KWOA-AM/FM, Worthington, Minnesota, a booster of the "Super" radio idea, called the outcome "predictable. There was too much turf to be given up by the association bureaucrats and people who'd been elected to posts in those nine organizations." Ironically, it was Bernie Mann who would give up the most turf ultimately.

Bev Brown, an NAB loyalist and member of its executive committee at the time, said the NAB had an active radio department, a big legal staff, a research department, a science and technology department (which included a laboratory that set industry standards for equipment) and a lobbying staff (at that time 12 people — now 20). He also argued that Congress and the FCC saw radio and television as one medium that broadcast programming free to the public. "You can't separate radio from television in their eyes," he said.

At the combined radio show, Bernie Mann made the leadership of NAB, the RAB (invited guests) and some of his own members uncomfortable with his opening remarks to the entire convention. He called advertising agencies "snake oil salesman." He claimed that the agencies don't give radio its "fair share because the agencies make more money buying television for their clients than they do buying radio for them." No one took issue with the truth of his statement.

NAB fired another salvo at NRBA during the fall, saying that it was doing research as to whether it would co-sponsor another fall convention with NRBA. A hasty release came out from NRBA that the location (New Orleans) and the dates (September) were firm. "There'll be a radio-only convention, whether or not NAB takes part."

Despite the friction between the two organizations, merger talks were being conducted quietly, behind the scenes. Interestingly, 75 percent of the NRBA members also held membership in NAB.

The debate apparently sparked some soul-searching at NAB. Quietly, an outside research firm was hired to determine the opinions of station operators as to the usefulness of membership in the trade associations. The results must have been disheartening at NAB headquarters. By and large, the stations owners saw RAB membership as most useful, followed by NRBA, their state association and NAB, in that order.

A merger was announced in early January 1986. It was ratified unanimously by both associations' boards in February. Under the terms of the agreement, there would continue to be a "Radio Only Convention" each fall, and the "Radio Sales Universities" inaugurated by NRBA would be continued and open, at low rates, to both NAB members and non-members. They would be conducted by Radio Advertising Bureau. Three NRBA directors would go on the NAB board for short terms, and one of them would be Bernie Mann. Radio would be free to go its own way in matters in conflict with TV. The Radio Office at NAB would be headed by an executive with senior vice president stripes.

Steve Trivers said recently: "I think the merger was a good thing. It almost had to happen. Abe Voran (NRBA senior vice president) was the driving force. Although nobody is indispensable, I don't know who could have or would have taken his place."

Voran had terminal cancer at the time of the merger. He could not attend the final board meeting, but wrote to them of his misgivings about the merger, saying: "The old guard ego and resistance to change will deprive radio of its independence and aggressive representation it deserves." Voran died shortly after the merger.

Trivers believes "the merger came at the right time and would not have happened had it not been for the good common sense and selflessness of Bernie Mann." In the years that followed the merger,

Mann would seldom be heard from. He, is at this writing, out of the radio business — in publishing. Contrary to rumors that NRBA was broke, the association had more than $150,000 in cash when it concluded its business. Half the money went to the All Industry Music Licensing Committee, which negotiates the ASCAP and BMI contracts for the radio industry. The other half went to fund a perpetual broadcast scholarship fund, named for Abe Voran.

It is a misnomer to characterize NRBA as a small market radio association. Its board had far more big group owners on it than the NAB Radio Board has had traditionally. When it came time to lobby the Commission for a preference for AM stations in "80/90" hearings, which would be mostly for small town facilities, NAB's proposal was far more favorable to small town incumbent AM owners than that espoused by NRBA. NAB asked for a "strong preference"; NRBA "a slight preference." NRBA got its small market-friendly reputation mainly by the services it provided, often crude-looking but full of helpful advice on the bread and butter operating strategies that spell profit or loss — even survival — in a small market station.

Ironically, there was a high-profile suggestion again in the early 1990s that radio and television should go their own separate ways. It came, not from the radio industry, but from television's Robert Wright, president of NBC's Television Network and Owned and Operated Television Stations. NAB President Eddie Fritts quickly spoke against the idea, issuing a news release with the intriguing headline "Wright is Wrong!" The idea was dropped quicker than the mid-'80s "Super" radio idea.

Eddie Fritts says: "I'm completely comfortable with NAB. The big guys fund much of our operation. They expect protection from us. The little guys give us our legislative muscle. They want services. Usually, when something comes up, we look good when the dust settles." Before Eddie Fritts became NAB president, the standard joke around Washington was that "NAB couldn't lobby its way out of a paper bag." You don't hear that much anymore.

80/90 or 7-Eleven

Early in the "80/90" proceedings, Randy Johnson, then co-owner/operator of KAAT-FM at Oakhurst, California, said: "This '80/90' program at the Commission would be better named '7-Eleven' — a radio station on every corner."

The idea had been initiated by the Charlie Ferris' FCC in 1980.

Since 1963, when an earlier Commission had issued an FM Table of Assignments, the commercial FM frequencies had been divided into classes: Of the 80 channels, 20 had been designated as "A" channels, on which stations operating with 3,000 watts or less could be built. The other 60 channels accommodated stations of 50,000 watts (Bs) or, in wide areas of the United States, powers of 100,000 watts (Cs).

The engineers at the Commission, prodded by private consulting engineers, found that there were wide-open spaces on the B and C channels where stations could be built at powers of less than 50,000 or 100,000 watts without interfering with existing stations. In addition to establishing 3,000-watt Class A stations on the B and C channels, 25,000-watt stations could be built on many B and C Channels and some 50,000-watt stations on the C Channels. Mixing the new As and B2s, C2s and C3s onto the B and C Channels had the potential of creating at least another 1,500 stations across the country.

The declining fortunes of AM radio (by the mid-'80s it accounted for only about 32 percent of radio listening) created a huge demand for FM stations. As soon as the FCC announced its intention of going forward with the "80/90" FM program, the promoters started coming out of the woodwork.

One of the most prominent was Edward M. Johnson at Knoxville, Tennessee. Johnson did not have a consulting engineering license (even a "First Phone"). He did have great advertising and promotional skills. Before "80/90," his firm had filed hundreds of applications for Low Power Television Stations.

In July 1983, Johnson staged an "80/90 Seminar" at Knoxville's Hyatt Hotel. The FCC declined to send a representative. Nevertheless, it attracted nearly 100 attendees. Instead of the low-profile, conservative dress generally associated with engineering professionals, Johnson's demeanor and dress would have been expected of a barker at an old-time burlesque show. There was little discussion of how an FM station could be operated profitably and serve the needs of a community. Instead, there were recitations of how much money could be made quickly — more often by "churning" stations than by operating them long term.

During a session on how to file an application, seminar attendees were told: "Check the question: Are you financially qualified 'YES.' If you get the license, you'll be financially qualified because you can use it to borrow money on."

There was also a session on negotiation, instructing how to "bow out of an application by negotiating a high-dollar settlement with a more qualified or determined applicant."

A list of likely "80/90" allocation was distributed at the seminar, even though the Commission two weeks earlier had said no such list would be issued until at least November 1983.

Again and again, the seminar-goers were told to "Get rich by thinking spectrum. There's only a small amount of it. Like land, there isn't going to be any more. Get your share of the spectrum 'pie.' "

Reports quickly circulated from AM station owners, anxious to get an FM station, about being taken by the "consultants" who were springing up across the country. One AM daytimer owner told of answering an ad in the trade press for an "80/90" search at $100. He ordered and was sent two channels "that might work" and a bill for $4,000. Despite advice from the Commission that spending money for "80/90" searches was imprudent, the promoters continued to do brisk business.

In early 1984, the state of Tennessee issued a notice of inquiry as to whether Johnson had the required credentials to head an engineering firm in the state. In March 1984, Johnson sold his firm to one of his lawyers — before the first "80/90" FM application had been accepted at the Commission. Johnson moved into promoting cellular telephone licenses, where he made millions.

Shortly after the "80/90" list was made public, the Commission issued a *Guidebook on Applying for the New FM Allocations*. Instead of the dry, dispassionate tone that might have been expected in such a publication, it resembled a borderline legal announcement of a speculative stock issue.

Page 1 of the introduction told readers: "This decision creates unprecedented opportunities for entrepreneurs interested in owning FM radio stations. This is particularly true for minority and female entrepreneurs who are able to take advantage of FCC policies designed to encourage ownership of stations by groups that are under-represented in the broadcast marketplace."

The next paragraph advised: "Broadcast ownership can be quite profitable. The value of FM stations has increased dramatically in recent years, and last year the average large market FM station reported an annual net profit of $750,000, while the average medium market FM station earned approximately $400,000 in net profits."

The publication did not cite any figures for Class A FM stations located in very small towns (10,000 and under). Only 84 of the 684 assignments on the "80/90" list were in towns of 25,000 or more (the medium and large markets which were turning in such stellar financial performances).

The *Guide* estimated the costs of building a Class A FM station (the vast majority of the assignments) at $120,000 to $275,000. It listed the average sale price of a small market FM station at $400,000. The chance to make a profit of 45 percent to 333 percent was the stuff that dreams are made of.

The lure for applicants was further enhanced by a statement that "Some applicants obtain a construction permit simply by paying all opponents to withdraw from the case. There is no limit on how much money can be paid to other applicants to abandon their applications." That was qualified in the text: "But, buyouts must be approved by the judge, who must find that the withdrawing applicants did not file their applications only to be bought out." That qualifying statement would quickly prove to be little deterrent to speculators who would overwhelm the process.

Just how unreasonable many of the "80/90" assignments were is shown by three such assignments in Fulton County, Ohio — overshadowed by Toledo, but too far out to be reached by a Class A FM station in that county. There was already one Class A FM in the county. The addition of three more would mean one station for each 9,575 people in an area under the umbrella of over-radioed Toledo. The county's retail sales base was $160 million. With radio advertising getting $3 per $1,000 retail sales, the four stations would have a potential revenue of just $10,000 a month each — at the most optimistic projection.

"80/90" came at the worst possible time. Many of the small towns where the allocations were located were in serious decline in the new service economy, where making things was being replaced by making deals. Old-fashioned hard work was losing favor to new-fashioned get-rich-quick schemes. Financial institutions, major stock brokerage firms, law firms and accounting firms, even religious organizations, would lose their former exalted places in the public mind as scandal after scandal surfaced.

The deregulated FCC in the mid-'80s seemed to believe that its mission had changed from making sure stations served the "public interest, convenience and necessity" to maximizing "investor returns." The 20-year-old "Three Year Holding Rule," which said that a license holder could not sell at a profit until he or she had operated for three years, had been repealed. A station no longer had to maintain a studio in its city of license (just a free telephone). The studio could be located in any community within the station "city grade signal." The longtime Commission "Berwick and Suburban" rules were put aside. They had been designed so that there would be a fair and equitable distribution of stations. The Commission had for years taken the position that if it didn't ration the location of stations, most would be located in the large cities, where they'd make more money than in small communities.

Prior to the Fowler commission, stations in small towns wishing to associate themselves with larger cities had to get permission to get dual city designations. That rule was eliminated. Stations could now identify themselves as being anywhere, so long as they identified their city of license first on the required on-the-hour identification.

As soon as the relaxation of the rules took place, many small towns and cities effectively lost their local station as it moved to the more fertile ground of one of the cities or "good towns."

In the months leading up to the acceptance of "80/90" applications, "application mills" sprang up and were widely advertising in the trade press. The conservative consulting engineering firms and communications law firms were more discreet but nevertheless were aggressively going after the business, advising clients and potential clients to "put us on retainer now. When this thing gets under way, there'll be a shortage of of engineering and/or legal talent. Rates are sure to rise. Lock in a good rate now."

Before the filings began, one Nashville operation sent letters to law firms in each of the "80/90" towns suggesting that the new FM stations would be excellent investments for clients they represented or for themselves. Other firms sprang up with other ideas to lure investment.

The Commission had increased its ownership caps from seven stations per service to 12. At the start of the "80/90" process, it warned that it would not accept more than 12 applications per entity (fewer if they already had licenses). As the application filing process got under way, it was obvious that neither filers nor the Commission paid much attention to the "12 application" rule.

Prior to starting on the "80/90" list, the Commission set up a 30-day filing window for 152 unapplied-for FM allocations. When the window closed 30 days later, 1,200 applications for the 152 channels had been filed — more than seven per allocation. One-third of the applications were seriously defective. Almost 10 years after the window, only 99 of those stations have been built, 22 are unbuilt CPs and three that went on the air have gone silent. There were no applications for 28 — about 20 percent.

The first "80/90" window opened on October 15, 1985 — Class A facilities on 96.5 mHZ in 13 communities across the country. Nine years later, it's interesting to see what happened to those assignments:

• At England, Arkansas, the facility went to the local daytime AM station.

• The Colusa, California, facility actually located at Chico, where it is one of 18 stations competing in a metro of 162,000.

• The Marsailles, Illinois, station was built, but at this writing is not on the air.

• The Corydon, Indiana, allocation operates out of Louisville, Kentucky — 30 miles away.

• The Breaux Bridge, Louisiana, allocation operates as an L.M.A. out of Lafayette, where it is one of 16 stations in a metro of 166,000.

• The Clarksdale, Mississippi, (pop. 20,137) station became the town's fourth radio station.

• At West Yellowstone, Montana, which already had an AM station, the FM is yet to be built.

• In Portage, Michigan (adjacent to Kalamazoo), there were 10 applicants. A sole-owner/minority, who had broadcast experience and promised to operate the station himself, was, on paper, a "sure winner." The other nine applicants withdrew without reimbursement. He put the station on the air "on the cheap," kept his Chicago employment and a year later sold out to the owner of other stations in the market for $700,000.

• Sparta, Missouri, operates out of Springfield, where it is one of 22 stations in a metro of 210,000.

• Fredonia, New York, a town of 11,000, saw its FM assignment ultimately picked up by the publisher-owner of the AM station at Dunkirk, population 16,000. It operates from there.

• The allocation at Pine Ridge, South Dakota, has not been built.

• The Harrogate, Tennessee, allocation is operated out of Middlesboro, Kentucky, where it is part of an AM-FM combination.

• The Moundsville, West Virginia, allocation operates out of Washington, Pennsylvania — population 15,864 — where three operators have four stations.

• The Algoma, Wisconsin, allocation was, by most accounts, the first "80/90" station on the air. It went on in the fall of 1986. It now has its third owner, who has gotten an upgrade from 3 kW to 50 kW. It is seeking to make a place for itself in the Green Bay market of 161,000 people and 17 stations.

The "80/90" program attracted all manner of scam artists, including a lot of kitchen table engineers. One young man in the Midwest held a half dozen CPs he was trying to sell. He was for a time in jail, because he couldn't make his court-assessed child support payments. A college professor in New York state was caught filing several applications for the same facility under different names.

The champion "80/90" scammer turned out to be Ralph Savage. In his mid-50s, he formed Sonrise Communications at Columbus, Georgia. His Washington lawyer was Tom Root. Together, they filed more than 160 applications, of which only three were granted. They took in $16.3 million they had gathered from more than 3,000 investors.

It was not the FCC that uncovered the Sonrise operation, but the attorney general of North Carolina. Root was fined and is serving a long prison term. Savage committed suicide before his sentencing.

With very few exceptions, the real money in "80/90" was not made by the operators of the stations but by lawyers, engineers, various kinds of consultants. The promise of bringing local service to communities without it occurred only occasionally. More often than not, they became an inferior facility that would find it very hard to compete in already overcrowded metros. In both the 1960s and the early 1970s, radio overpopulation had been the subject of serious Commission inquiry. That concern quickly changed during the Ferris, Fowler and Dennis Partick commissions. When Partick succeeded Fowler, he said flatly: "The public has never had so many choices. More is better."

In the "80/90 Guide," the Commission said that the policy would encourage ownership of stations by minority and female owners. Since 1985, about 2,000 new stations have gone on the air. The National Association of Black-Owned Broadcasters (NABOB) says that there were 75 minority-owned stations in 1985. At this writing, there are just 85 more.

At this writing, of the 684 stations on "Docket 80/90," 71 had not been applied for; 110 were still unbuilt CPs; 12 had gone on the air, then off; 407 were operating. Eighty-four of the allocations were in towns of more than 25,000. Seventy-two daytimers got FM stations that could not have had them under the old rules that kept stations off the B and C channels. From 1977 through 1984, 849 stations were built in small markets. From 1985 through 1993, 684.

How Much is Too Much?

Since World War II, regardless of the party occupying the White House, FCC policy has generally let the laws of physics dictate the creation of radio stations. In the early 1960s and 1970s, the Commission had studied "overpopulation." Nothing came of it.

With the breakdown of the heretofore B and C FM channels, allowing lower-power stations on them, the top 20 markets, where the dial was already filled up, did not generally feel the impact of overcrowding. It was the markets below and the small markets that felt the greatest impact.

Before 1981, astute small market station builders generally believed that a station had to have 10,000 listeners weekly, which generally meant about 1,000 average listeners at a given time. Radio advertising on small town radio stations could be expected to yield about $3 per $1,000 of home county retail sales (1975 NAB *Future of Radio* study).

Radio has clearly overbuilt itself since 1985. Attractive tourist areas, where there has always been an inducement other than just the promise of a good business, filled up quickly. Lake Tahoe, California, with just 28,000 permanent residents in its metro, has nine commercial radio stations, one for each 3,111 residents; the Aspen/Glenwood Springs, Colorado, market of 40,700 permanent residents has seven commercial stations, one per 5,815 population. On the Florida Keys, where the signals cover more water than land or people, there are 18 commercial stations and a permanent population of 67,200, one station per 3,739 residents.

Overbuilding has not been confined to tourist areas but also reaches unglamorous places like Valdosta, Georgia (one station per 3,676 people), Mankato, Minnesota (one station per 4,000 residents), Scottsbluff, Nebraska (one station per 6,183 people), Kalispell, Montana (12 stations in a "metro" of 50,100 — one per 4,275 people), Roswell, New Mexico (13 stations, one per 3,983 residents).

Just how overbuilt some small markets are is shown by examining the Scottsbluff, Nebraska, market. According to information published in the 1994 *M Street Journal Directory*, in addition to the local stations, two commercial stations at Alliance, Nebraska, get 3.7 percent and 13.8 percent of the listeners in the Scottsbluff market.

Additionally, a non-commercial public FM station at Alliance attracts 1.3 percent of the audience. (The ratings estimates are by the well-regarded Willhight radio surveying firm.) If you add those three stations to the six stations in the market, you have an average of 3,455 population per station.

By the late 1980s and into the early 1990s, the overbuilding had created a new phenomenon: silent stations.

Glenn Olsen tells of the educational process through which he took his small town banker when he was building his Webster City, Iowa-based small market radio group. "When I'd go in to see him about borrowing money for a station acquisition, he'd always ask, after looking over the balance sheet and inventory: 'What are you buying? It looks like a lot of money for what you're getting.'" Glenn then would tell him about radio station cash flows, etc. "Finally, I'd ask the banker, 'Have you ever heard of a radio station going out of business?'" He only half chuckles now, saying: "I'm glad I don't have to ask him that now."

The 1980 FCC Radio Station Financial Report reported that "no stations had gone silent in 1980." By 1989, 112 stations were silent. In 1990, the number was nearly twice that, 210; in 1991, 308; 1992, 352; 1993, 345; 1994, 408.

Of the 1994 stations reported silent in the *M Street Journal*, 154 were in Arbitron-rated markets, 254 were in the small non-rated markets. (More than 25 percent of the silent"stations were FM.)

A Word from Our Sponsor

In 1927, the newly installed Federal Radio Commission made the following pronouncement: "Such benefits as derived by advertisers must be incidental and entirely secondary to the interest of the public." Two years later, the infant radio industry's trade association, NAB, gathered to write a code of industry practices. One of the ideas advanced was that there should be no commercial announcements between 7 p.m. and 11 p.m., then radio's most-listened-to time period. That suggestion was dropped. However, as an advertising medium, radio was doing business with its hands tied behind its back. In early radio, the big advertising successes were being scored by national and regional products — the principal revenue sources of the radio networks and the majority of radio stations, which were located in metropolitan areas.

The numbers of listeners reached and the small amounts of

money in the small markets saw few national and regional product advertising dollars going into them. All through its history, national and regional advertising accounted for little more, and most times less, than 10 percent of a station's revenues. The small market station operator had to take his wares to Main Street.

A retailer advertises for a variety of reasons: To bring customers into the store to inspect goods and services being offered; to introduce new goods, styles and services; to stimulate demand for a product; to teach customers new uses for a product; to prepare the way for personal selling; to keep the business name in front of the public; to reassure customers about previous purchases; to create good will; to promote a business's distinctiveness; to promote special events and/or to promote good prices.

Scores of retailers in small towns found that they could satisfy the goals of their advertising on the local radio station. The majority of chain retailers did not share the local independent store's enthusiasm for radio advertising.

The chain retailer's office, hundreds or even thousands of miles away, was more comfortable with newspaper advertising: Copies of the ads could be read in the home office. Audited circulation figures gave the chain store executive comfort that he knew where his advertising dollars were going. If manufacturer co-operative dollars were being used, that money was easier to obtain in print.

Policy regarding the use of radio advertising traditionally has varied from company to company, even locality to locality, often local manager to local manager. For most of radio's history, business from the chains was small in relation to the market share they enjoyed in the communities. The real money in the small town radio business has always been in the sale of advertising to locally owned retailers — spending their own money.

Long-term, those decisions were not made on the basis of rating points. As Dean Sorenson, owner of a group of small town stations in the Dakotas, Minnesota and Iowa, often says: "Our advertisers take their own rating — customers through the door and money in the drawer."

Depending on small merchants for most of its income made small town radio a very tough business in most places pre-World War II. In 1939, there were about 1 million retail stores (one for each 132 people in a country of 132 million). The average salary was $107 per month. Unemployment was 17.2 percent. Fewer than 2 percent of the nation's retail stores took in more than $200 a week.

A social scientist at the time said of retail merchants: "The economic existence of small merchants, if not solitary, certainly tends to be poor, nasty, brutal and short." The prosperity of the war years and the years following would greatly improve the lot of the independent merchant, like his customers. Small town radio shared that prosperity.

The Chains

Chain retailing had started after the Civil War when A&P began a group of grocery stores. A&P started discounting by establishing what it called "Economy Stores" in 1912. Kroger, Safeway and National Stores followed A&P into discount grocery chain retailing in the 1920s.

In 1902, John Cash Penney operated a department store in Kemmerer, Wyoming. By 1929, he was operating 1,000 stores in small cities and towns. He proved that the chain concept worked, not only in the grocery business, but in other lines as well. Chains of apparel stores, drugstores and general merchandise stores popped up across the country. Catalogue merchants Sears and Montgomery Ward opened chains of retail stores beginning in the 1920s.

During the 1930s, as the Depression ravaged small merchants nationwide, the chains were seen by many as a threat to the settled lives and the respect and standing enjoyed by small merchants. The merchants' small town bankers, suppliers and landlords joined in the growing anti-chain store movement, whose ranks included no less a personage than Supreme Court Justice Louis Brandeis. He thought chain stores were "a threat to democracy."

In 1933 alone, anti-chain store legislation was introduced in 42 state legislatures and passed in 13. A national tax on chain stores was introduced in Congress. It didn't pass.

The general public liked the often-lower prices and wider merchandise selections offered by the chains. They were not buying the argument "pay more — it's good for America." Independent merchants were divided. The chains' pulling power brought increased traffic to town, increasing the potential for sales in their generally smaller stores.

Storm Clouds for Independents

A Chinese proverb says: "Nothing improves the crop like the owner's footprints." However, a one-man or one-woman show has always been challenged by one basic problem: The business depends on the owner's ability and desire to change with factors inside (the aging of the owner, loss of energy and enthusiasm for it) and outside the business (changing lifestyles and demographics, competition, etc.).

The changes in the retail marketplace started in the late 1950s into the 1960s as President Eisenhower's ambitious road-building program changed the face of America. Small town residents were brought within an hour of shopping centers along those new highways. Thousands of square feet of merchandise in climate-controlled surroundings awaited eager shoppers — and, there was parking in front of the store, luring many shoppers out of unattractive downtowns where it was often hard to find a parking space.

As increasing numbers of married women entered the work force, small town merchants stubbornly clung to 9 to 5 store hours, when "customer hours" were now evenings 'til 9 and Sundays. As inflation crept into the economy in the '60s and '70s, a new breed of merchant came on the scene. Discount prices had been a part of the retailing mix for years, but these new discount stores offered generally good merchandise at lower prices. Instead of buying from middle men who added 20 percent to 25 percent to the price they paid manufacturers, the discounters were buying direct from the source in huge quantities. Early discounters operated at low-rent locations without fancy fixtures and only a minimal amount of labor. They sold at prices (at a profit) generally lower than traditional retailers. They were open nights and Sundays. Their unique selling proposition was "stack it high and sell it low."

Initially, much of the merchandise offered was slightly imperfect or leftover merchandise. Brand-name merchandise was not plentiful in the early discount house operations. Major brand-name manufacturers wanted to protect their traditional outlets and the prestige and value they had built into their goods with millions of dollars in advertising.

That changed as the manufacturers couldn't resist the high volume the discounters could offer. It accelerated in the late '70s and early '80s, when the companies were bought up in highly leveraged deals that required enormous cash flow to service mountains of debt. Name-brand merchandise in the discount stores was offered to the customers at prices that were often lower than independents were paying for it.

The high interest rates of the late 1970s and early 1980s caused many small merchants to take a new look at their businesses. Many of the longtime bank relationships evaporated in bank failures and purchases by regional and national bank holding companies. The new bank owners' loan requirements were often more stringent.

In addition to the thousands of well-publicized bankruptcies, many small retailers decided it made good business sense to sell off their buildings (or sublease them at a profit) and liquidate their stock and fixtures, investing the proceeds (at high interest rates) to enjoy an easier, less-hectic life. In 1983, there were 69,000 fewer independent stores than six years earlier. There were 72,000 more chain retailers.

Some entrepreneurs still wanted to be in business for themselves. Increasingly, they were investing in franchised business, where the odds of succeeding were far better than going it alone. They were willing to sacrifice a degree of independence for access to the systems and managerial experience afforded by many franchises. As with the chain stores, many of the advertising decisions were made out of town. Soon, in many small radio markets, chains and franchises accounted for two-thirds of the advertising potential.

The Agencies

John Wannamaker, who spent millions advertising his department store, has often been quoted as saying: "I know half of my advertising money is wasted. The problem is, I don't know which half."

Hard-nosed business people have often seen advertising as a necessary evil. Its success or failure, in their view, is often subject to mystifying intangibles. Time spent creating and placing good advertising, in the view of most business people, is better spent on the other 97 percent of the business. (Retailers, on average, spend 2 percent to 3 percent of their gross on advertising). While print is normally handled in-house, the much smaller portion of advertising expense is most often turned over to an advertising agency.

Agency buying has increasingly been reliant on audience ratings. The accuracy of broadcast ratings has been a controversial subject since radio's earliest days. The truth is that in broadcasting, the number of people who hear (or see) a message is not the issue. The success of the message is determined by a combination of who hears the message, where he or she is, how often he or she hears the message and how compelling the message is.

Advertising is far more art than science. The continued success of an advertising agency lies in retaining clients. Rating numbers give the agency security. If a campaign doesn't meet the customer's expectations, the agency can say that the copy was researched and the schedule reached so many people. If it didn't work, it may be that: Your product may not be right; your price may not be right; your distribution may not be right; your competitor may be outspending you; your competitor may be "dealing or couponing you to death." Buying by the numbers clearly favors large-market radio stations and television stations. Media buying is, even in the age of computers, the most expensive part of the operation of an advertising agency. Pure "dollars and cents" sense tells us that a $150 spot that reaches 15,000 people is cheaper than 10 spots at $10 each on 10 different stations.

Agencies also complain that "radio is hard to buy." It's not just the number of stations and the disparity of the quality of the stations, it's the fact that rates vary from station to station — and often month to month. A buyer no longer can pick up a Standard Rate and Data Service book and know what a spot costs on a particular station. Many stations don't publish their rate. Ironically, many agencies that complain about this brought about the situation. As increasing numbers of stations started "Grid Pricing" based on the demand for time, many ad agencies renamed their time buyers "negotiators" in the 1980s.

Buying time is not the end of the complications and the high cost of doing business at an agency. Getting billing and documentation from stations that the schedule was run as agreed is another complaint of agencies.

The stations often have an equally valid complaint that when an agency takes over a former direct account, the station schedule is often cut — and, although the agency generally gets paid by the client by the 10th of the month, stations wait 90 days or more.

Stuart Sharp, owner of Regional Reps, believes things could be vastly improved by strong, regional representative firms. They could eliminate a lot of the burdensome paperwork if the stations priced their time through them at the same price "they sell direct on Main Street," and refrained from undercutting the rep when an agency wants to make a direct buy. That situation, which has always existed in radio, is like other historic problems in the business — it won't go away until most station operators are making enough money to be able to walk away from a buy if the price is "off the card" and in keeping with a station's agreement with its rep.

The "Wal-Marting" of America

No one person has had as much impact on small town retailing and consequently on the fortunes of small town advertising media as a country merchant from Arkansas named Sam Walton.

Walton, and the firm he founded in 1962, Wal-Mart, is blamed for the disappearance of more small town merchants than any other retailer. Walton and Wal-Mart, after the mid-1970s, turned out to be the realization of a small town newspaper publisher and radio station executive's nightmare: A business that came to town and was phenomenally successful while spending very little money on advertising. In the late 1980s, Walton was chosen "Advertiser of the Decade" by the advertising industry's leading trade publication *Advertising Age*. Wal-Mart at the time was spending less than $1/2$ of 1 percent of sales revenues on advertising, while its principal discount store competitors were spending more than four times as high a percentage of their sales revenues.

In his autobiography, Walton says of advertising: "From the very beginning, we never believed in spending much money in advertising, and saturation helped us save a fortune in that department. When you move like we did from town to town in mostly rural areas, word of mouth gets your message out to customers pretty quickly without advertising." He also said: "We usually ran a circular a month instead of a lot of newspaper advertising."

What he did not say was that, in its early years, Wal-Mart was the largest customer of the local radio station. Dub Wheeler, longtime owner of KHOZ-AM/FM, Harrison, Arkansas, remembers vividly the arrival of Wal-Mart store No. 2 in his town. The first had opened two years earlier at Rogers, Arkansas.

"Wal-Mart was our biggest advertiser. Their bill ran $1,000 to $1,200 a month (at $1.25 a spot). The store manager bought the advertising. One of our disc jockeys, who called himself the 'Old Country Boy,' broadcast a lot of shows direct from the store."

When Sam Walton made one his famous "unannounced" visits to the Harrison store, "He would sit down with the 'Old Country Boy' during his broadcast. I don't think he ever discussed his radio advertising. Instead, he asked him what the customers who shopped the store were saying. I don't think Sam ever appeared on the air during those visits.

"Sometimes, he'd stop by the station to 'visit.' He never talked about advertising. He left that up to the local manager. He'd usually ask me about what I was hearing about his store," Wheeler says. "He was always very interested in the economic progress being made in the town. Even after Wal-Mart virtually quit advertising with us, Sam would still stop by the station for a visit with me."

The big advertising expenditures on KHOZ-AM/FM, like elsewhere, ended, in Wheeler's words, "abruptly and without explanation in the mid-'70s.

"Harrison," Wheeler says, "is a very strong business town and Wal-Mart has been here as long, or even longer, than most of the other businesses in town. Nobody, not even Wal-Mart, gets all the business. There are a lot of businesses here making good money. Wal-Mart is now tripling its size into a 'Supercenter.' That may make a difference."

Wheeler's station is doing record business as this is being written. "In 1965, I spent about $400 getting a Class C license. At first, all we had to show for it and the thousands of dollars it cost to build it was a stack of high power bills paid with revenue from our AM station. When Branson, Missouri, developed (30 miles away), I built a high tower halfway between and established a branch operation there. Next to Harrison, it's our second-best revenue-producing area. In addition to that, our presence there has gotten us an audience base and business 50 miles in every direction from the tower — but only a 'dribble' of business from Wal-Mart."

The dropping of big schedules on radio stations seems to have coincided with Sam Walton's resignation as chairman, at age 57, in 1974. The success of his enterprise and the stock price its shares brought on "the big board" had, in Walton's words, made him and his family far wealthier "than I'd ever imagined it could be. I really didn't see how I could reasonably expect more out of life."

In 1976, Walton decided that his retirement had been a mistake for him. He took back his old job. One of the owners who had been a beneficiary of those big Wal-Mart schedules in the early days happened to run into Walton on one of his frequent visits to the stores. He asked: "Sam, we sure miss your business. Did we do something to make you mad?"

In typical Walton fashion, Sam told him: "No, that decision was made by some of the people in our headquarters during the time I'd stepped back. They were doing such a good job, I just didn't feel I could question their judgment."

The 1970s and 1980s were just right for the Wal-Mart formula. In the 1970s, real family income grew less than it had in any period since World War II. In the 1980s, it actually shrank by 2 percent for the first time since the Depression. It was fertile ground for discounters, as families struggled to maintain their standard of living and enjoy a dizzying array of new time- and labor-saving devices and diversions that appeared: microwave ovens, handy vacs, home VCRs, compact disc players, big-screen television, video games, camcorders, wireless telephones, telephone answering machines.

The Wal-Mart strategy was simple. In Walton's own words: "K mart wasn't going into towns of less than 50,000. Even Gibson (a smaller discount chain based in Texas) wouldn't go into towns much smaller than 10,000 to 12,000. Our formula was working in towns less than 5,000." In those towns, he didn't have to vie with entrenched mass merchandisers who would fight the discounters with a heavy bombardment of advertising and low-priced merchandise. The merchants that Wal-Mart came up against in those "one-horse towns" were no match for Wal-Mart's extraordinary buying clout, distribution system and management controls. In 1968, there were 20 Wal-Mart stores in four states. By 1988, there were more than 1,000 Wal-Mart stores operating into 18 states. By the mid-1990s, Wal-Mart was operating nationwide.

Wherever Wal-Mart located in a small town, the story seemed to be the same as what occurred in Waverly, a town of 8,500 in northeast Iowa. After Wal-Mart had been there for three years, Coast-to-Coast and Pamida, both discounters, closed because they couldn't compete with Wal-Mart's even-lower prices. A shoe store, a fabric shop and a sporting goods store had all closed their doors. A strip shopping center was virtually vacant as one anchor tenant, a department store, closed and the other, a supermarket, moved to a location next to Wal-Mart to cash in on its traffic.

In the mid-'80s, Ted Snider assembled the managers of his Arkansas Radio Network for a daylong sales seminar in Little Rock. The sales consultant who conducted the seminar told attendees that there was "one things worse than having Wal-Mart in town — that was not having Wal-Mart in town."

Towns bypassed by Wal-Mart for "better opportunities" in nearby towns were hurt even more. Those towns tend to empty out as customers leave to shop at Wal-Mart. In the Wal-Mart towns, businesses not in competition with the giant retailer — such as furniture stores, service stations, building supply dealers and restaurants — tend to benefit from Wal-Mart's drawing power. Retailers in merchandise lines also carried by Wal-Mart often carve out a profitable niche by selling higher-style goods — even if it costs more. Other retailers compete by offering services that are not practical for Wal-Mart to offer.

There is not a small market radio operator in the country whose business has not been impacted, sometimes devastated, by the arrival of a Wal-Mart store in his town or nearby. His brethren at the local newspaper are affected as well. In 1975, there were 850 daily newspapers in towns of under 25,000. By 1980, the number was 829. By 1990, 696. Circulation of such papers was 7.5 million daily in 1975. By 1990, it was 6.3 million.

Unwittingly, the small radio stations and the newspapers may have helped Wal-Mart get its story across with millions of dollars of free advertising. Wal-Mart's slogan, printed in its circulars and featured in its television spots, is "Always the low price — Always."

When a Wal-Mart store opening in a new town is announced, the local merchants and their allies predictably try to block the entry of the feared newcomer, appearing before Chambers of Commerce, city councils and zoning boards. In one way or another the message, carried prominently in the local newspapers and on the radio station's local news, is that "Wal-Mart's prices are so low, the local merchants won't be able to compete with them." By the time Wal-Mart opens, their story is so well told in the newspaper and on the radio that little advertising is required. In the fall of 1994, when Wal-Mart opened in Calais, Maine, it bought a schedule of just 35 spots on WQDY-AM/FM to announce its grand opening.

In 1980, the Radio Advertising Bureau conducted a survey of its membership to learn which business categories accounted for the average small station's advertising income. Six business types accounted for 51 percent of the average small station's sales: auto dealers (10.2 percent), banks (9.1 percent), clothing stores, department/discount stores and supermarkets (8.1 percent each), furniture stores (7.3 percent). Six other categories accounted for another 30 percent of the business: restaurants (6.1 percent), appliance stores (5.2 percent), bottlers (4.9 percent), lumber yards (4 percent), savings and loans (3.9 percent) and drugstores (3.4 percent).

In addition to the havoc in the retail business, small market radio's two biggest categories were also impacted. The number of new car dealerships (small market radio's No. 1 advertising category) dropped by more than 3,000 during the 1980s — more than one in 10. In radio's No. 2 category, 2,100 banks either went out of business or were merged into other banks.

Radio had to re-invent itself when television arrived in the late 1940s and the early 1950s. Forty years later, in the small towns, radio clearly had to re-invent its customer list.

Many small market stations were replacing lost retail dollars with new service dollars, including a lot of categories of business that had not used the medium before: health care services, accountants and lawyers, temporary help agencies, animal health care providers, financial services, auto repair, travel agents and a host of other businesses that had not been called on in simpler times.

Sales efforts such as telemarketing small businesses to help further a local cause or event, or offering traded merchandise on radio auctions, had been shunned by most small market stations as being "sleazy." By the mid-'90s, they were found on the best small stations across the country.

In addition to more stations competing for a shrinking traditional advertising base, formidable competition was coming from local cable systems selling local advertising and from a proliferation of free circulation print media. As they had done before, technology and innovation stepped in to assist stations in dealing with the new realities of the marketplace.

Technology and Innovation

It is hard to believe that, between 1948 and 1958, radio industry revenues dropped from $46 million to $41 million, while the number of stations doubled. The average revenue per station on the air was less than half what it had been 10 years earlier. Thanks to the improved reliability of the equipment and the invention of a remote control unit that could be operated by an announcer with an easily obtained "Restricted License," three or four salaries were eliminated from the operating expenses of a radio station.

The new economies of operating a radio station not only helped the profit margins of the stations on the air, but paved the way for profitable stations in communities much smaller than had been economically viable for station location previously.

Technology again in the 1980s and the 1990s would be a paramount issue in allowing more radio stations to exist on what, by any measure, was a shrinking retail advertising market in most small towns.

Computerized Logging and Billing

The computer had made its appearance in the United States around 1950. Computers for much of their history were very expensive. In 1970, it was estimated that the cost of a computerized logging and bookkeeping in a radio station was equal to the salaries of 10 people. By the early 1990s, the cost was less than the cost of one person.

In 1978, Pete Charlton, who had worked in various capacities for small stations in Texas and Oklahoma, started working on a program that would run on an inexpensive Radio Shack computer. In 1980, when he was ready for the market, he started showing up at state and national conventions, demonstrating "The Management" computer program.

Not much for the social part of conventions, Charlton could be found in his room (not a suite) demonstrating his innovation, often until the wee hours of the morning. Not a "sales type," Charlton answered questions from station operators, only some of whom had ever seen a computer, let alone operated one.

Some of the operators were fascinated with computers — most had only one thing in mind, getting their daily log done quickly and accurately. They also wanted to get their bills and affidavits done within hours, rather than the days that task had required all through radio history. The system also promised to re-cap the monthly tally by salesperson.

Rather than the $60,000 to $80,000 such systems had cost since the late 1960s, Charlton's program cost just $1,750, and it was run on a Radio Shack computer, available from a retailer in almost any town for just $2,968 — a total of under $5,000. Within two years, "Management" bookkeeping was running in more than 125 stations. Dozens of competing systems quickly came on the market.

The inexpensive computer system obsoleted the mundane but necessary tasks. The time saved turned a full-time job into a part-time job. The bookkeeper, in many stations, was no longer a "dead expense," but a productive one.

At one station, the bookkeeper was filling her newly found extra hours by conducting telephone sales campaigns. She got a raise: 10 percent of the $1,700 in new revenue the call-outs were generating.

In another small station, collections improved greatly when the bookkeeper set up and managed an ongoing, systematic collection system.

In still another station, the bookkeeper became sales support, spending the extra time the computer system created by taking over much of the salespeople's paperwork and preparing written presentations.

The inexpensive computers contributed to station profitability and replaced tedious chores with satisfying work.

Out of the Sky

Since the 1950s, radio stations had utilized automated programming with varying success. It worked best in AM/FM combos, where generally the AM announcer kept his eye on the automated FM station. In stand alones, it was necessary to have someone on premises to baby-sit the automation because of the short "walk away times" (between loading reel-to-reel music tapes and the cartridge playbacks that carried the non-music elements).

In August 1981, WHRT, Hartselle, Alabama, became the first affiliate of the Satellite Music Network. From then on (until this writing), the national news, the music and the disc jockeys heard on the station were more than 1,000 miles distant. The programming was uplinked to a satellite thousands of miles in the sky and transmitted from there to a satellite dish at the station.

Like conventional radio network programming, there were windows in the 24-hour-a-day programming into which the station inserted its local ads, news and features. The station filled 18 local minutes per hour — the rest came off the "bird."

WHRT was on Satellite Music Network's *Country Coast-to-Coast* format. A second format, *Star Station*, adult contemporary programming, was launched the same day, without a single affiliate. John Tyler, SMN's founder, recalls: "We didn't tell the *Star Station* disc jockeys that they were broadcasting only to the themselves that first day." By the second day, *Star Station* got its first affiliate — a station in Boise, Idaho.

By the end of its first year, SMN had signed up 100 stations and a rival had emerged, Transtar (later Unistar — now Westwood One).

By the mid-'90s, more than half the radio stations in small towns were receiving the majority of their programming from SMN (now a division of ABC), Westwood One, Jones Satellite Networks or one of several other full-time satellite networks whose offerings include all-news, all-talk, programming for children under 12, all shades of religious programming, all-sports, jazz, classical music.

Tyler, who had spent most of his pre-SMN career in television, says he got the idea for satellite radio programming while running a comparatively small TV station in Texas. "At a network television station, you came on in the morning with a little local programming, then carried the network most of the day. Only about three hours a day was programmed by the local station. It was easy to make money. You had plenty of time to concentrate on sales and promotion — the things that make you money. I believed if the same thing could be done in radio, almost any radio station, anywhere, could make money."

Candidly, he says: "There was a lot of resistance to the idea in the early days. A lot of operators thought satellite programming robbed them of their localism. Some still do. I'd hear such things as: 'When the mayor scores a hole-in-one, I want my disc jockeys to talk about it on my station.' " With a chuckle, John asks: "Do those minimum wage disc jockeys really do that?"

John, at this writing a consultant to Jones Satellite Network, says of his idea: "Satellite programming has saved a lot of stations. There are some who just 'ride the bird,' but a lot of our stations do a great job on local news and community programming. Without the savings of being on satellite, they couldn't do that."

Gene Blabey, whose WVOS-AM/FM, Liberty, New York, is on a satellite network and does an outstanding job on its local programming, says: "I guess we've turned the clock back. In the years just before, during and immediately after World War II, small stations got most of their programming from the Mutual Network or one of the other networks. Only a relatively small part of the station's programs were done locally. Much of an announcer's time was waiting to do station breaks. Today, that announcer has been replaced by a computer — as it has been done for more than 25 years in television stations."

Going Network — Staying Local

When satellite programming came, some stations had personnel manually inserting the network breaks. Some others assigned a staffer to make up a reel-to-reel tape on which each local break was recorded in sequence (a job that took at least three hours a day). The tape played when it was signaled by the network system tone. Some put their old automated carousels to work filling the breaks or bought a system that would do that.

The most innovative and least expensive system came from Decatur, Illinois, where the owner of longtime station WDZ developed a system on which local spots were recorded on inexpensive

214

cassettes. Steve Bellinger called his innovation Systemation. Bellinger had left college in his late teens to pursue his first and still major love — radio. He hired on at minimum wage as an announcer when WTCJ, Tell City, Indiana, went on the air in 1948. In short order, he bought his first small station. A series of station ownerships followed.

Bellinger's system, powered by an inexpensive consumer-grade computer, utilized inexpensive consumer-grade cassette decks. It offered satellite-programmed stations almost unlimited walk away time. The system sold initially for about $8,000 — compared with cartridge systems that cost two and one-half to three times as much. Bellinger's slogan: "LIVE is EVIL spelled backward."

A better system emerged in late 1989. It was the brainchild of the chief engineer at a college station, WCAL, Northfield, Minnesota. Tim Valley called his system Audisk. Material was recorded onto and played back on hard disc automation, with initially three hours' storage capacity.

Tim Valley tested his system on FM stand alone WBWA in remote Washburn, Wisconsin. Charlie Jenkins was Valley's first customer. He put it to work at WQKC/WZZB (formerly WJCD-AM/FM) Seymour, Indiana, in February 1990.

Blair Trask, manager of the Seymour stations, recalls the early days of the Audisk installation. "It was hectic. We had taken over the operation of the station just a month before. In addition to the challenges which go with a new purchase that would have to be quickly improved to justify Charlie's and his stockholders' investment, we were dealing with something brand new to us and the industry.

"After we got used to the system and Tim worked out a few flaws, it ran virtually without upkeep or recurring cost, unlike re-purchasing cartridges or cassettes in earlier automation systems." The success of the Audisk at the Seymour stations is best demonstrated by the fact that Jenkins installed the same system at his Jeffersonville, Indiana, station, WXVW, and Louisville, Kentucky, station, WAVG.

Digital automation spread quickly. By March, Bellinger introduced his digital system at the Country Music Radio Seminar. By April, a half-dozen digital systems were being demonstrated at the NAB Convention. One of those systems came from Pete Charlton's Management, called Digital D.J. It interfaced Pete's computer logging and bookkeeping.

Fifteen years after he demonstrated his computer logging/bookkeeping system at the NAB, Charlton has dozens of competitors, but his formerly one-man business has grown to 25 employees. He says:

"Not being a salesman, I would have been scared to death if I'd known how many competitors I'd have — but the business has grown and prospered far beyond anything I'd dreamed of."

Other Innovators

To allow unattended operation, two portable remote control units came on the market in the 1980s, from Burk Technologies in Pepperell, Massachusetts, and Genthner Electronics in Salt Lake City. The portable units made it possible to monitor and make routine transmitter adjustments from virtually any telephone, anyplace in the world. Many small market operators put the equipment to work from police stations, hospitals, motel lobbies, 24-hour convenience stores and telephone answering services. This made it possible for the stations to operate on weekends and evenings without anyone in the station. It also made it practical for many small stations to operate 24 hours a day.

As the '90s came, Ray Reich, owner of WDXY/WIBZ, Sumter, South Carolina, diversified by setting up a nationwide transmitter monitoring service. His firm, Southern Communications, monitors a station's transmitter, makes necessary adjustments, takes required readings and faxes a copy of the station transmitter log the next morning. His on-duty engineer activates EBS messages and notifies station personnel of any emergency that requires attention. The service costs stations $275 a month for monitoring 12 hours a day.

George Marti, who freed station owners of much of the financial burden of leased telephone lines with his Marti short wave system in the 1960s, came up with a technical system that could keep stations alive in dying towns.

With a Marti two-way microwave system, KCLE, Cleburne, Texas, resurrected two small town Texas stations:

Hamilton, Texas, 30 miles from Cleburne, had taken a real beating during Texas' mid-'80s economic downturn. The county's 8,600 population shrank to just 7,700 by 1990. Retail sales retreated 16 percent from their pre-bust level.

San Saba, 40 miles farther out, was even smaller and in worse economic shape. By 1990, its county population was just 5,400, with retail sales of only $26.6 million.

It was obvious that neither community could support a conventional radio station, even with a bare-bones staff of four or five low-paid employees. Instead, with Marti's help, the KCLE owners, Lloyd and Gary Moss, came up with a system that could put KBAL, San Saba, and KCLW, Hamilton, on the air with just two full-time, comparatively well-paid people. Both sell time and handle other chores like covering local news and other local programming, calling play-by-play sports and taking part in community activities.

All but the local programming would be the KCLE programming. Breaks for local commercials and community service would be recorded and inserted at Cleburne like a network.

Hamilton and San Saba had local radio stations again. Lloyd and Gary Moss recovered their investment in three years. In Marti's words: "Those radio stations are important in those communities. If somebody dies or loses a dog, the stations are there. In addition to the programming, the two-way Marti microwave system also connects the community by telephone toll-free to Cleburne when the studio is not manned. Copy and orders are faxed between the two locations. Those stations are good for the communities and have been good to the owners. That's good for everybody."

One-Woman Radio Station

When KPAH, Tonopah, Nevada, went on the air in 1982, it had a staff of seven. The immediate market area had a population of 4,000, with a total of 150 business licenses. It lost a lot of money quickly.

A year and a half into the venture, in early 1984, the station's non-broadcaster absentee owners (a former Nevada governor and two Las Vegas advertising men) decided drastic steps had to be taken to stop the losses — or they'd have to take the station off the air.

The station became affiliated with Satellite Music Network. Systemation was installed to insert the local ads and other local programming. A Management computer logging and billing system was installed. A Burk System was installed at the reception desk of a local 24-hour-a-day gambling casino. The attendant on duty made the required readings, made necessary adjustments and monitored the station. The casino got a schedule of ads in return for providing the service.

The staff was reduced from seven to just one person, who had been at the station just two months. Her only previous radio experience was conducting a talk show on a station her former husband owned in Alaska.

A typical day for Eula Ray at the one-woman station started with an hour spent programming Systemation and recording local spots and programs, such as a classified ad program, a job market broadcast and community bulletin boards.

She then left for a local restaurant for the small town's "coffee klatsch." In her words: "You could get most of the local news there and see a lot of station customers." She then made the rounds of in-person sales calls. Others were made by phone.

Late afternoons, she checked the automation system print-out of what had run that day. She entered the results into the station's computer bookkeeping system, which produced bills and affidavits at the end of the month.

To broaden the station's potential advertiser base, translators were established in 12 communities that did not have radio stations — some up to 100 miles from Tonopah. After six months, one additional person was hired to do play-by-play sports and work the translator-served communities.

At this writing, the station's call letters have been changed to KHWK, "The Hawk." It still operates on SMN with the Systemation gear, and the computer logging and billing systems are still in place. The Burk System is still at the gambling casino. The one-time one-woman station now has two employees: the owner-manager and an operations man.

That the station is still on the air is a tribute to modern technology. It has survived two changes of ownership. (Eula Ray left the station during one of them.) What's more, Tonopah, which in 1984 had a population of 4,000, is estimated to be 25 percent smaller now as a result of a decline in the mining economy and defense cutbacks.

1990 Radio Financial Report

The FCC had discontinued having radio stations file an annual financial report in the early 1980s (a de-regulation action). The best available tally of the radio industry's financial health came in annual reports issued by NAB, tabulating the results of voluntary questionnaires it sent to all stations. Only about 20 percent of the stations responded. The 1990 NAB Report was, to say the least, glum. It showed that grosses and cash flow margins were down in almost all categories of stations:

	Revenues	Cash Flow
AM Daytimers	-.01%	-3.4%
AM Fulltime	-17%	-45.7%

FM Stand alones	-16%	-34%
AM/FM Combos	+4.5%	-21%

Financial information from other sources included a tally of 1990 station sales with an average price than was more than one-third below 1989's average.

A report showed that 30 percent to 40 percent of all stations purchased during the five years between 1985 and 1989 were not making their payments as agreed.

Total industry radio advertising ad sales were down 2.7 percent, for the first decline since the 1950s. It was estimated that more than 60 percent of stations were losing money — double the number in the 1980 FCC Report.

In a year, the number of stations off the air had nearly doubled, from 112 to 210. That number would rise to 308 in 1991, 375 in 1992. It would drop slightly to 363 in 1993, then rise again to 408 in late 1994. It was not just an AM problem — almost 30 percent of the stations that went dark were FM stations. In 1980, no stations were reported off the air.

In the cities, much of the financial problem could be traced to overly optimistic projects that led to overpaying with too much high-interest borrowed money. In the small towns, the stations off the air and in financial distress were generally operated by inexperienced or inept operators whose finances were so limited they couldn't afford to install the new technological innovations that had come on the market in the 1980s. It took a lot more ability and energy to stay afloat in markets where more stations and other media were chasing fewer traditional advertising dollars.

Al Sikes Arrives at the FCC

When Al Sikes came to the FCC in mid-1989, he found a radio industry more chaotic than any since 1927, when the Federal Radio Commission came into being.

Sikes, like Mark Fowler, had a background in radio. Unlike Fowler, who had spent his early years mainly as on-air talent, Sikes' radio experience had been in management for nine years. He'd also held numerous government posts, including a four-year term as head of the National Telecommunications and Information Administration at the Commerce Department.

Clearly, the "80/90" mess had gotten out of control. The Sikes

Commission returned to the pre-Reagan policy that withdrawing applicants could receive no more than reimbursement for their documented, prudent expenses. His Commission further ruled that an applicant going to hearing stage could get no reimbursement. As an attorney serving a conservative president, Sikes knew that many of the ideas being put forth by the industry were not do-able under Communications Act and longstanding Commission precedent. Very simply, the Commission has always favored as many choices as possible for the listener, and a variety of voices within a community.

Ideas advanced by the industry included a freeze on grants for new stations and a showing that the economic vitality of a community could support a new radio station. Although there was an economic hardship rule on the Commission books that could be used by an existing station, it usually caused a delay and quite an expense for a prospective station builder who wanted to enter a market. It never stopped the building of another station. What's more, historically, towns that were thought to be too small for one station, or a second or third, proved otherwise, if not immediately, then over time.

In 1990, the country was seriously overpopulated by radio stations, but the country was also over-office built and over-stored. Nobody was seriously advancing a federal law that would freeze building office buildings or stopping new stores from being started. There was no place for a station-building freeze in a Republican, "let-the-marketplace-decide" administration. In Congress, which has oversight responsibility over the FCC, there was no enthusiasm for protecting incumbent licensees from new competition.

The Sikes Commission thought that an industry with bigger potential would attract and keep well-financed and well-managed companies. The 12-station ownership cap was increased, first to 18, now 20, stations in each service (AM, FM and TV).

In early 1991, Local Marketing Agreements (leases) were entered into at Scottsbluff, Nebraska, where Michael Tracy, owner of KOAQ-AM and KMOR-FM, leased KOLT-AM, which was about to go off the air because of financial problems. (He since bought the station.) Shortly after, Bob Neathery, owner of KWPM-AM and KSPQ-FM, West Plains, Missouri, entered, with Commission approval, into a lease of his grandson Brad's 50,000-watt FM station, located 20 miles away at Willow Springs. KGAR simulcasts the AM station's programming. The AM station on 1490 did not adequately cover the West Plains trade area, particularly early morning and nights.

The Neathery idea got the attention of *The New York Times*, which gave it a half-page of space in its business section in the spring of 1991. The idea quickly spread to large and medium markets, where it saved a lot of owners struggling with large amounts of debt to service.

If the Commission rules permitted leasing, why not allow broadcasters to own two or more stations in the same service in the same market? It had been allowed up to 1941.

The idea was not popular industry-wide. Strong objections came from minorities. NAB endorsed the idea. Station brokers also saw such rules changes as a possible boon to the station trading market, which was suffering as financing dried up because of the widespread financial problems stemming from the highly leveraged deals of the station-buying frenzy of the mid to late-'80s.

Fearing a backlash in Congress over what might be termed "undue concentration of control," the big players in the industry wanted what came to be known as duopolies limited to the larger markets. Sikes, who had earlier had ownership interest in small markets, knew there needed to be consolidations there, too. The rule enacted allowed a single owner in a small market to own up to 50 percent of the stations serving that market. The rule was crafted so that almost any station could be part of a three-station mix of two AMs and one FM or one AM and two FMs.

Three years after the rule went into effect, almost every state has several small town duopolies — and the number is growing steadily.

Group Ownership

When ownership limits were raised, first from 7-7 to 12-12, then to 18-18 and now 20-20, there were widespread fears inside and outside the industry that a few big companies might expand their holdings — and that small town radio might well go the way of the drive-in restaurant on the outside of town being replaced by McDonald's and Burger King. Apparently, small town radio is still dominated by the mom-and-pop operations that characterized it since nearly the beginning. Apparently, radio in the small towns is less attractive to group owners — not more.

In 1960, there were 30 groups operating stations at three locations exclusively in towns of 25,000 and under. Although the number of small town stations has grown from 1,618 to 5,000, the number of licensees holding licenses in three or more markets under 25,000 grew to just 41. Their holdings in 1960 equaled about 10 percent of such stations. In the mid-1990s, such groups account for less than 4 percent of the stations. Of the 1960 group owners, only three survive as small town group owners in three or more locations: Bob Ingstead and the Linder family in the Midwest and Cary Simpson in Pennsylvania. A few of the other 27 have scaled down their operations. Few of those who left found satisfactory buyers for their groups. They found that the parts were equal to more than the whole. Often, the buyer of the individual station was the manager. He perhaps couldn't pay as much as someone else would have, but he was a known quantity to the seller, who generally was going to carry a note on the station.

Dean Sorenson, who started building his group of stations in the early 1970s, believes the "small market business will always be dominated by owner-operators. It's a business that's made for that — not usually for chain operation. The threshold for a group owner to make money with a small station is much higher than it used to be. First, it takes a station big enough to pay the manager a very good income. If the station can't do that, the manager will either go in business for himself or be stolen. There are more stations in small towns that need good managers than there are good managers."

Sorenson, whose group now includes stations in eight markets and could conceivably add as many as a dozen more markets, says: "There are plenty of stations for sale, but I have perimeters in which I'm interested: The Dakotas, Minnesota and Iowa. We're not going to spread beyond that, because I've spent my whole life and entire career in this area. I think I know it pretty well."

Secondly, Sorenson says: "We'll pay eight times cash flow if the property includes a 50-kW or more FM, if we see some upside. We are confident we can do all right with a station like that, if the market is right. We get offered something almost every week — but we haven't bought a lot lately."

Sorenson, unlike some group owners, has shown by his record that he goes into a market to stay. As friends say: "He's an operator, not a speculator. He enjoys seeing his stations grow and yield good operating profits, rather than getting a big payoff at sale time."

Sorenson has sold just two stations during his group-operating years. He recalls: "One station was in a very small, isolated market. It would have worked if I had found someone to manage it who, with his family, would have been happy living there. We sold it — I lost some money."

The other Sorenson sale involved an AM-only "a good distance from our other stations. On a visit there, I told the manager I wanted to sell it. The station was doing very well. My manager said that he'd like to buy it." In typical Sorenson fashion, he said: "Let's look at the books and see what you can pay me for it." The station, in Sorenson's words, is still doing well. Sorenson's manager ultimately bought out his FM competitor.

Sorenson was a widely quoted, vocal critic of the change that allowed a single owner to build more than one AM or one FM in a single market. Three years later, he says: "I always knew that the rules change was good for a lot of operators from a business standpoint, but I didn't believe it was going to promote program diversity, as many duopoly adherents were promising. What I thought would happen is happening in a lot of big markets. An owner is using his second AM or FM, not to bring something new into the market, but to put on another station in the same format as a competitor to cut into the competitor's market share (audience and revenue).

"I think," he says, "it can work for everybody's benefit in overcrowded small markets. We're seeing some of this now. We'll see still more in the future: One operator buying out his financially stretched competitor across town — or down the road. A lot of stations won't survive unless that's done. The buyer gets the opportunity to do more business and make more money. The public gets the benefit of having more stations from which to choose."

Sorenson, who got his first managing job in the late 1960s at KGFX, Pierre, South Dakota, has been both a manager and a group operator. "Obviously, I like this better; as you can see, that's what I'm doing."

Sorenson explained the difference in a 1993 edition of the *Small Market Radio Newsletter*.

"Running a small market radio station is fun, especially because you can 'fix' things many times each day. But running one station is a far cry from running a bunch of them. You have to forget 'fix it' and 'get into business.'

"When you're running a station, you wake up listening to it while shaving, making notes of improvements you would like to make on the morning show — or you do the morning show, with a Dictaphone in the control room. I always did that so I could capture those many ideas and improvements which raced through my mind while I was doing the show. It's exhilarating.

"It's so much fun," he continues, "that you might decide to buy two or even four more stations — so you can have two or four times more fun.

"But moving into the position of small market head puts you 'two memos and two weeks away' from any decision. You now become involved in motivating other people, counting on their progress and growth for your success. And, frankly, many of those folks fail to see the exciting big picture you do. So, you become a hand-holder as you bring them up to speed, helping build that new picture and helping them to buy into that big picture. Often, they never do.

"Where do you start? You build rules and policies into your company. Keep in mind that your policies will be bought into and followed by your staff when you follow them first and best. Because, you need to set the example. You need to make fewer impulse and knee-jerk decisions and actions. It's clearly not as much fun or as daring as when you were the flying, growing entrepreneur station-builder."

Finally, Sorenson said: "You also need to remove yourself from the 'show biz arena' to become a business operator. Running a group is a business focusing on financing and financial relationships, recruiting, training and building people and providing an environment for your staffs to excel. Being on the air, on the street, being 'Mr. Radio' in a small town is a pretty good life — but, so is this."

A Buyer's Market

Until 1960, small market radio stations generally sold for 1-time their gross sales. The law of supply and demand pushed that figure up to 1.5-times to 2-times gross. Those figures were subject to adjustment for various reasons, but they were a good starting point.

In the 1970s, when inflation came into play, some stations were bringing as much as 2.5-times to 3-times gross. In 1983, Chapman Company, based in Atlanta, was the country's largest broker of small market stations. One of the firm's vice presidents said then that AM/Class A FM Combinations were bringing 2-times to 2.5-times, full-time AMs 1.5-times to 1.7-times, AM daytimers 1.25-times to 1.5-times. As small market station prices dropped and listings and qualified buyers for small stations declined in the later '80s, the 35-year-old Chapman Company went bankrupt. The number of small station brokers shrank.

In the 1970s, a potential small market buyer most often found that the asking prices would seldom support the payment schedule financing required. Stations sold because buyers then could look forward to 8 percent to 10 percent increases.

By the mid-'80s, as sections of the country in turn suffered economic problems and competition increased from new stations and FM stations that increased their coverage, buyers were reluctant to pay what was described as "an opportunity premium." So many buyers had been disappointed by their failure to reach what often turned out to be overly optimistic expectations, that multiples of gross largely became a thing of the past. The important consideration became "trailing cash flow" — how much money was there available to service debt?

Bob Kimel, a former station owner and for many years the senior partner in New England Media, a media brokerage firm, says that under selling conditions in the 1990s, many good properties that might have come on the market in his area are being kept by the owners. The current 5-times to even 8-times cash flow multiples are not very attractive, since sale profits are now taxed by the federal government at regular rather than half the ordinary rates at which capital gains were taxed prior to the 1986 Tax Reform Act.

Missouri broker Ralph Meador sees the market for small market stations improving. Small Business Administration guarantees will make it easier to finance them. He also believes that "the market at this time is very good for young people who can get into a station of their own a lot easier than they used to."

Jerry Johnson, a Minneapolis-based media broker who covers what has been traditionally the best small market area in the country, says: "It's now a buyer's market. Values are rising, but we're not concentrating as much on getting listings as qualified buyers. When we find them, we can usually find them a station."

Caught in the Low Market

Phyllis Rice spent the first years of her working career as a bookkeeper in an automobile agency. When she heard there was an opening at the Tomah, Wisconsin, radio station, WTMB, for a copywriter, she decided she might like a change.

Mrs. Rice enjoyed the new job. She particularly liked dealing with the customers by phone, first getting their copy changes then calling back, reading the finished product for approval. Some accounts she saw personally.

Her boss, Hugh Dickey, encouraged her to try her hand at selling. "You're doing most of what needs to be done now. Why not make some more money?"

When Dickey decided to sell his station, he found an eager buyer for his 100,000-watt FM station — a Milwaukee-based non-profit religious group. He sold the companion AM daytimer to Mrs. Rice for $125,000 with an SBA-guaranteed loan from a local bank.

"The AM station had been here long before the FM station (AM 1959, FM 1965)," she recalls. "Now that I was selling just AM radio, everybody said: 'I sure wish you were on FM, like you used to be.'"

Mrs. Rice hired a consulting engineer to find her a frequency. When it was assigned, she promptly filed for it. So did others. Quickly, she petitioned for another FM frequency. Again, there were competing applications.

In addition to Mrs. Rice's mounting legal bills in her quest for an FM license, her market was hurt by a declining farm economy, "The Wal-Marting" of the town and an ambitious street re-building project in the central business district that for more than a year brought retail activity to a near-standstill. Mrs. Rice was forced to seek Chapter 11 protection from her creditors. She held on.

By 1992, the farm economy was turning up, the street work was completed and many of the local businesses were finding that "there was life after Wal-Mart." Although she now had two FM competitors, WTMB-AM was doing well enough to emerge out of Chapter 11. She had beaten the odds, which traditionally saw only one-and-a-half of 10 businesses that go into Chapter 11 come out of it. Then, the worse loss of all came.

In 1992, Phyllis Rice's son, John, was an enthusiastic worker in the movement to elect independent presidential candidate Ross Perot. John had driven to a big Perot rally 100 miles from Tomah. He was killed in an auto accident on his way home from the rally.

When a broadcaster friend called to offer his condolences, she thanked him, saying: "In the small town radio business, you get to know more people well than in any business I can think of. You find that a lot of bad things happen to good people. When something like this happens, all you can do is pick up what you have left — and keep going."

One of the FM licenses had been awarded to son John and his fiancee, Jamie Westpfahl. Mrs. Rice inherited John's share. The two survivors decided to move the FM station to the WTMB studios to share expenses. "It wasn't great, but we were doing a lot better together and the future looked pretty good," Mrs. Rice says.

The second Tomah FM license went to an unemployed small town policeman. He had immediately put the CP up for sale. As his extensions were close to running out, he found a buyer, a young satellite network salesman, Dave Magnum.

Magnum built a state-of-the-art FM station, installed one of his company's formats — "oldies" — put his wife in charge of the day-to-day operations (while he continued with the network) and put a well-trained sales effort on the street.

Two years after he put WBOG on the air, Magnum was ready to expand. He looked downtown to main street, where WTMB-AM and WZFR-FM were housed together in second-floor quarters that were easily large enough to accommodate his station. He approached Mrs. Rice and Ms. Westpfahl about buying their stations.

At 66, Mrs. Rice was ready to slow down. Jamie had become, in Mrs. Rice's words, "a very good air talent." She was interested in pursuing that talent on a bigger station. "So, we agreed to sell."

About selling in a down market, Mrs. Rice says: "No, I'm not disappointed. I never thought about retiring. I didn't know whether I'd live to be 66. I bought WTMB with $125,000 borrowed money. Obviously, I'm leaving with more than I came in with. Jamie will have a nice nest egg for a young woman.

"Eleven years ago, when I was Hugh Dickey's sales manager at WTMB-AM/FM, the last year before the sales, we did nearly $500,000 gross. I'm sure that the three stations here now aren't doing that kind of business, but I think one operator with three stations might do even better. The customers will have two fewer radio salesmen calling on them. They'll have more time for other business things. The community will have three local stations from which to choose. It will have to be better for everybody."

Hard Times at a High Gross Station

Vincennes, Indiana (population less than 20,000 — home county about twice that) has, since 1940, been home to the state's 12th oldest radio station, WAOV.

The station was put on the air by group newspaper owner Eugene Pullium (former Vice President Dan Quayle's grandfather). Pullium's newspaper holdings included the *Vincennes Sun*.

Although few newspaper publishers admitted it, they built radio stations in radio's early days to protect the advertising base of their newspapers. Through the 1940s, WAOV was content to cash the monthly affiliation checks from the Mutual Network and to run a lot of national and regional business, much of it generated by Pullium's Indianapolis station, WIRE. The station generally followed an unwritten policy that it would not "disturb" the *Sun's* big local customers.

Things changed quickly in the 1950s. The Mutual checks stopped coming. Much of the national and regional business went to television. The station was not doing well when Pullium sold it to his publisher at the *Sun.* Howard Greenlee couldn't afford to continue the station's less-than-aggressive stance on selling local advertising. He also was reasonably sure that a better radio sales effort at WAOV might ultimately help create more business for the newspaper.

During the 20 years Greenlee owned WAOV (and ultimately its sister 3,000-watt rock FM station), the stations paid for themselves several times over, made Greenlee money along the way and turned a handsome profit when they were sold to local contractor-entrepreneur Bob Green.

As Green had done in his other businesses, he installed strong management to "think and do big." They did! Through much of the 1980s, the country AM Class IV and its rock-formatted FM billed close to a million dollars a year.

Green, a close observer of other businesses like his, saw the remarkable success enjoyed by high-powered WSTO-FM at Owensboro, Kentucky, where one of his four Executive Inn Hotels was located. Green decided his radio station could enjoy a similar success by acquiring 50,000-watt WFML-FM at Washington, Indiana — 20 miles from Vincennes.

Because of the overlap rules then in effect, Green had to dispose of his lower-powered FM station at Vincennes and the daytime sister station of the Washington FM. In Green's tax bracket, his CPA advised him that it made sense to donate the stations to Vincennes University. The advice turned out to be just the opposite.

The university changed the donated FM station to full-time country, doing serious damage to the audience of WAOV-AM. It hired the WAOV sales manager to manage its FM station.

Vincennes got another FM station in 1988 when Mark Lange, a professor of radio management at the university, built WZDM. Lange had made a lot of money in and out of a small market turnaround.

Still another FM station went on the air 10 miles away at

Bicknell — WUZR. The owner of that station was a former WAOV manager who, in Mark Lange's words, "knew all the Vincennes businesspeople — and all of WAOV's 'secrets.'"

All along, Stu Lankford's WAKO-AM/FM, 30 miles away in Lawrenceburg, Illinois, was selling actively in Vincennes. There were strong ties as WAOV, before WAKO went on the air in 1957, had for years maintained a branch studio/sales office there.

In 1992, Green, then in his 80s, was still a "hard-driving workaholic." He died in an early-morning auto crash on his way home from an inspection trip to his Evansville, Indiana, Executive Inn.

Two years later, WAOV and its 50,000-watt FM station were doing less than WAOV and its then 3,000-watt FM sister were doing in the 1980s. They were consistently showing cash flow deficits of $17,000 a month. The Green heirs decided it was time to bail out.

When Lange heard that the Green heirs wanted to sell, he and his partner, Dave Crooks, went to see them. The price was $250,000 (half in cash). In Lange's words: "We bought it in 10 minutes."

The lawyers worked out an LMA to take effect immediately, which would give Lange and his partner ownership of the FMs and WAOV. The formal sale took place shortly.

The WZDM operations were moved into the WAOV studios atop the Green family's Vincennes Executive Inn. Much of the WRBT satellite-delivered programming is also operated out of the Vincennes location.

"We still maintain a studio and offices in Washington — and we always will," Lange says. The three-station "tri-opoly" offers listeners Satellite Music Network's "traditional country," a format exclusive to its huge coverage area. It also carries schedules of college and professional sports — many also exclusive in its area — and an area-wide "High School Game of the Week."

WZDM continues its established adult contemporary format and some play-by-play sports. WAOV carries a lot of news, talk and sports — plus Westwood One's "AM Only" adult standards music format.

Eight salespeople sell all three stations, with the help of one sales support person, in Vincennes and Washington. There are a total of six other staffers — "always a live body on duty 24 hours a day in Vincennes," in Lange's words. "The other stations in the area have gone to unattended operation most evenings and overnights. Having a live announcer available to broadcast news updates and handle emergencies

— and answer the phone — gives us a competitive advantage.

"When we took over two of our competitors, we debated whether to have a separate sales staff for each station," Lange recalls a year and a half later. "We decided that one of the greatest contributions we could make to the business community would be to cut the number of salespeople the merchants had calling on them. Our salespeople have the advantage that an old-timer talked about during his presentation at a state broadcasters meeting. Like the old days of block programming, our salespeople have something to sell everybody. We don't have to pass up anybody."

Courage

Small market broadcasters are, for the most part, optimistic people. They are so consumed by their everyday activities that there is little time for planning for the future — or thinking about contingencies in the event of the unexpected.

Fred Hirsch, owner/operator of WDME, Dover-Foxcraft, Maine, said in 1987 that had pretty well described him until January 3 of the year before. He and his then-wife, Vicki, had taken an after-Christmas break — a skiing trip. During that trip, he suffered a skiing accident that made him perhaps permanently crippled. He was away from the station, which he had owned for five years, until late December, almost 12 months.

His full-time station, which had just five full-time employees, managed a 3.8 percent sales increase during a year in which RAB said radio sales industry-wide had grown by 3.5 percent.

Upon his return to work, only short hours initially, he credited his stations' performance in his absence to the efforts of the station's sole salesperson and his wife, who gave up her job as manager of the local Chamber of Commerce to pitch in at the station while the boss was gone.

The medical expenses were tremendous, but mostly covered by insurance. One expense, not covered by insurance but very high, was making the WDME-AM/FM facility friendly to the wheelchair of its owner-operator.

Fred, an imaginative man, had moved his station from the tiny 2½-room suite in which it was located when he bought it to a surplus sleeper-lounge railroad car. The lounge served as the station's principal office/reception area. The sleeper compartments were utilized as studios, a production room and control room. The car had cost him $6,250. The move to Dover-Foxcroft cost $3,500. Another $2,500 had been spent to make renovations and redecorate it. In the railroad car, the town not only had a radio station, but what quickly became a tourist attraction. WDME-AM/FM had the distinction of being the only radio station in the nation housed in a railroad car.

That railroad car was a challenge to the workmen who would convert it to being wheelchair-friendly. A large door had to be cut through the heavy steel wall. A ramp had to be built. Carpet had to be replaced by tile. Also, Marti equipment had to be purchased to allow Hirsch to do some broadcasting from his home when bad New England weather made a trip to the station impossible.

People who come in contact with men and women with infirmities similar to Fred's often find those people demanding and self-centered. That was not Fred. Soon after he found that his disablement was probably permanent (barring a scientific breakthrough), Hirsch told his wife Vicki that she was too young, too attractive and too talented to be tied down to a man with his disability. He says: "She protested that, but I insisted. This was something that I felt I should deal with alone." Vicki left to start life over, with Fred's full blessing. As a result of her experience during his absence, she got a management job at a station in a larger market.

Fred still recalls, with not a small measure of pride: "While I was gone, a flood swept the area, causing a major emergency. Vicki and the small staff stayed on the air 24-hours-a-day keeping listeners abreast of conditions and relaying emergency messages. The area won't ever forget that event — or what my radio stations did."

Fred is a caring man, too. Shortly after he returned to his station in the wheelchair, he learned that the 23-year-old top-billing salesperson of another Maine small market station had been killed in an auto accident. Dave Tudor, owner-operator of WHOU at Houlton, Maine, remembers Fred was the first to call him, asking: "Is there anyway I can help you?"

Although Fred says the station was never much of a financial success, it was an outstanding small market radio station from a programming and community service standpoint: It annually did a three-hour remote broadcast from the state capital on "Moose Day," when 900 hunters were awarded the right by drawing to hunt for the limited number of moose; it broadcast the graduation ceremonies of high schools in its area; it got an AP award for Fred's Saturday morning *Radio Talk* program, on which he discussed his station and radio generally from the listeners' point of view. In 1990, WDME-AM/FM was one of five small stations nationwide nominated for an NAB Marconi Award.

Fred, who had started his radio career as a desk assistant at NBC News, credited his "close to the community" programming to his three years with Bill O'Shaunecy at WVOX, New Rochelle, New York. Of him, Fred said: "His views on industry affairs have made him somewhat of an enigma to many in the business, but he's one of the great community broadcasters."

By 1994, 13 years after he'd come to Dover-Foxcroft and eight years after his paralyzing ski accident, Fred decided to sell WDME. "I knew the timing wasn't quite right from a financial standpoint, but I knew it was right for me."

Like other markets, Dover-Foxcraft had been impacted by the new realities in radio. WRQB at Brewer, Maine, had become a giant country music success, earning numerous nationwide awards and, in Fred's words, "quite a bit of business out of my area." And an "80/90" went on the air eight miles away at Dexter (WGUY) with, in Fred's words, "an oldies satellite format and good sales effort." The new stations, plus the New England economy, had taken WDME's grosses from their high in 1989 to about 10 percent less.

Fred, contemplating a sale, found that instead of the 2-times gross ($55,000 x 2 = $110,000) he had paid in 1981, he would be lucky to get 1-time gross (1 x $210,000) in 1994. He didn't. He sold at a published price of $150,000 (20 percent down — balance over six years).

He does not blame his personal infirmity, the new competition or the New England economy. He says: "I spent my time doing the things I liked doing (news and programming) instead of putting the effort into the sales I should have. But, it was a great 13 years."

Fred has moved to a larger city, near a "female companion" he met during her time as editor of a weekly newspaper in the WDME area. He says: "I met her after my accident. She volunteered — she didn't inherit my problem. That's very different."

Fred is out of radio, "sort of." He is a public relations consultant with clients including a university. He is also a free-lance writer, often called on to author articles on radio and television. About plans for the future or unexpected emergencies, he says: "I guess I'm still a small market person by temperament. I'm busy with my everyday activities. I don't take much time to plan for the future or concern myself with what might happen. We'll deal with what might happen — when it happens."

The Public Interest, Convenience and Necessity

During the 1980s, when there were widespread predictions of the demise of small towns and the stations in them, John Carl, the longtime owner/operator of KCOB-AM/FM, Newton, Iowa, said: "Growing up in a small town has been a wonderful experience for my children. I would hate that my grandchildren wouldn't have that same opportunity. And, not just because I've done it, I think good local radio stations make an invaluable contribution to small town life."

Commission policy over the years has favored the creation of such small stations in small towns for a very good reason: Good local radio stations do the things for a community that outside stations can't do. They most often give locals, newcomers and visitors a sense of place that no other station or communications medium can offer. They generally stand for the things that improve the life of a community. Successful managements not only involve their stations but involve themselves in the civic and religious movements that enhance the quality of life there.

Much of what they do goes unnoticed outside the community and may not always be fully appreciated within the community — until, as has happened more often in recent years, the station goes silent or is moved out.

In many small towns, it is only the local radio station that carries the fact that a friend has passed on, or that a neighbor or relative has had a new baby, or that a neighbor's barn burned, or that the county or city board is planning an increase in the property taxes. These stations are the vehicles that carry urgent pleas for a blood donation to save a youngster's life, that the high school band needs a donation to march in the president's inaugural parade, that the school system is deficient in a vital but not-budgeted area.

When Gerry Boos, his partner Todd Hale and the family of a deceased partner sold KRFO-AM/FM, Owatonna, Minnesota, after owning it for more than one-third of a century, the townspeople organized a reception to say "Thank You" for what the station had done for them. Hundreds upon hundreds came. In Boos' words: "We never won any state or national awards. We were so busy, we never had time to enter contests." (KRFO, bought in 1956 for $30,000, "by the hardest," sold for a total of $1,050,000 35 years later, which Boos termed "pretty good pay for doing good.")

More often than not, important contributions to a community

go largely unnoticed outside:

A pre-Christmas fire in Exeter, New Hampshire, in 1991 at the town's Family Service Agency destroyed the entire stock of clothing, food and toys destined to go to the community's needy. The town's radio station, WERZ, quickly broadcast an appeal for donated replacements. The effort was successful and many needy families had a Christmas they would not otherwise have had.

In 1992, when town budgets were stretched to the limit by the bad economy in the eastern United States, it was announced that Leesburg, Virginia, and three nearby communities would not have 4th of July fireworks. WAGE manager Chuck Thornton and morning man Todd James sparked a fund-raising effort they called "Light Up The Sky." The sky did light up with fireworks in the four small communities, thanks to more than $8,000 the effort quickly raised.

In Norwalk, Ohio, owner-operator Jim Westerhold has broadcast a daily call-in now called *Sound Off* on WLKR/WVAC. In the spring of 1992, that show ignited a protest at the local courthouse as citizens voiced their outrage at the light sentence given a local businessman convicted on a drug charge. That program runs, despite the fact that the owner's license is not dependent on providing such a daily public affairs program.

KELK/KLKO has brought major cultural experiences to the remote town of Elko, Nevada, including a performance of the *Nutcracker Suite* by the Portland (Oregon) Ballet Company and a concert by the United States Air Force Band. Paul Gardner, who bought the stations from his father, Ray, says: "We don't make any money on those events, but we feel they're good for the community. We can afford to do things like that and feel we should."

Don Martin, the ingenious longtime owner-operator of WSLM, Salem, Indiana, says: "Our station doesn't sound like any other station — anywhere else." It sends a dramatic but simple message for miles around each Christmas season. For years, he has installed a large, lighted cross near the top of his 360-foot tower.

Sometimes, little stations confound conventional wisdom by providing services far beyond anything that can be rationalized by their size or the numbers (rating estimates) of their stations:

When the 1993 Midwest floods hit, at Spirit Lake, Iowa, where Paul Hedberg lives and owns KUOO, his station not only covered the disaster, but quickly raised more than $100,000 to provide emergency help for residents and to supplement government loans to rebuild their property and their lives.

Nineteen hours after the 1993 California earthquake, KBET, Santa Clarita, California, returned to the air and was immediately declared by the city government "The Official Disaster Information Station." In owner Chuck Goldman's words: "People were in shock and needed more than just information — they needed support. Our local station gave them that as no out-of-the-area station could. Red Cross trucks arrived at odd times. KBET would call for 20 strong men to help unload them. The requests were always over-subscribed. The local library had been damaged beyond repair, and 100,000 books had to be removed before rains came. Within a minute of the radio announcement, a basketball coach called to volunteer his team for the effort. Price-gouging was non-existent in the area, as listeners called in quickly to alert the community of any incidents."

When his community's adult education program ran out of funds, Francis Nash at WGOH, Grayson, Kentucky, raised more than $5,000 to keep it going until more funds were available.

When a tornado struck an area near Union, South Carolina, WBCU canceled a sponsored game to allow listeners to call in to tell concerned friends and family that they were OK. The calls came in for three hours. The local radio station stopped a lot of people's anguish.

WFOB, Fostoria, Ohio, raised funds for an impoverished murder victim's family so they could give him a decent funeral.

KMIT, Mitchell, South Dakota, achieves two worthwhile objectives: by sponsoring a New Year's Eve dance that provides young people with a safe way to ring in the New Year, and by raising more than $3,000 each year to aid the local art center.

During the worst winter storm in history in DuBois, Pennsylvania, WDBA went to work covering the emergency. An announcement was made that the electric power life support of a listener was out. A generator was quickly delivered by a listener who donated it. Two years later, the person who was aided is still living — reportedly in better health.

The holding of a radio license does not require a lot of public service. Small market radio station operators, like their fellow small town insurance agents, professional people and retailers, have found that being a good citizen is good for business, but it may not be, in strict accounting, cost-effective. But those are the kinds of people they tend to be. Small market radio people include "do-gooders" in numbers far beyond their numbers compared to other businesses.

Every day, they and their stations provide little services that make people's lives better. Sometimes, when the occasion rises, they perform far beyond their own strength and the apparent strength of their stations.

Mid '90s Small Market Radio Financial Report

Data of sufficient accuracy is not readily available as it was in the days when the FCC required licensees to submit under penalty of perjury detailed information on the financial standing of their stations. Almost 100 percent of the stations complied. Now, the best information available comes voluntarily from less than 20 percent of total stations.

Shortly before this book was completed in the fall of 1995, the author sent questionnaires to a cross section of small stations across the country — some daytimers, AM full-timers, AM-FM combos, FM stand alones and a few 50,000- and 100,000-watt FM stations (generally the blessed among the small market stations). No claim is made that these findings or the author's conclusions are statistically correct — but the author believes they paint a pretty good picture of the financial side of small market radio at this writing in the mid-1990s:

First, the *M Street Journal*, the industry's best source of ongoing information about stations' formats and which stations are operating or are off the air, reports the total number of stations at this writing in the fall of 1995 is 9,880 — about 50 percent in the metropolitan areas, the other 50 percent in the non-metropolitan areas. There are, at this time, 342 stations off the air, about 3.4 percent of the total — 70 fewer than the year before. Of these, 64 percent are in the non-metro areas, 36 percent in the metropolitan areas — 244 AM and 98 FM. There are 577 permits for new stations.

At this writing, there is one metropolitan radio station for each 38,500 people living within the "metro."

There is one non-metro radio station for each 11,200 people living outside the "metros."

On a historic basis, population per station:

	1946	1950	1960	1980
Non-metro	117,500	65,180	33,407	14,848
Metro	145,325	49,813	50,794	38,809

Although there have been a lot of complaints about the problems the station building of the 1980s and early 1990s caused, the number of new metro radio stations increased by only 13.5 percent — while the population there increased by 15.4 percent. The metropolitan areas look even less crowded when you eliminate about one-third of the stations there — they do not command enough audience to be listed in the Arbitron books. A station with as little of the 12+ audience as 1/l0th percent "makes the book."

The population of the non-metro" areas of the United States did not grow during the 1980s, but station population grew by 42 percent.

The best estimates say that radio advertising gets, on average, .003 percent of retail sales ($3 per $1,000). On that basis, there is $208,835 average available to each non-metro radio station. Counting an AM-FM combination as two stations, the number rises to $417,670; for a three-station duopoly to $626,505. The .003 percent of retail sales is a national average. Some stations and markets do better, some less, depending on the perceived value of radio in the market, the number of stations competing and the quality of the stations and their sales efforts.

Taking its toll on the stations in our sample is all the new competition from new stations and Class B and C FM stations that have polished their programming and selling skills, as well as new competition from cable advertising sales and the replacement of loyal station customers by chains, most notably Wal-Mart, and franchises.

Another factor is that many areas that experienced "bust" economies in the early to late '80s are slowly recovering or rebuilding. During the years of high inflation, new yearly records were a given in most stations. Now, in a period of low inflation, increases more often come hard.

The high-billing years for the stations in our survey:

1980 · 0	1985 · 6%	1990 · 12%
81 · 0	86 · 0	91 · 3%
82 · 3%	87 · 6%	92 · 9%
83 · 3%	88 · 6%	93 · 6%
84 · 3%	89 · 15%	94 · 27%

Of the stations that reached their billing high water mark between 1980 and 1984, the average station reports it is currently doing 87.9 percent of its historic high. Of the stations that topped in 1985 through 1989, the average is doing 83 percent of its record billing. Of the 1990 through 1993 records, the average station has worked its way back to 85 percent of its record.

Hardest-hit since 1990 were stations on the West Coast, followed by stations in New England. Some of those stations saw their grosses drop by 25 percent or even 50 percent.

Technology and innovation have replaced "live bodies" in every station the author checked. A typical response, from the owner of a station in upstate New York: "I had 14 people here in the mid-'80s. I now have two more competitors working my market, cable is selling and there's a lot of new print competition. I now have seven people here, thanks to the satellite and hard disc automation. I would call four people here now well-paid. The others, a little better than I used to pay. My station is doing 25 percent less than its peak year, but I'm not making 25 percent less. This is still a very good business."

In the Last of the First 75 Years

The radio marketplace is overbuilt, moreso in the small markets than the large markets. Many stations have been built by people without experience or ability to run a radio station. Station building has been generated by greed — not need. Often heard in broadcasting circles: "The FCC is building too many stations." The fact is, the FCC doesn't build stations — people do. Since the beginning, broadcasters have insisted that there be no ceiling on how much a station can earn. Therefore, there is little likelihood that the Commission would ever set a floor on the amount of money someone can lose. The laws of physics promise an end to the station-building orgy. In simple language, barring government-sponsored technical changes, the dial won't hold many more stations in most parts of the country.

Good small market operators will be consolidators. Some who are less-talented and less-dedicated will be consolidated. For better or worse, that's what happens in any mature business: Radio is 75 years old, one-third older than the age for AARP membership.

In addition to the quality of a station and its management, there is also the overriding issue of the quality of the marketplace. Things are definitely coming back and looking up in many small towns. Since 1990, the population of non-metropolitan America is growing faster than that of metropolitan America. The non-metropolitan population shrank in the 1980s. That 1993 Census Bureau information is probably not a mirage.

Roper Organization surveying, published in 1992, shows that 83 percent of non-metropolitan residents say they are family-oriented; 69 percent identify themselves as having a strong commitment to their community (only 5 percent of metropolitan residents do). Rural residents are much more likely to give their communities high marks for personal values, friendliness, cost of living, police protection, recreational facilities, low pollution and quality of life for themselves and their children. Sixty percent of rural residents think their community is moving in the right direction; only 36 percent of urban residents do.

That Roper survey shows that $33^1/_3$ percent of Americans believe that rural America is the ideal place to live — and 35 percent of all Americans say they would like to be living in a small town in 10 years.

Tom Robson, owner-operator of KAWL-AM/FM, York, Nebraska, may sum it up best: "I'm a native of this town, married a local girl. I guess this is a typical small town kid's story. I thought happiness would be seeing the town in the rearview mirror. I went off to school, worked for Associated Press, got into TV with a CBS station in Missouri, then a station in Omaha, finally Baltimore, where I was local-regional sales manager at WBAL-TV. We were there for four years.

"Our Baltimore years were a great experience. Our kids were exposed, for the first time, to cultural diversity in the schools — 23 different countries represented. But Pat and I realized the kids were growing up with such a lack of space and freedom.

"This is the station where I broke into broadcasting during my high school years. When it came up for sale, I decided it was just right for me — and Pat and I agreed, this town was just right for our family."

KGCX 1995

The town of Vida, Montana (population 27) is, according to reporter Floyd J. Ell of the Sidney *Herald Leader*, no longer in existence. And the radio station that was born in the back room of the local bank on a Sunday in 1925 is also no more.

In 1925, the station operated without a license. It became 7.5-watt KGCX in 1926. It moved twice in its lifetime, first to Wolf Point, then to Sidney, where it operated for over 50 years. In 1992, it was taken off the air for "financial reasons."

A granddaughter of founder Ed Krebsbach, 33-year-old Jennifer Krebsbach Forbis, and her 38-year-old husband, Phil, stepped forward to "bring it back from the dead" in 1994. The couple met at KERR, Polson, where her father, Clair, finished his more than 60-year radio career as manager.

The young couple's ambitions for KGCX (and its sister FM

license) were frustrated by several things, she says: "I don't think we'll be able to rescue the station. Instead, we'll look for an opportunity somewhere else."

Meantime, Charles Scofield, owner of KEYZ/KYYZ, Williston, North Dakota, who "cut his radio teeth" at KGCX in the 1940s, has bought the equipment of another failed Sidney station, KSDY, and has made application to the FCC to build a new Class C FM station on its facilities, 100,000 watts at 95.1 mHZ. Under the relaxed ownership rules, he was granted a construction permit in 1995.

KGCX may well be gone forever, but, in Scofield's view: "We'll give Sidney its own radio station again — and I'll be back over 50 years later where I started in this business. Life is funny, isn't it?"

In a business like small market radio that is constantly changing, it is foolish to dwell on the good old days — how good or, for some, how bad it was. The justification for a book like this is a simple one: It's impossible to know where you are, let alone where you're going, unless you know where you've been.

In 1992, after FCC Chairman Al Sikes announced rules changes that were sure to dramatically change the face of the radio industry, Fairfield, Iowa-based radio station consultant Jay Mitchell commented on those changes in a widely circulated letter to clients and potential clients.

Those rules would allow stations to buy each other and, in the case of AM stations, allow an AM owner to take his station off the air and get paid for making it possible for another AM station to improve its coverage. Obviously, what scholars call "Economic Darwinism — the Survival of the Fittest" was about to begin in the radio business.

Mitchell says he never heard of *Radio Digest*, let alone saw the 1927 article that is quoted in Chapter 1 of this book. A reader has to be impressed by the similarity of the two articles published 65 years apart. In 1992, Mitchell said:

> "We hope and believe that most of the operators who will be hurt by market concentration are those very operators who find their struggle frustrating and who will be ultimately better off doing something else.

> "We are not so much concerned about the loss of people from our industry as that we are about to lose GOOD PEOPLE from our industry because we are not able to pay them their just deserts, because we have so many people to pay. When the dust settles, our dream is that radio will be populated by fewer people, but good peo-

ple who enjoy their work and are well rewarded for it."

Something for Everybody Everywhere

Primary Program Formats in Small Markets

1995 M Street Radio Directory

Country	36.8%
Adult Contemporary	15.9%
Oldies	7.1%
News, Talk	6.2%
Soft Adult Contemporary	3.6%
Adult Standards (nostalgia)	3.2%
Spanish	3.2%
Religion (Teaching/Variety)	2.6%
CHR (Top 40)	2.5%
Southern Gospel	2.4%
Adult Hits	2.3%
Classic Rock	1.9%
Urban (R&B)	1.0%
Rock	1.0%
Variety	1.0%
Easy Listening	0.8%
Contemporary Christian	0.8%
Alternative Rock	0.7%
Gospel	0.6%
Black Gospel	0.5%
Urban Adult Contemporary	0.2%
All-Sports	0.2%
Ethnic	0.2%
R&B Oldies	0.1%
New Rock	0.1%
Classical, Fine Arts	0.1%
Jazz	0.1%
Pre Teen	Just 1 Station

The top six formats are programmed by 72.8 percent of small market stations. Those six formats are programmed by 52.1 percent of stations within Arbitron markets.

Regardless of primary format, small market stations tend to program more local news, community involvement and play-by-play sports than their counterparts within or close to the central cities of the 316 Census Bureau-designated metropolitan areas.

EPILOGUE

"I blame most of small market radio's current problems on 'experts.' They're spreading a lot of bad news and forecasts. Radio's like the bumblebee. A good aerodynamics engineer can make good argument that a bumblebee can't fly — but they do."

Charlie Wright
WBYS-AM/FM
Canton, Illinois

EPILOGUE

This is a story that obviously had a beginning but hopefully will not have an end. The radio story may have been a small town story from the beginning. Many locals in Calloway County in far-western Kentucky claim that an eccentric, Nathan B. Stubblefield, actually broadcast there before Marconi made his broadcast. Historians argue the point, but WNBS, the original station in Murray, the county seat,was founded in 1948 and is named for him. (The station is now part of a three-station duopoly owned by Dr. Sam Parker, a broadcasting professor at the local state university.) Murray calls itself "The Birthplace of Radio."

The future history of small town radio will be written by, more than anyone else, the station operators. The author surveyed a cross-section of them with the following questionnaire:

Sparks Out Of The Plowed Ground Questionnaire

Name _____ Years In Radio _____

Station(s) _____ Operator _____

City/State _____ This Station _____

If I had known radio would be the way it is in the mid-'90s, I would have _____ would not have _____ gotten into radio. Why?

_____

_____

_____

I see the future of the community where my station is located as:

_____

_____

I see the future of my radio station as:_____
_____
_____
_____

Other comments: _____
_____
_____

PLEASE ANSWER EACH QUESTION. If you do not wish to be quoted on a particular question, just mark "DON'T QUOTE" with your response. The following will not be quoted but will be used in formulating a "state of the business" item:

My station's best year was_____ .

Past 12 months +/- _____ % of my best year.

Please return ASAP to:

Bob Doll

1746 Rosewood Street

Seguin, Texas 78155

FAX: (210) 372-2905

Thanks!

Beyond 1995

Of the people surveyed, only two said they would not have gotten into small town radio if they had known it would be the way it is in the mid-1990s. One said he wasn't really sure.

While the markets surveyed span the country from coast-to-coast and border to border — and even into Hawaii — all see the future of their individual markets as positive. They see their radio stations changing, but their belief in its future is best evidenced by the fact that, under "other comments," none said he or she would like to sell.

Their own words, I believe, best tell the story:

Gene Blabey, WVOS-AM/FM, Liberty, New York (in radio 25 years, owner of station 11 years):

"My greatest fear is that radio, like much of the restaurant business, will become homogenized — stations will have a McDonald's-like sameness, carrying the same music hosted by the same disc jockeys, in every community. If that happens, there's not much of a future. Stations can carry the satellite and be successful if they continue to provide the local information and services that earn them their place in the community. We're doing that, and I am guardedly optimistic about our future."

Rich Wachtel, WRNR, AM only, Martinsburg, West Virginia (21 years in radio, 18 years as owner-operator):

"I believe overall the future of local radio is bright across the country. Print continues to decline. There's a slight decline in television viewing, which is fragmenting even more than radio. Our talk, news, sports format is growing with our community (75,000 in the county with just three local stations). We're a good business in a good place to be. I am confident that will continue."

Bob McRaney Jr., WROB-AM/WKBB-FM, West Point, Mississippi (30 years in broadcasting, one year with WROB/WKBB):

"My father predicted many years ago that eventually every town in America would have its own TV station and a lot of radio stations. That prediction has come true with the evolution of cable and the multitude of radio signals.

"I spent 30 years in television and recently came home to take care of the family business and 'stop jumping through corporate hoops.' Small market radio is still fun; folks depend on us for local events and information, sports and religion — and our advertisers still get results. I see the future of our stations as bright. Many operators have failed to adjust to the changing small market radio economy: new competition, fickle listeners, demanding clients. Many of them have 'turned off the lights and gone home.' But we're here to stay."

Don Bennet, KREW-AM/FM, Sunnyside, Washington (52 years in radio, 41 at KREW):

"The AM-FM battle was nearly lost, but AM is making a slow but sure comeback. That's good! We play music on our FM station and talk a lot on our AM station. I think our two stations are doing what I used to do — reaching most of the market. Whether it's on AM or FM, you have to be a 'service station' to survive."

Paul Tinkle, WCMT-AM/FM/WCDZ-FM, Martin, Tennessee (25 years in radio, 14 years at WCMT/WCDZ):

"I believe the future of my stations will be profitable, but I have to be careful about how I spend my dollars. I have to continue to be in a promotional mode and interested in my customers and stay active in the community — but the bottom line will need a lot of attention."

Len Robinson, WPAX-AM/WTUF-FM, Thomasville, Georgia (15 years in radio, nine years at WPAX/WTUF):

"I like what I'm doing and I can't think of anything I'd rather do. I'll continue to do all right if I'm not regulated out of business. If I have the freedom to operate my station as I believe best, the community will be served and I'll have a good life."

Lyle Irons, KDUN-AM, Reedsport, Oregon (in radio 37 years, at KDUN 10 years):

"This is the most challenging, versatile service business in the world. Few of us will ever get rich, but we'll get along and will have the satisfaction of performing an appreciated service by serving the community and by being a helpful advertising entity to the local businesses. That's a combination of both money and pride. I don't think it can be beat."

Lou Vito, WBLL, Bellefontaine, Ohio (in radio 11 years, at WBLL/WPKO seven years):

"We need to be confident in what our station is. We need to ask for enough money to be important to our customers and to make our customers important to our audience. If we do that, our future will be bright; so will our audience's and our customers' futures."

Dick Gleason, WOXO/WTBM FMs/WKTQ/WTBM AMs, Norway, Maine, area (in radio 30 years, at WOXO 18 years):

"This is a relationship business — relationships with the audience and the advertisers. Traditional retail has always been weak in our operations. Wal-Mart coming is providing opportunities for 'niche' retailers and service business, where we've traditionally done well. I don't see any fewer ambitious risk-takers in the future. As long as we do our job of finding and helping them, our business will be good."

Art Cooley, WHKP-AM, Hendersonville, North Carolina (37 years with station, owner for three):

"All of us here at WHKP have a feeling of community. As well as making a good living, we have always looked upon ourselves at the station and out in town as community leaders. It's more than just a profession, it's a calling. I don't see anything on the Information Highway that's going to do for Hendersonville what we do. As long as we don't change, or feel differently about what we do, I think the future is very bright."

Walter E. May, WPKE-AM/FM/WDHR-FM, Pikeville, Kentucky (in radio 39 years, at WPKE/WDHR 33 years):

"Pikeville is now, and has always been, the No. 1 city in eastern Kentucky, although the population is just 6,324. We've been judged one of the best 100 small towns in America.

"I have a lot more competition now. It's such a good business town, that had to happen. But as long as I keep my stations No. 1, the future has to be even better than the past."

Tom Anderson, KOAL/KARB-FM, Price, Utah (in radio 35 years, at KOAL 29 years):

"With fewer things to regulate, the FCC is regulating the hell out of these small stations. We live in constant fear of being fined. Aside from that, I believe my stations, like my community, will enjoy steady growth.

"When I graduated from college, the best jobs were with IBM, AT&T and Sears — big firms like those. People who went with them now have less security than I do. It used to be that government jobs were the bad jobs — now people who took them have all the security and benefits."

Kevin Doran, WLEA/WCKR, Hornell, New York (in radio 41 years, at WLEA 24 years):

"Whatever this business is, the one thing it is not is dull. There's nothing like being a big frog in a little pond. In a big station, you may be able to report what's going on — here you can be part of making what's going on.

"I am concerned that my stations may lose value in the future what with all the new stations coming on. Who can predict what the government will do with our lives and our communities? It is unfortunate that we've let our government grow so big. But, whatever happens, I'm sure we'll deal with it. And, as history has clearly shown us, tomorrow is usually better than today and a whole lot better than yesterday."

Wally Christensen, KLOH-AM/KISD, Pipestone, Minnesota (in radio 30 years, at KLOH 22 years):

"My marketplace is not the best — we're going down in population and retailing is shrinking — but I see the future of my stations as great, because this business, like no other, is always as good as YOU make it."

Ray David, KLTC-AM/KRRB and KCLI FMs, Dickinson, North Dakota (in radio 32 years, at KLTC 25 years):

"The radio business has changed a lot in the 32 years I've been at it, but so has everything else. It all has to do with the good old free enterprise system. Not everybody makes it every time, but when you do it feels mighty good."

W. Don Sports, WCLA-AM/FM, Claxton, Georgia (in radio 39 years, at WCLA 37 years):

"It is much better to receive satellite programming so a few good people can spend their valuable time selling and servicing advertisers and preparing local programming. In that way, small town radio has improved."

Jim Roper, KRTN-AM/FM, Raton, New Mexico (in radio 46 years, at KRTN 30 years):

"My daughter, Mary Lynn, is vice president and general manager of KOAT-TV, Albuquerque. My son Mark, 32, is president and general manager of KRTN. The broadcasting business has been mighty good to the Roper family. I still call on some of my old accounts, cover local news stories when I'm needed and call a ballgame when it looks like it's going to be a good one. Our area is growing with new industries, and retirees, like myself, are discovering it. The future looks good for the area and our stations."

John Goeman, KJAM-AM/FM, Madison, South Dakota (in radio 34 years "and 343 days," owner for 16 years):

"I see moderate growth in my area's future and therefore for my station. Radio is busy, exciting, changing, innovative, effective and listened to. There can't be anything wrong with something like that."

Eugene Puffer, WYKR-AM/FM, Wells River, Vermont (in radio 24 years, at WYKR 28 years):

"After an economic recession in '89/'90, things are coming back here — and things point to a growing future. Things would be better if FCC was more supportive — a 'friend' instead of an enemy. They should slow down the building of stations to allow present owners to do more for their communities."

Joe Jindra, KNCK/KCKS, Concordia, Kansas (in radio 15 years, at KNCK/KCKS four years):

"We do a lot of local programming here. That wouldn't be possible if it weren't for the satellite, hard disc automation, FAX machines, shortwave remote pickups, etc. Those technologies have made it possible to give our listeners more, our customers more and to allow us owners to keep more. I wasn't around in the old days, but I'm sure I wouldn't want to go back."

Rick Charles, WRJC-AM/FM, Mauston, Wisconsin (in radio 30 years, at WRJC nine years):

"People want and need more information than ever before. A local station can provide it. My area is growing. The last half of the '90s, I believe, will be better than the first half."

Bill Taylor, KQSS, Miami, Arizona (in radio 39 years, at KQSS eight years):

"Small town radio is the only place I know where one person can create a concept, go out and sell it, then come back and produce the final product — one person start-to-finish. In other media and larger stations, ideas go to a committee first. After they're done with it, you probably won't recognize it."

Craig Donnely, KLMJ, Hampton, Iowa (18 years in radio, one as owner of KLMJ):

"I started out with my mother and dad's station (Frank and the late Carol Donnely, KTLB, Twin Oaks, Iowa). I have never known any other life, but I can't imagine anything that could get in your blood like this does. I'm just starting here, my first station on my own. It's going good, and I'm sure it'll get better as I do."

Don Steese, WVLY/WMLO, Milton, Pennsylvania (30 years in radio):

"I see consolidation as the only answer to overcrowded small markets like ours. I think we'll end up with three or four operators, rather than the eight we have now. I intend to be one of the three or four left."

Gary Johnson, WLDY/WJBL, Ladysmith, Wisconsin (in radio 20 years, at WLDY/WJBL three and one-half years):

"We can get our music from Dallas or talk from New York, but we'd better give the school closings, obits, weather and ballgames, and it's got to be professional."

Bill Buchanan, KSHN-FM, Liberty, Texas (in radio 40 years, at KSHN {formerly KPXE-AM} 19 years):

"Like a lot of the people who've been around this business for a while, there's a lot about the old days I miss — but a lot more of it I don't — like absent announcers, aspiring Larry Lujaks playing music outside the format, high line charge bills. The 'good old days' that we'll be talking about 25 years from now are right now. I'm enjoying them."

Bill Dahle, KUAI-AM, Eleele, Hawaii (in radio 32 years, at KUAI 30 years):

"We'll continue to place local events ahead of state and national issues. We do more in small markets than stations in large markets do, with a lot less people, and I think we do it well. The economic viability of our market is a major concern, but it is not the overriding factor. It's what we do and how well we do it."

Tom Land, WFIW-AM/FM, Fairfield, Illinois (in radio 49 years, at WFIW 41 years):

"Monetary success was not my primary inducement to come here — or build WFIW. As early as high school, I wanted to be part of this — being of service. That aspiration has remained undiminished all these years. I'm glad I passed that along to my son Dave, who now runs the station and keeps busy doing the right thing in the community."

Steve Blair, WFIS-AM, Fountain Inn, South Carolina (in radio 37 years, at WFIS six years):

"As much as I hat to say it, I see my future as doing more with less people, in order to stay in business. Doing more with less people is hard, but the income has to be better than the outgo. No technology has come along that builds strong relationships with the local businesses, schools, churches, clubs, governments. People will always do that. We'll always need 'a few good ones.' "

Dennis Voy, KMAQ-AM/FM, Maquoketa, Iowa (in radio 36 years, 24 as owner of KMAQ):

"Costs continue to rise, even with new labor-saving (or eliminating) technologies. New costs include a mandated AM carrier test $350, FCC annual fee $800, time-consuming and therefore expensive EEO reports to file. Local radio will remain a good business — tough, but good."

Col. Bill Willis, WFLQ-FM, French Lick, Indiana (in radio 20 years, at WFLQ 11 years):

"My very small market is having the same problems as the same kinds of stations are having across the country — some shrinkage in our retail section, an increase in chains who do not do much radio. I am confident our station will continue to do well, but it will probably be necessary to look to some new revenue sources like expanding into travel (selling tours) and providing services direct to consumers by utilizing our FM sub-carrier or other new technology."

Art Sutton, WBCU-AM, Union, South Carolina, and WCRS-AM/WSZC-FM, Greenwood, South Carolina (in radio 12 years, at WBCU three years, at WCRS/WSZC one year):

"I have confidence in the growth and future of small towns. Personally, I believe the town is better off if it's within about one hour's drive of a medium-size city, as both of my stations are. Young business and professional people who are necessary to the vitality of a business community, and a community overall, like the way of life a small town offers if good entertainment (theater, dining, sports) are convenient to the town. I am willing to put up with the competition for listeners posed by city stations. I think it's a good tradeoff."

Ray Lockhart, KOGA-AM/FM, KMCX-FM, Ogallala, Nebraska (in radio 35 years, at KOGA-AM/FM 35 years, at KMCX one year):

"The future of my stations and other small market stations is bright, if the operators are willing to embrace the new technologies, and if those of us in the leadership are able to pass the 'vision' along to those that follow."

Jim Stewart, WHEP-AM, Foley, Alabama (in radio 40 years, at WHEP 33 years):

"The future will be better than the past, if we keep getting better."

Thurman Hamilton, KHBM-AM/FM, Monticello, Arkansas (all 10 years in radio as co-owner of KHBM):

"I have a new FM competitor and cable is selling in our small town, but we're only a little off in our business. My station is going to survive and, I think, thrive. The chain mass merchandise retailer for whom I managed a store before I bought the radio station didn't."

Ken Orchard, KVVQ-AM/FM, Victorville, California (in radio 37 years, at KVVQ 15 years):

"I worked my way through college at one of the early McDonald's restaurants. Ray Kroc had just bought the founders out. On one his visits, he tried to talk me out of going into radio and going with him in his new enterprise full time. 'I'll make you a millionaire,' he promised. He probably would have, but I can't believe serving Big Macs and french fries could be as much fun as this.

"We're having tough times here now, but we've got something that can't be distributed to other places — the world's greatest weather. People will continue to come here — start businesses and professions. The economy will turn up. When it does, my stations' finances will turn up, too!"

Bill Warren, WMCR-AM/FM, Oneida, New York (in radio 51 years, at WMCR 25 years):

"I'm sorry that Main Street seems to be drying up. It's very likely that it's just in a period of change. Even if the worst is true, we'll find new customers to take its place — we always have. Remember when the dimestore and the drive-in theater were good customers?

"I am not concerned that my radio station is not as valuable to a buyer as it was 10 years ago. It's worth a lot more than I paid for it. Vivian and I did not come here 25 years ago to build a fortune; we came here to build a life. We have."

Broadcasters' Prayer

Small market broadcasters are a unique group of people. They are in the business for more than just making a living. How most feel about their businesses is well-stated in the *Broadcasters' Prayer*, whose author has broadcast it at signoff for more than 40 years on his radio station:

"As we close this broadcast day, we pray that we have not offended any person of any race, religion or politics.

"We pray that our guests, rich and poor, have been treated alike.

"We trust that our words have been as impartial as our radio waves, which enter the homes of rich and poor without discrimination.

"We pray that we have said something that might have prevented at least one traffic accident and saved at least one life.

"We pray that we have said something to cause someone to contribute to a worthwhile charity and that perhaps we have said something that has added an extra pint of blood at our blood bank.

"We pray that we have caused one shut-in to forget his or her troubles today, and through our efforts someone has decided to go to church this Sunday, and that perhaps at least one person has saved his soul before it's too late. And, Dear Lord, we pray that we have caused the tears to fade from at least one small child today.

"That is our Broadcaster's Prayer. If we can accomplish part of this goal each day, our efforts will not be in vain, because this station's success depends upon the service it can offer this and surrounding communities. We shall always strive to maintain this type of service, because we believe sincerely that this is broadcasting in the fullest sense of the word."

Don Martin, WSLM-AM/FM, Salem, Indiana

table

SMALL MARKET RADIO STATIONS

table

SMALL MARKET RADIO STATIONS

**(Currently On Air —
Dates Indicate Period Established)**

		1920-1927	1928-1945	1946-1950	1951-1960	1961-1968	1969-1976	1977-1984	1985-1992
AL	am	0	3	29	23	7	8	12	0
	fm	0	0	5	3	6	12	8	18
AK	am	0	1	1	3	3	2	4	2
	fm	0	0	0	3	0	1	4	3
AZ	am	0	0	3	5	3	4	8	1
	fm	0	0	0	0	1	1	17	19
AR	am	2	2	16	19	5	6	4	0
	fm	0	1	1	2	4	8	33	13
CA	am	0	2	14	1	2	6	3	3
	fm	0	0	0	0	8	17	32	38
CO	am	2	1	7	7	3	1	4	0
	fm	0	0	1	0	0	15	15	14
CT	am	0	0	0	3	0	0	0	0
	fm	0	0	0	0	0	1	1	0
DE	am	0	0	0	3	0	0	0	0
	fm	0	0	0	0	0	4	0	2
FL	am	0	1	8	29	10	5	1	0
	fm	0	0	0	0	6	12	21	24
GA	am	0	10	26	35	21	10	12	1
	fm	0	0	2	0	12	21	22	27
HI	am	0	1	1	0	3	0	0	0
	fm	0	0	0	0	0	1	6	3
ID	am	0	1	6	8	0	1	2	0
	fm	0	0	0	0	0	5	6	4
IL	am	3	3	18	22	10	3	2	2
	fm	0	0	5	6	23	20	20	16
IN	am	0	1	12	12	9	4	1	0
	fm	0	0	4	4	24	17	13	15
IA	am	3	2	14	12	5	3	3	0
	fm	0	0	2	1	8	20	21	7
KS	am	0	6	11	10	5	0	2	0
	fm	0	0	0	1	8	9	23	10
KY	am	0	3	17	33	9	13	10	2
	fm	0	0	2	3	24	231	14	7
LA	am	0	0	8	20	9	9	4	0
	fm	0	0	0	1	9	15	18	17

257

		1920-1927	1928-1945	1946-1950	1951-1960	1961-1968	1969-1976	1977-1984	1985-1992
ME	am	0	0	4	12	3	1	2	0
	fm	0	0	0	0	4	14	7	8
MD	am	0	2	3	8	4	1	0	0
	fm	0	0	1	1	5	4	4	6
MA	am	0	2	3	5	0	1	3	0
	fm	0	0	2	0	4	2	3	6
MI	am	0	6	16	25	11	4	1	3
	fm	0	0	1	1	17	29	24	20
MN	am	1	3	20	15	8	5	3	1
	fm	0	0	0	2	9	24	29	16
MS	am	0	4	15	22	6	9	2	0
	fm	0	0	0	3	11	29	14	15
MO	am	0	3	17	26	13	6	5	0
	fm	0	1	3	3	10	24	31	14
MT	am	2	1	7	5	5	4	1	3
	fm	0	0	0	0	2	7	12	9
NE	am	2	4	7	14	6	3	1	0
	fm	0	0	0	1	5	8	18	14
NV	am	0	0	2	2	0	0	0	1
	fm	0	0	0	0	0	0	7	0
NH	am	2	1	3	7	5	1	1	0
	fm	0	0	1	0	2	6	0	12
NJ	am	1	1	0	6	3	2	0	0
	fm	0	0	3	2	2	8	0	3
NM	am	0	2	8	8	5	0	2	1
	fm	0	0	0	0	0	7	8	6
NY	am	1	5	14	22	9	8	4	0
	fm	0	0	7	1	11	15	19	30
NC	am	0	7	42	33	26	9	8	1
	fm	0	1	7	3	12	12	9	20
ND	am	1	2	4	3	4	2	3	0
	fm	0	0	0	0	2	1	7	2
OH	am	1	2	16	14	10	3	0	0
	fm	0	0	7	7	17	18	12	18
OK	am	0	5	16	7	3	3	1	1
	fm	0	0	0	1	5	12	19	12
OR	am	2	8	12	20	2	2	2	2
	fm	0	0	0	0	4	7	19	13
PA	am	0	5	28	34	8	7	7	1
	fm	0	0	7	6	16	17	14	21
SC	am	0	1	18	18	15	6	4	0
	fm	0	0	0	2	9	13	8	16
SD	am	2	1	4	9	6	1	2	0
	fm	0	0	0	0	2	9	5	6
TN	am	0	1	16	41	18	9	12	1
	fm	0	0	0	0	19	25	14	19

		1920-1927	1928-1945	1946-1950	1951-1960	1961-1968	1969-1976	1977-1984	1985-1992
TX	am	0	8	54	34	11	1	9	1
	fm	0	0	1	6	10	23	53	41
UT	am	0	2	3	3	1	3	2	0
	fm	0	0	0	0	1	4	5	3
VT	am	0	3	2	6	0	2	1	0
	fm	0	0	0	2	0	6	7	10
VA	am	0	4	17	26	11	7	2	2
	fm	0	0	3	4	11	14	11	22
WA	am	2	2	11	13	6	4	5	1
	fm	0	0	0	0	4	4	12	15
WV	am	0	6	16	11	7	5	2	0
	fm	0	0	3	0	2	10	19	11
WI	am	2	5	9	22	9	9	6	2
	fm	0	5	4	6	6	11	11	17
WY	am	0	3	5	6	3	1	0	4
	fm	0	0	0	0	0	5	11	6

The above table includes stations in towns of 25,000 and under. It does not include stations established in towns of less than 25,000 whose population rose above that in a later census.

Source: Standard Rates and Data Service *Small Markets Edition* October 1993 (cities of license 25,000 and under).

Note: This table is divided into parts corresponding with chapters 1, 2, 3 and 4. From 1961 onward, it is divided into eight-year periods for comparison with the first eight years of the FCC "80/90" Docket (1985/1992). Data later than that on this table is found elsewhere in this book.

RESOURCES

RESOURCES

George Brooks

John David

Charlie Harper

Susan Hill

Sherri Lackey Jeffers

Lynn McReynolds

Lori Morgan

Francis Nash

National Association of Broadcasters Library

Jerry Papenfuss

Pavlick Library

Bill Peake

Radio Advertising Bureau

Sue Tate

Robert Umacht

Bill Wertz

American Chronicles — Lois and Allen Gordon (Atheneum)

Best 100 Small Towns — Norman Hampton (Prentice Hall)

Best Seat in the House — Pat Weaver (Alfred Knopf)

Bing Crosby — Donald Shepherd and Robert Slatzer (Pinnacle)

Broadcasting Magazine

Broadcasting in America — Sidney Head and Christopher Sterling
    (Houghton-Miflin)

Broadcast Pro-Files, Hollywood, California

Empire — Louis J. Paper (St. Martin's Press)

Facts on File

Fifties, The — David Halberstam (Villard Books)

History of Broadcasting — Eric Bernouw (Oxford Press)

History of Kansas Broadcasting — (video) Sherwood Parks

History of Minnesota Broadcasting — Minnesota Broadcasters
Association

KMA — *First 60 Years* — Robert Barkley

M Street Journal (weekly) and *M Street Directory* (annual)

Made in America — Sam Walton (Doubleday)

New and Improved — Richard S. Tedlow (Basic Books)

Only Yesterday — Frederick Lewis Allen (Bonanza)

Radio Advertising — Bob Shulman (NTC Business Books)

Radio Digest — onetime weekly publication

Radio's Golden Years — Vincent Terrance (Barnes)

Radio Ink — semi-monthly magazine

Radio Man — Gayle Stone (unpublished authorized biography of
the late Robert Rounsaville)

Radio Mirror Yearbook — former annual publication

Radio World — twice-monthly newspaper

Rand McNally Road Atlas

Reagan's America — Gary Wills (Prentice Hall)

Rebel in Radio — Elliot Sanger (Hasting House)

Regions of Opportunity — Dr. Jack Lessinger (Times Books)

Retail Merchandising — Susal, Little and Wingate (South Western
Publishing Co.)

Sam Walton — Vance Trimble (Dutton)

Since Yesterday — Frederick Lewis Allen (Bonanza)

Small Market Radio Newsletter (weekly)

Smithsonian magazine (monthly)

Standard Rate and Data Service — Small Market Edition

Statistical Almanac of the United States

This Incredible Century — Dr. Norman Vincent Peale (Tyndale
House)

Welcome South Brother — WSB, Atlanta, Georgia

Whatever Happened to Madison Avenue? — Martin Mayer (Little Brown)

When We Were Young — Ruth Lang Klemfeld (Prentice Hall)

SNAPSHOTS OUT OF THE PLOWED GROUND

SNAPSHOTS

OUT OF THE PLOWED GROUND

Ed Krebsbach started broadcasting his band, The Vida Syncopators, on an unlicensed station at Vida, Montana. He licensed KGCX in 1926, owning it until his death in 1971.

Clair Krebsbach worked for the family radio station until he was 49, selling KGCX two years after his father's death. He later managed KERR, Polson, Montana, until his retirement in the early 1990s.

Bob Compton called his 1919 amateur station at Carthage, Illinois, "BOB."

It started in a corner of Bob's Battery Shop.

It became WCAZ in 1922.

Dana McNeil built 9ZP, Land License #12, at Pierre, South Dakota, in 1916.

It became KGFX, operating from the Dana and Ida McNeil residence at 203 W. Summit, Pierre, South Dakota, in 1927.

The founder's wife, Ida, broadcast a steady stream of news and information across the prairies for 40 years.

Ida McNeil retired at 74, selling out to Bob Ingstead. A young Dean Sorensen got his first managing job. Pictured, Dean Sorenson, KGFX station manager, at controls of new transmitters.

"Dr." J.R. Brinkley had an audience over a wide part of the U.S. from his station, KFKB, at Milford, Kansas.

The nation's most popular radio announcer, selected by *Radio Digest* in 1925 — Henry Field, KFNF, Shenandoah, Iowa.

The most popular *Radio Digest* announcer in 1927, Field's seed company and radio rival, Earl May, KMA, Shenandoah, Iowa.

Hoyt Wimpy started building and selling radio receivers in the early 1900s.

"The Wimpy Radio Sets" were displayed in his auto repair business.

Karl Stefan took a break from his newspaper duties to broadcast the Noontime News on WJAG, Norfolk, Nebraska, beginning in 1922. He called himself the Printer's Devil. He did the broadcast until 1936, when he was elected to Congress. The program continues to this day.

WJAG enjoys the longest continuous ownership in American radio — 73 years. Its founder, Gene Huse, started it as a hobby.

His son, Jerry, serves as the station's second and current president. He is publisher of the *Norfolk Daily News*.

Art Thomas, WJAG's first manager.

Bob Thomas, his son, WJAG's second manager.

Rob Thomas, Art's grandson, Bob's son, WJAG's
third and current manager.

The 1937 flood turned the seven-year-old WPAD,
Paducah, Kentucky, "popular and profitable."
It spawned the Lackey family's small town
radio empire.

The Lackey brothers in 1965 (l-r): Pierce, Prewitt
(a WPAD executive), Dutch and Hecht.

State Sen. Henry G. Lackey followed his father
and uncles into radio and politics.

Charlie Persons in 1926. His career spanned 69 of radio's first 75 years. He built a dozen radio stations.

A Persons-designed 160-foot wood tower at WHLB, Virginia, Minnesota. It was taken down after 31 years' service.

Charlie Persons retires at 87. He retains his airplane pilot's license.

A young Gordon Capps reporting an election right off the tally sheets at KSRV, Oregon, in the late '40s.

His righthand man, John Powell, would go on to become the 30-year manager of KHAS, Hastings, Nebraska.

Doing it big in a little place: WDLB, Marshfield, Wisconsin had a staff of 17.

Radio learned to live alongside TV in the '50s as Todd Storz launched Top 40.

Gordon McClendon brought excitement and drama to music/news programming.

Elmo Ellis didn't rock 'n' roll 'em — he entertained and informed them.

One of the first blockbuster rock acts, the Everly Brothers (Phil and Don), started with their mother and father, Ike and Margarite, at KMA and KFNF, Shenandoah, Iowa.

It wasn't all music. Art Taylor, Tony Kehl and Red Davis doing a ballgame on KOLT.

In Willmar, Minnesota, June Marshall introduces new arrivals on Harry Linder's KWLM.

Eddie Fritts at 22 bought his first radio station, WNLA, Indianola, Mississippi, in 1963. He became NAB President/CEO in 1982.

His father, Edward M. Fritts, followed his son into radio station ownership, buying WPAD, Paducah, Kentucky, in 1967.

In the late 1960s and in the 1970s, Jerrell Shepherd was showing small market stations how to do big billing.

In the '80s and early '90s, high-tech innovators like Steve Bellinger were showing them how to reduce overhead in overcrowded markets.

Westwood One's Jim Bohannon breaks into radio at 15 in his hometown of Lebanon, Missouri, on KWLT.

Paul Harvey, in his teens at KFBI, Abilene, Kansas.

Rush Limbaugh in the 1960s, when he was a part-time announcer on KGMO (now KAPE), Cape Girardeau, Missouri.

Willie Nelson — back to his roots at KDOP, Pleasanton, Texas, where he was a disc jockey in the early 1950s.

The prestigious *Radio Ink* magazine Radio Wayne Awards are presented by publisher B. Eric Rhoads annually to outstanding broadcasters and are open to managers of all-size stations in all-size markets. The first three awards attest to the fact that small station managers are in a unique position to involve themselves and their stations in a meaningful way in their communities:

1993 — Cary Simpson, founder/owner/group manager of the 45-year old Allegheny Mountain Network of small town stations in Pennsylvania.

1994 — Lou Vito, President/General Manager, WBLL/WPKO, Bellefontaine, Ohio.

1995 — Art Sutton, President/General Manager, WBCU, Union, South Carolina.

INDEX

A

AARP. 237
A&P 202
A&P Gypsies, The 6
Abbott and Costello. 70
Acme Flour Mills, Hopkinsville, Kentucky. 29
Adventure Media 38
advertising. 5-7, 15, 25, 43, 52, 53,
56, 57, 61, 77, 83, 86, 90, 96, 98-101, 105, 114, 115, 119, 121, 129, 131,
132, 141, 149, 151, 152, 154-158, 160, 164-166, 179, 180, 184, 190, 193,
195, 199-201, 204-210, 216-218, 227, 236
Advertising Age 206
affiliates 153
Ain't That a Shame. 145
Air Force. 77
Alaska Radio and Service, Ketchikan, Alaska 28
"album rock". 147
Alford Radio Company, Belvidere, Illinois. 28
All Industry Music Licensing Committee 51, 192
Allegheny Mountain Network, Pennsylvania 279
Allen, Fred 27, 97
Allen, Frederick Lewis. 5, 8
Allen, George i
Allen, Gracie 27
Allen, Mel 96
Allen, "Pink" 81
Allison, Fran 58
AM. 67, 69, 76, 83, 87, 98, 99, 113, 114,
120-124, 133, 146-150, 154, 166, 167, 173, 182-184, 189, 192-194, 197,
218-221, 228, 239
AM-FM combos. 167, 174, 197, 212, 223, 235, 236
Ambler, Frena 32
American Broadcasting Company (ABC) 37, 57, 96, 97,
108, 109, 153, 154, 212
American Chronicles 31
American Dream, the 106
American Electric, Iron Mountain, Michigan. 29
American Legion 86
American Women in Radio and Television 190
America's Town Meeting. 58
Amos and Andy 61, 112
Anderson, Ann. 119
Anderson, Reed. 117-119
Anderson, Tom 56, 247
"application mills" 196
Arbitron. 200, 236, 240
Arkansas Radio Network. 208

Arlington Hotel, Hot Springs National Park, Arkansas. 28
Armed Forces Radio 65
Armstrong, Edwin 127
Arnold, Eddy. 102, 134
Arrowhead Network, Duluth, Minnesota 53, 82
Arthur Godfrey Talent Scouts 112
As Time Goes By. 64
ASCAP. 9, 50, 51, 89, 192
Ashback, Karl L.. 29
Ashtabula Newspapers, Ashtabula, Ohio. 53
Associated Press, The (AP) 52, 53, 89, 117, 230, 238
Associated Transcription Service 100
Astoria Hotel, Astoria, Oregon. 54
AT&T 5, 57
Atlantic Automobile Company, Atlantic, Iowa 28
audience participation programs. 58
Audisk. 214
automation 146, 166, 179, 212-215, 217, 237
Avery, Sewell 75

B

Bagely, Carl. 7
Bailey, Jack. 73
Baker, Dr. Norman 21, 29
Banash, Ann. 55
bankruptcies. 150, 204, 225
Banner, Logan, West Virginia. 53
Bar Bear Clothing Company, Decorah, Iowa 29
Barkley, Alben 62
Barret, Pat 58
Barry Seed Company, Clarinda, Iowa 28
Bartlett, Tommy 69
baseball game of the day 130, 131
Bass, Harold 113
Bates Radio & Electric Co., Cedar Grove, Louisiana. 29
Baxter, C.C.. 31
"beautiful music" 131
Becker, Aurelia 66
Becker, Frank B.. 66
Beale, Horace A.. 30
Beemer, Bruce 57
Behling, Bob. 79-81
Bellefontaine Chamber of Commerce, Bellefontaine, Ohio 30
Bellinger, Steve 214, 215, 278
Bennet, Don 245
Benny, Jack 27, 112
Berle, Milton 110

Bert Wick Presents 13
Bidin' My Time 41
Bill Stern Sports Newsreel. 109
"Birthplace of Radio". 243
Bissell, George F. 55
Bissell, George F. Jr.. 55
Bissell, Judy 55
Blabey, Gene 213, 244
"Black Friday". 41
black programming 95-97, 153
"Black Friday". 41
Blackburn Company 151
Blair, Steve 251
Blue Network 37, 43, 52, 57, 58, 68
Block, Martin 96
block programming. 169
Blueberry Hill 125
Blum, George. 116
BMI 51, 89, 90, 192
Bob and Ray 109
Bob Jones University, Cleveland, Tennessee 92
Bohannon, Jim 278
Boone Biblical College, Boone, Iowa 16
Boone, Pat 134
Boos, Gerry 81, 232
"boxcar hoppers" 46
Boy Scouts. 111
Brandeis, Supreme Court Justice Louis 202
Brandywine, Nat 102
Breakfast Club 58
Breathitt, Edward T. 63, 64, 142
Brinkley, Dr. J.R.. . . . . 9, 20-22, 29, 272
Broadcast Advertising Bureau (see also Radio Advertising Bureau)
. . . . 99, 100
Broadcast Financial Management 190
Broadcast Information Office. 99
Broadcast Promotions Managers Association. 190
Broadcasters' Prayer 253
Broadcasting in America. 22, 129
Broadcasting magazine 56, 88, 90, 127, 145, 189
Broadcasting Yearbook. 44
Brown, Bev. 189, 190
Brownell, Boyd 82
Browning King Orchestra, The. 6
Bryant, Slim. 102
Buchanan, Bill 171, 181, 182, 250
Bucknell University, Lewisburg, Pennsylvania. 54
Budget, The, Astoria, Oregon 53, 54

Bunker Hill Company, Wallace, Idaho 177
Bureau of Navigation 3
Burger King. 220
Burk Technologies, Pepperell, Massachusetts 215-217
Burkhardt-Abrams 147
Burns and Allen 109
Burns, George 27
Bush, James F. 12, 28
Bush, President George 176
business news 156

C

cable 82, 84, 101, 114, 118, 210, 236, 237
Calumet News, Calumet, Michigan 53
Campbell, Marianne 123
Canadian CBC network 36
Cantor, Eddie. 27
Capital Cities 100
Capital Comments 78
Capitol Times, The, Madison, Wisconsin 13
Capps, Gordon 84-87, 275
car radio
    first 31
Carl, John 232
Carmen, Frank 55, 56
Carrell, Charles E. 24
Carrell, Adelaide. 24
Carter, President Jimmy 175, 182, 183
Carthage College, Carthage, Illinois 15
Cashion, John 145, 146
Census Bureau. 237, 240
Central Radio Co., Muscatine, Iowa 29
Central Radio Electric Co., Central City, Nebraska 29
CFRB, Toronto, Canada 121,122
Chandler, A.B. "Happy" 63, 130
Chapman Company, Atlanta, Georgia 223
Charles, Rick 249
Charlton, Pete 211, 214
Chicago Tribune, The 6
CHR (contemporary hits radio) 152
Christensen, Wally. 248
Christian Science Monitor 47
church broadcasts 54
Church of God, Cleveland, Tennessee 93
"churning" 111, 193
cigarette advertising 154, 155
Cincinnati Reds 130, 135

Civil Defense 62
civil rights 140
Civil War 140, 202
CKRC, Winnipeg, Canada. 36
classical music. 212
classified ads 132
Clear Channel Broadcasters Association (CCBA) 121, 122
Clear Channel Communications 164, 165
clear channel stations. 67, 124, 184
Cleveland Broadcasting Company 17
Cliquit Club Eskimos, The 6
Close, Joe 54
Coast-to-Coast. 208
code of good practices 44
Cold War. 175
college stations. 16
Collins, Gov. LeRoy 185
Columbia Broadcasting System (CBS) 37, 43, 52, 57, 58, 62, 68, 75, 84, 98,
108, 109, 115, 147, 153, 154, 238
comedy/variety programs 58
commercials. 26, 109, 150, 151, 155, 157, 166, 200
    first 5, 6
    first singing 6
commission 52, 160, 161
Commonwealth Reporter, Fond Du Lac, Wisconsin 31
Communications Act 219
Communist world 74
community needs 150, 216
Community Service Radio, Sulphur Springs, Texas. 33
Compton, Robert 14, 15, 270
Compton, Robert Jr. 15
Compton, Zola 15
computerized logging and billing. 210-212, 214, 217
computers 213
Concept, The 158
Concordia Broadcasting Company, Concordia, Kansas. 29
Congress 22, 23, 175, 185, 190, 202, 219, 220, 273
Conn, Jacob. 30
Connell, Dr. D.D. 30
Conrad, Dr. Frank 4
Cook, Fred 162
Cooley, Art 247
Coolidge, President Calvin 23
copyright. 9, 52
Corliss, George. 102
Cornett, Marshall 84, 87
Country Coast-to-Coast format. 212
Country Music Radio Seminar 214

Courier-Post, Hannibal, Missouri 53
Cox Broadcasting 128
CPs 83, 196, 198, 226
crime programs 58
Crocker, Betty 69
Crooks, Dave 228
Crosby, Bing 27, 51, 112
Crosley, Powel 122
Crowder, G. Paul 137
Cumberland Electric Company, Cumberland, Maryland 38
Cummings, Ira 32
Cutler Radio Broadcasting Service, Brookings, North Dakota 30

D

Dahle, Bill 250
Daily Courier News, The, Blytheville, Arkansas 14
Daily Telegraph, Bluefield, West Virginia 38, 53
Dakota Radio Apparatus Company, Yankton, South Dakota 12
Dale, Martha 187
Darwinists 183
David, Miles 100
David, Ray 106, 248
Davis, John 178
Davis, Red 277
Daytime Broadcasters Association 122-124
daytimers. 23, 38, 39, 66, 69, 94, 95, 120-125, 147, 148, 163, 181, 184, 188, 194, 197, 198, 223, 225, 227, 235
Dean, Dizzy 131
December Bride 142
De Forest, Dr. Lee 6, 127
deficits 175
Democratic Party 43, 60, 61, 162
Department of Justice 51
Depression, The Great. 15, 16, 31, 37, 41-43, 45, 46, 75, 106, 141, 202, 207
depression, postwar 74, 75
deregulation 182-184, 217
Dickey, Hugh 224-226
Digital DJ 214
Dinner Bell 10
Dinner Winner 97
Dispatch, Cordele, Georgia 53
Dix family 115
Dixon, Mason 89, 90
Dr. IQ 91, 109
Domino, Fats 125
Donnelly, Tom 160, 161
Donnely, Carol 250

Donnely, Craig 250
Donnely, Frank 250
Don't Get Around Much Anymore 64
Doran, Kevin 247
Dorsey, Tommy 96
double billing 151, 152
Dow Jones 41, 42
Drake, Bill 147
Drake, Galen 69
drama programs 58
drive-in theaters 131
drought 59
DuMont Network 114
duopoly 38, 220, 236, 243
Durante, Jimmy 27
dust storms 59

E

early morning broadcasting 11
Ebel, Jim 45
"Economic Darwinism" 239
economy
    1920s 8
Economy Light Company, Escanaba, Michigan 29
editorializing 97, 119, 125
Edwards, Ralph 97
8XK, Pittsburgh, Pennsylvania 4
"80/90" FM list 83, 192-198, 218, 231
Eisenhower, President Dwight 106, 143, 176, 203
Electric Farm, Poynette, Wisconsin 13, 31
"elevator music" 147
Elks 118
Ell, Floyd J. 238
Ellis, Elmo 127-129, 276
Eppel, Ray 115, 116
equal opportunity 97
evangelists 88
Evans, Billy 148
Everly Brothers, the 125, 126, 276
Everly Ike 126, 276
Everly Margarite 126, 276
Ewing, Clay 55
Ewing, P.K. 55
Executive Inn Hotels 227, 228
Experimenter Publishing Company, Coteysville, New York 30

F

F.A. Battery Company. 29
Fairmont Sentinel, Fairmont, Minnesota 7
Fairness Doctrine. 161, 162
Fantasia, Nick 38
farm news 156
Federal Communications Commission (FCC) 16, 19, 36, 43, 54, 56, 65-68,
75, 76, 83, 84, 89, 90, 97, 108, 112, 116-124, 126, 127, 132, 133, 142, 143,
145-147, 150, 151, 153, 157, 162, 163, 174, 181, 183-186, 190, 192-196,
198, 199, 218-220, 232, 235, 237, 239
      "Berwick and Suburban" rules 196
      Guidebook on Applying for the New FM Allocations. 194, 195
      1945 financial report 67
      1954 financial report 120
      1955 financial report. 101, 102
      1960 financial report. 132, 133
      1970 financial report 154
      1980 financial report 167, 200, 218
      1990 financial report. 217, 218
      seven-station limit 95, 196
      Table of Assignments 146
      "Three Year Holding Rule" 195
      12-station limit. 196, 219
Federal Radio Commission (FRC) 12, 15, 17, 20, 21, 23, 24, 27, 35, 38, 39,
45, 59, 143, 200, 218
Federal Reserve Board 175
Fellows, Harold. 185
Felker, Lloyd L. 78-82
Ferguson, Lina 32
Ferris, Charles. 124, 183, 184, 192, 198
Fetzer, John 9, 46
Field, Frank 49
Field, Henry 8-12, 49, 50, 272
Field Seed Company 9-11, 29, 49
Fields, Shep 102
Fifties, The. 106
"52-20 Club" 74
fines. 150
First Bank of Vida, Vida, Montana 3, 4, 29, 139
First Congregational Church, Springfield, Vermont. 54
First Trust and Savings Bank, Harrisburg, Illinois 17
Fitzgerald, Harold 109, 110
5YM, Fayetteville, Arkansas 15
Flatwoods Broadcasting Association, Kalispell, Montana. 29
Fleming, Clarence "Red" 76, 77
"floaters" 144-146
floods. 59-61, 233, 274

FM . . 69, 76, 81, 83, 84, 87, 98, 99, 101, 110, 111, 113, 121, 124, 132, 133, 140, 146-150, 153, 154, 166, 167, 173, 179, 181-184, 188, 189, 193-200, 214, 218-222, 224, 225, 227, 228, 235, 236, 238
    first 66
FM Association 99, 188, 189
FM Table of Allocations 16, 147, 193
Folkvold, Mr. and Mrs. Olaf 174
Folkyard, Borghild 139, 140
Folkyard, Olaf 139, 140
Forbis, Jennifer Krebsbach 238
Forbis, Phil 238
Ford, John 69
Ford, President Gerald 175, 182
Foreign Exchange (FX) 90
Forrest, J.F. 13
Forrest, William 13
Fort Campbell, Kentucky 63
Fortas, Abe 75
Fowler, Mark 183, 184, 196, 198, 218
Fox, Robert A. 30
fraudulent billings 152
Freberg, Stan 109
Fred Harvey Restaurant 47
Freed, Alan 126
Freeland, Mike 148-150
freeze on radio station building 64, 65, 92, 108, 116, 219
freeze on TV station building 112
frequency monitors 45
Fries, Gary 100, 101
Fritts, Edward M. 62, 186-188, 277
Fritts, Edward O. (Eddie) 62, 185-188, 190, 192, 277
Fritz, Alene Wendel 162, 163
Fritz, Norbert 162

G

Gaarenstroom, C.G. 7
Gabbard, Jim 189
Garbo, Greta 97
Gardner, Paul 233
Gardner, Ray 1, 233
General Mills 6
Gensch and Sterns 31
Genthner Electronics, Salt Lake City, Utah 215
G.I. Bill 75, 85, 117
Gibson 208
Gilbert, Galen 33
giveaways 97, 131

Gleason, Dick. 246
goat gland operation. 20
Goeman, John 249
Goetz, Nathan 82
Gold Medal Flour 3
Goldberg, Mel. ii
Golden Age. 27, 31, 35, 37, 41, 66-68, 71, 73
Golden Mike. 26
Goldman, Chuck 234
Goldwater, Barry 162
GOP. 162
Gordon, Lois and Alan 31
government regulation 22
Great Empire Group, Wichita, Kansas 21
Great Northern Railroad. 25
Great Plains. 59
Green, Bob. 227, 228
Green Hornet. 109
Green Mountain Ballroom 64
Greenlee, Howard. 227
Grenada College for Women, Grenada, Mississippi 55
"Grid Pricing". 205
Griffin, Gov. Marvin. 142
gross national product 41, 140
ground conductivity. 149
"ground screen". 118
group ownership 220-222
Grove City College, Grove City, Pennsylvania 16
Gurney, Chad. 12
Gurney Seed and Nursery Company, Yankton, South Dakota 12, 30
Gurney, Thompson L. 29
Guterma, Alexander 109

H

Hackman, Jack 82
Halberstam, David 106
Hal Roach Studios. 108, 109
Hale, Todd 232
Haley, Bill and the Comets. 125
Halverson, Faye 139, 140
Halverson, Oscar 139, 140, 173, 174
Halyard, O.C.. 130
Hamilton, Thurman 252
Hampshire, Earl W. 30
Hanneman, Dick 81
Hansen, Bob 98
Harding-Cox presidential election 4

Harding, President Warren G. 5
    adminstration 23
Hargis, Billy Joe 162
Hart, Ken 77, 78
Haroldson & Thingstad 30
Harris, Edgar 14, 28
Harris Newspapers 186
Harvard Business School 152
Harvey, Paul 21, 278
Hayloft Hoedown 70
Head, Sidney 184
Hearst Newspapers 52, 53
Heatter, Gabriel 73
Hedberg, Paul 233
Henderson, W.K. 10, 11, 143
Herald, Big Spring, Texas 53
Herald Leader, Sidney, Montana 238
Hercules Powder Plant, Cleveland, Tennessee 92
Higgins, Hugh M.P. 100
Hilger, Andy 49
Hill and Sullivan Mining, Kellogg, Montana 29
"hillbilly music" 125
Hindenburg, the 38
Hirsch, Fred 229–231
Hirsch, Oscar 98
Hirsch, Vicki 229, 230
Hirsh Battery & Radio Company, Cape Girardeau, Missouri 29
"Hit Parade" 147
Holiday, Jon 146, 176
Holt-Rowe Novelty Company, Fairmont, West Virginia 37
Home Auto Company, Dell Rapids, South Dakota 30
Home Electric Company, Burlington, Iowa 28
Hoosier Hot Shots 58
Hoover, Herbert
    President 43
    radio conferences 22
    Secretary of Commerce 3, 6, 10, 13, 22, 37
Hope, Bob 112
Horne, C.R. 155
Horne's Department Store, Pittsburgh, Pennsylvania 4
Hotel Pennsylvania 6
Hound Dog 125
Howard, Eddy 102
Howdy Doody 142
Hoyt, Waite 135
Huddleston, Walter "Dee" 148
Hummer Furniture Company, La Salle, Illinois 28
Hunter, Gerald K. 28

Huse family. 7
Huse, Gene 273
Huse, Jerry. 273
Husing, Ted 96
Hyatt Hotel 193
hypnosis 149

I

IBM 160
I.G.M. system 146, 147
Illinois School for the Blind, Jacksonville, Illinois 65
Indiana Publishing, Indiana, Pennsylvania. 53
industrialization 107
Infinity 154
inflation . 74, 85, 101, 140, 141, 154, 167, 174, 175, 182, 183, 203, 223, 236
Ingersoll, Charles. 18, 82
Ingstead, Bob 26, 221, 271
Inner Sanctum 109
institutional advertising 155-157
interest rates 175, 203
International Apple Shippers Association 41
International Harvester, Canton, Illinois. 178
International News Service (INS) 52, 53, 56
Ipana Troubadours, The. 6
Irons, Lyle 246
It Pays To Listen. 128

J

Jack Armstrong. 70
Jacobs, Joe and Marcellous 3, 4
Jacobs, Lee 84-87
James, Todd 233
Jaren, Charles. 18, 19, 44, 47, 48
Jaren Drug Company, Barrett, Minnesota. 29
Jaycees 5
jazz 212
Jeffers, Roger. 64
Jeffers, Sherrie 64
Jenkins, Charlie 214
Jindra, Joe 249
jingles 156
John Brown University, Siloam Springs, Arkansas 16
Johnson, Edward M.. . . . . 193, 194
Johnson, Gary. 250
Johnson, George W. 28
Johnson, Jerry. 224

Johnson, President Lyndon Baines 150, 151
Johnson, Randy 192
Jolson, Al 27
Jones, John Wilburn 30
Jones, Rogan 146, 147
Jones Satellite Networks 212, 213
Jurgens, Dick 102

K

K and B Electric, Webster, Massachusetts 29
K mart 208
KAAL-TV, Austin, Minnesota 115
KAAN-AM/FM, Bethany, Missouri 160
KAAT-Fm, Oakhurst, California 192
KABC, Los Angeles, California 153
KABL, San Francisco, California 131
Kaddatz Hotel 45
Kadow, Francis Mangain 25
KADS, Elk City, Oklahoma 42, 132
KAGO, Klamath Falls, Oregon 9, 25, 40, 54
KAPE, Cape Girardeau, Missouri 278
Kaplan, Sis 189
Kaplan, Stan 189
KARB-FM, Price, Utah 247
KARV, Russellville, Arkansas 155
KAST, Astoria, Oregon 53, 54
KATL, Miles City, Montana 37, 53, 105
KATQ, Plentywood, Montana 174
KAUS, Austin, Minnesota 115
KAUS-TV, Austin, Minnesota 115
KAWL-AM/FM, York, Nebraska 238
Kaye, Sammy 69
KBAL, San Saba, Texas 215, 216
KBET, Santa Clarita, California 234
KBKR, Baker, Oregon 84
KBRF, Fergus Falls, Minnesota 40
KBST, Big Spring, Texas 53
KCCR, Pierre, South Dakota 27
KCKS, Concordia, Kansas 249
KCLE, Cleburne, Texas 215
KCLI-FM, Dickinson, North Dakota 248
KCLW, Hamilton, Texas 215, 216
KCOB-AM/FM, Newton, Iowa 232
KCOJ, Sapulpa, Oklahoma 163
KCOR, San Antonio, Texas 97
KCRI, Helena, Arkansas 188
KDKA, Pittsburgh, Pennsylvania 4, 18

KDLR, Devils Lake, North Dakota 13, 30, 49
KDLT-TV, Mitchell, South Dakota 116
KDOP, Pleasanton, Texas 278
KDSR, Williston, South Dakota 174
KDUN-AM, Reedsport, Oregon 246
KDWB, Minneapolis, Minnesota. 150
KDZN, Glendive, Montana 174
KEEL, Shreveport, Louisiana 132
Kehl, Tony 277
KELK, Elko, Nevada 1, 233
Kelly, David 83
Kennedy, President John F. 140, 142, 150, 175
Kennedy, Robert 140
Kentucky Broadcasters Association (KBA) 75
Kentucky Fried Chicken 113
Kentucky State Senate. 63
KERR, Polson, Montana 140, 238, 269
KEUB, Price, Utah. 55
Keynes, John Maynard. 41
KEYZ, Williston, North Dakota 105, 239
KFBB, Havre, Montana. 29
KFBM, Greenville, Texas 31
KFBI, Abilene, Kansas 21, 278
KFDI, Wichita, Kansas 9, 21
KFEQ, Oak, Missouri/St. Joseph, Missouri 9
KFEY, Kellogg, Montana. 29
KFGQ, Boone, Iowa. 16
KFGZ, Berrien Springs, Michigan 9
KFIZ, Fond Du Lac, Wisconsin 31
KFJB, Marshalltown, Iowa 8, 29, 45, 53
KFJI, Astoria, Oregon/Klamath Falls, Oregon 9, 24, 30, 40, 54
KFJY, Fort Dodge, Iowa 29
KFKB, Milford, Kansas. 9, 20, 21, 29, 272
KFLU, San Benito, Texas. 9
KFLZ, Atlantic, Iowa 9
KFMQ, Fayetteville, Arkansas. 15
KFNF, Shenandoah, Iowa 8, 10-12, 29, 49, 126, 272, 276
KFPM, Dublin, Texas 31
KFPW, Fort Smith, Arkansas 15
KFQU, Alma, California 28
KFVN, Fairmont, Minnesota 29
KFVN Broadcasting, Fairmont, Minnesota. 29
KFVN, Welcome, Minnesota/Fairmont, Minnesota. 7
KFVS, Cape Girardeau, Missouri 29, 38, 98
KFXD, Jerome, Idaho 28
KGAR, Willow Springs, Missouri. 219
KGAS, Carthage, Texas 189
KGBU, Ketchikan, Alaska 28

KGBY, Columbus, Nebraska 30
KGBZ, York, Nebraska. 30, 39
KGCA, Decorah, Iowa 29
KGCG, Newark, Arkansas 28
KGCH, Wayne, Nebraska 30
KGCL, Seattle, Washington 40
KGCN, Concordia, Kansas 29
KGCR, Brookings, North Dakota 30
KGCU, Mandan, North Dakota 30
KGCX, Vida, Montana/Wolf Point, Montana/Sidney, Montana . . 3, 4, 29,
35-37, 39, 73, 74, 105, 139, 173, 174, 238, 239, 269
KGDA, Dell Rapids, South Dakota. 30
KGDE, Barrett, Minnesota/Fergus Falls, Minnesota 18, 29, 40, 44-49
KGDJ, Cresco, Iowa 28
KGDW, Humbolt, Nebraska 30
KGDY, Oldham, South Dakota 30
KGES, Central City, Nebraska 29
KGEU, Lower Lake, California. 28
KGEZ, Kalispell, Montana 19, 20, 29, 168
KGFF, Alva, Oklahoma 30
KGFF, Mitchell, South Dakota 30
KGFK, Hallock, Minnesota 29
KGFL, Trinidad, Colorado/Raton, New Mexico 40
KGFM, Trinidad, Colorado 28
KGFM, Yuba City, California 28
KGFN, Aneta, North Dakota. 30
KGFN, LaCrescenta, California 28
KGFW, Ravenna, Nebraska/Kearney, Nebraska 30
KGFX, Pierre, South Dakota 26, 27, 30, 222, 271
KGGF, Coffeyville, Kansas 42
KGGH, Cedar Grove, Louisiana 29
KGGP, Picher, Oklahoma 30
KGIN-TV, Grand Island, Nebraska 46
KGIW, Trinidad, Colorado/Alamosa, Colorado 40
KGLE, Glendive, Montana. 174
KGMI, Bellingham, Washington 146
KGMO, Cape Girardeau, Missouri 278
KGMP, Elk City, Oklahoma. 42
KGNO, Dodge City, Kansas. 42
KGO, San Francisco, California 153
KGRI, Henderson, Texas 142
KHAS, Hastings, Nebraska. 53, 86, 115
KHAS-TV, Hastings, Nebraska 115, 275
KHBM-AM/FM, Monticello, Arkansas 252
KHMO, Hannibal, Missouri 53, 156
KHOZ-AM/FM, Harrison, Arkansas 206, 207
KHSN, Eugene, Oregon/Marshfield, Oregon/Coos Bay, Oregon 40
KHWK, Tonopah, Nevada 217

KICD, Spencer, Iowa. 89-91, 156
KICK, Atlantic, Iowa. 28
KIDW, Lamar, Colorado 40
"Kills Gloomy Dull Evenings". 18
KIMB, Kimball, Nebraska 158
Kimel, Bob 224
Kincaid, Garvice D.. . . . . 77, 78
Kincaid, George 24, 25
King, Dr. Martin Luther 140
KIOI, San Francisco, California 189
KIRK, Lebanon, Missouri 160
Kirksey Bros. Battery and Electric Company, Breckenridge, Texas . . 30, 31
KISD, Pipestone, Minnesota. 248
Kitson Country Enterprise, Hallock, Minnesota 29
KIUP, Durango, Colorado 48
KIVL, Garden City, Kansas 53
KJAM-AM/FM, Madison, South Dakota. 249
KJEL, Lebanon, Missouri. 160
KLBZ, Foxcroft, Maine. 29
KLCN, Blytheville, Arkansas. 14, 28
KLER, Lewiston, Montana 66
KLGA-AM/FM, Algona, Iowa i
KLIF, Dallas, Texas. 131
KLIK, Jefferson City, Missouri 156
KLKO, Elko, Nevada. 1, 233
KLMJ, Hampton, Iowa 250
KLMR, Lamar, Colorado 40
KLOH-AM, Pipestone, Minnesota 248
KLTC-AM, Dickinson, North Dakota 106, 248
KMA, Shenandoah, Iowa. 10-12, 29, 32, 39, 42, 49, 50, 126, 272, 276
KMAQ-AM/FM, Maquoketa, Iowa 251
KMAR-AM/FM, Winnsboro, Louisiana 188
KMCX-FM, Ogallala, Nebraska. 252
KMIT, Mitchell, South Dakota. 234
KMM, Clay Center, Nebraska 29
KMOR-FM, Scottsbluff, Nebraska 219
KNAF, Fredericksburg, Texas 162
KNCK, Concordia, Kansas. 249
KNEL, Brady, Texas 65
KNOP, North Platte, Nebraska. 115
KNOP-TV, North Platte, Nebraska. 115
KNPT, Newport, Oregon 56
Knox Battery & Electric Co., Brookville, Indiana 28
KOA, Denver, Colorado 22
KOAC, Corvallis, Oregon 16
KOAL, Price, Utah. 55, 56, 247
KOAQ-AM, Scottsbluff, Nebraska 219
KOAT-TV, Albuquerque, New Mexico 248

KODY, North Platte, Nebraska. 42
KOEL, Oelwein, Iowa. 156
KOGA-AM/FM, Ogallala, Nebraska. 252
KOLN-TV, Lincoln, Nebraska. 46
KOLO, Durango, Colorado. 28
KOLT, Fergus Falls, Minnesota. 40
KOLT, Scottsbluff, Nebraska. 42, 219, 277
KOLV-TV, Olivia, Minnesota. 116
KOOS, Coos Bay, Oregon. 40
Kopp Radio Company, Sisiht, Wisconsin. 31
KORD, Pasco, Washington. 150
Korean War. 80, 106, 116
KORN, Minneapolis, Minnesota. 115
KOVM, LaGrande, Oregon. 84, 87
KOWH, Omaha, Nebraska. 129
KOWN, Walla Walla, Washington. 31
KPAH, Tonopah, Nevada. 216
KPGM, Prescott, Arizona. 28
KPNP, Muscatine, Iowa. 29
KPQ, Seattle, Washington/Wenatchee, Washington. 40, 66, 168
KPXE-AM, Liberty, Texas. 181, 182, 250
KQEH, Coos Bay, Oregon. 40
KQKL, Apple Valley, California. 142
KQSS, Miami, Arizona. 145, 249
KQW, San Jose, California. 87
Krebsbach, Clair. 74, 105, 139, 140, 238, 269
Krebsbach, Ed. 3, 35, 37, 73, 74, 105, 139, 174, 238, 269
Krebsbach, Keith. 74, 105, 139
Krebsbach, Paul. 35
KREI, Farmington, Missouri. 160
KREN, Spokane, Washington. 66
KRES-FM, Moberly, Missouri. 158
KREW-AM/FM, Sunnyside, Washington. 66, 245
KRFO-AM/FM, Owatonna, Minnesota. 81, 232
KRGE, Weslaco, Texas. 9
KRJH, Hallettsville, Texas. 160
Kroc, Ray. 252
Kroger. 202
KRQ, Wenatchee, Washington. 146
KRRB-FM, Dickinson, North Dakota. 106, 248
KRTN-AM/FM, Raton, New Mexico. 40, 248
KRUK, Roseburg, Oregon. 53
KSCB, Liberal, Kansas. 142
KSDY, Sidney, Montana. 239
KSHN-FM, Liberty, Texas. 171, 182, 250
KSO, Clarinda, Iowa. 28
KSPQ, West Plains, Missouri. 219
KSRV, Ontario, Oregon. 85-87, 101, 102, 275

KSTP, Minneapolis, Minnesota. 3
KSTV, Stephenville, Texas. 139
KTHS, Hot Springs National Park, Arkansas 28
KTJJ, Farmington, Missouri 160
KTLB, Twin Oaks, Iowa 250
KTNT, Muscatine, Iowa. 21, 29
KUHI-AM, Eleele, Hawaii. 250
Kukla, Fran and Ollie 58, 110
KUMV-TV, Williston, North Dakota. 139
KUOA, Fayetteville, Arkansas/Siloam Springs, Arkansas. 15, 16, 39
KUOO, Spirit Lake, Iowa 233
Kuralt, Charles 84
KVBR, Brainerd, Minnesota 82
KVCK, Glendive, Montana 174
KVVQ-AM/FM, Victorville, California. 252
KWAL, Wallace, Idaho. 177
KWED, Seguin, Texas 185
KWIX, Moberly, Missouri. 156-158
KWKH, Shreveport, Louisiana 10, 143
KWLC, Decorah, Iowa 16
KWLM, Willmar, Minnesota 69, 70, 277
KWLT, Lebanon, Missouri. 278
KWOA, Worthington, Minnesota. 124, 190
KWPM-AM, West Plains, Missouri 219
KWSU, Pullman, Washington. 16
KWUC, LaMars, Iowa 10
KXGN, Glendive, Montana. 105, 174
KXRO, Aberdeen, Washington 31
KXYO, Breckenridge, Texas 30
KYSM, Mankato, Minnesota 64
KYTC, Glendive, Montana 174
KYTE, Newport, Oregon 56
KYYZ, Williston, North Dakota 173, 239
KZIM, Cape Girardeau, Missouri. 38

L

labor unions. 107
Lackey, Bonnie 63, 64
Lackey, "Dutch" 61-65, 274
Lackey, Hecht 60-63, 65, 274
Lackey, Henry 63, 274
Lackey, Pierce. 59-62, 65, 168, 274
Lackey, Prewitt 274
Ladies Home Journal. 26
Lamb, Dr. J. Arthur 19
Land, Allan 113-115
Land, Dave. 251

Land, Tom 251
Landon, Gov. Alf. 21, 123, 142
Lange, Mark 227, 228
Lange, Mr. and Mrs. Paul. 13
LangWorth transcriptions 36
Lankford, Ray 112, 113
Lankford, Stu 228
Larson, Jeanie 82-84
Last Picture Show, The 161
Leafstedt, Ray. 156
Lee, Carl 46
Liberty Network, The. 130, 131
Liberty Theatre, Astoria, Oregon 24, 30, 54
license . . 3, 4, 13, 14, 17, 21-24, 26, 51, 65, 76, 82, 117, 143, 145, 150-152,
157, 173, 181-183, 193, 195, 207, 210, 216, 220, 226, 233, 238
Limbaugh, Rush. 278
Linder family 221
Linder, Harry. 277
Lintzenich, Dutch. 14
Lions Club. . . . . *i*
Littick family 17, 113, 115
Livermore, Ed 163, 164
Livesay, Level. 121, 123
Livesay, Ray. 12, 71, 120-125
Livesay Stations, Mattoon, Illinois 71
L.M.A. (Local Marketing Agreement) 197, 219, 228
Local Development Districts 177
Lockhart, Ray 252
Loesch, J. Albert 30
Lone Ranger, The 57, 70
Lopez, Vincent. 6
Love, Stan and his 12-piece orchestra 21
Lotowana, Lower Lake, California. 28
low-frequency transmission lines. 163
Low Power Television Stations 193
Lucas, Nick 18
Lujaks, Larry 250
Lum and Abner 42
Luther College, Decorah, Iowa. 16
Lytle, Chris 165

M

M Street Journal Directory 199, 200, 235, 240
Mackenzie, Stan 185
Magnum, Dave. 226
Makadow Theatre, Manitowoc, Wisconsin 25, 31
Make Believe Ballroom 96

"man on the street" 48, 65, 97, 119
"Management, The" 211, 214, 216
Mandan Radio Association, Mandan, North Dakota 30
Mann, Bernie 189-192
Mansfield, Sen. Mike 183
Marconi, Guglielmo 127, 243
"Marketing Bridge, The" 158
Marsh, E.E. 24
Marshall Electric Company, Marshalltown, Iowa 29
Marshall, June 277
Marshall, Rex 142
Marti, George 215, 216
Marti short wave system 215
Marti two-way microwave system 215, 216, 230
Martin, Don 233, 254
Marx, Groucho 27, 112
Masonic Temple Building, Kalispell, Montana 19
Matmair, Bill 18
May, Earl 10-12, 32, 42, 49, 50, 272
May, Earl W. 10
May, Edward W. 10
May Fairways 42
May Seed Company 10, 29, 49
May Tire Orchestra 11
May, Walter E. 190, 247
Mayfair Theatre 11, 12, 42
"Mayflower Decision, The" 97
Mayola Orchestra 11
Mays, Lowry 164, 165
McCallum, Shelby 117
McCarthy, Al 109
McClendon, Gordon 130-132, 276
McDonald's 221
McGlone, Louise 32
McNeil, Dana 25, 26, 30, 271
McNeil, Ida 25-27, 271
McNeill, Don 58
McRaney, Bob Jr. 245
Meador, Ralph 224
media buying 205
"media mix" 158, 165
Medley, M.L. "Luke" 65
mental hospitals 42
Meredith, Don 142
merger of NAB and NRBA 191
Merideth, J.B. 30
Metropolitan Opera 58, 69, 70
Meyer, George 79, 80

Michener, James 142
middle of the road 153, 156
Miller, Bob 106, 174
Miller, David 56
Miller, Dean. 142
Miller, Dr. George R. 30
Miller, Justin. 185
Miller, Neville 185
Mills, Elmo 148
miniature golf 42
minimum wage. 44, 75
Mining Journal, Marquette, Michigan 53
Minnesota Broadcasters Association (MBA) 7
minority ownership 198, 220
minority programming. 97, 123
Minow, Newton 142, 150
Miss Hush 131
Mississippi Broadcasters Association. 188
Mister District Attorney 109
Mr. Professor 91
"Mitch's Pitch" 99
Mitchell Broadcasting Company, Mitchell, South Dakota 30
Mitchell, Jay. . . . . *i*, 239
Mitchell, Maurice B. "Mitch" 99, 100
M.M. Johnson Company, Clay Center, Nebraska 29
Monitor 109
monopolies 53
Monte American 69
Montgomery Ward 75, 202
Moore, Frank A.. 31
Moore Motor Company, Newark, Arkansas 28
Moose. 145
Morning Gazette, Houghton, Michigan. 53
Morrison, Herbert 38
Moses, Bill. 112
Moss, Gary 215, 216
Moss, Lloyd. 215, 216
"move-ins" 39
Muchmore family. 24
Muchmore, Tom. 24
music libraries 100
Mutual Network. 36, 57, 58, 73, 105, 108, 109, 131, 153, 154, 227
My Three Sons. 102

N

Nash, Francis 234
National Association of Black-Owned Broadcasters (NABOB). 198

National Association of Broadcasters (NAB) . . . 6, 50, 51, 62, 99, 100, 111, 124, 151, 184-186, 188, 189, 191, 192, 217, 220, 277
    code of industry practices. 200
    conventions 9, 99, 123, 142, 150, 156, 214
    Daytimer Committee. 124
    Distinguished Service Award. 186
    Future of Radio study 199
    HDTV Task Force 46
    Marconi Award 231
    merger with NRBA 191
    "Program Conference". 190
National Association of Recording Artists 51
National Broadcasting Company (NBC) . 27, 37, 43, 52, 57, 58, 64, 66, 68, 108, 109, 115, 153, 154, 192, 231
National Radio Broadcasters Association (NRBA) 124, 189-192
    merger with NAB. 191
    "Radio Show". 9, 190
National Recovery Agency (NRA) 44
National Stores. 202
National Telecommunications and Information Administration. 218
Nationwide Insurance. 38
natural disasters 59
Navy 162, 163
Navy Signal Corps 14
Neathery, Bob. 219, 220
Neathery, Brad. 219, 220
Nelson, Willie. 278
network programming. 153-155, 181
New Deal 184
New England Media. 224
New Furniture Company, Greenville, Texas 31
New Republic 98
New York Times, The 220
news. 90, 108, 113, 119, 131, 132, 158, 176, 183, 212, 216
    newcasts 7, 47, 52, 58, 66, 83, 93, 129, 153, 156, 157, 228
    news service 46, 181
News, Clarksburg, West Virginia 53
News-Review, Roseburg, Oregon. 53
newspapers 52-54, 78, 98, 101, 114, 115, 117, 122, 127, 152, 157, 163, 164, 173, 179, 184, 201, 209, 226, 227
Newsweek. 98
9CLS, Pierre, South Dakota 25-27
9EJ, Carthage, Illinois 14
9ZP, Pierre, South Dakota 25, 26, 271
1986 Tax Reform Act 224
Nightbeat 128
Nit Wit Club. 70
Nixon, President Richard 174, 182

Nolte, Vernon. 114
Nolting, Earl. 148, 149
non-commercial stations. 8
Norfolk Daily News, Norfolk, Nebraska. 7, 30, 53, 273
Norton, George V. 61
Nutcracker Suite. 233

O

O'Connor, Harry. 176
Office of Price Administration. 75
Ohio River. 59
"Ole Miss". 187
"Old Scotchman". 130
oldies format. 226
Olsen, Glenn. 200
Olsen, Paul. 80
On the Road. 84
Only Yesterday. 5
Orchard, Ken. 252
Oregon Station Agriculture College, Corvallis, Oregon. 16
O'Shaunecy, Bill. 231
overbuilding. 199, 200, 219, 222, 237
owned-and-operated stations . . 43, 57, 58, 67, 69, 109, 133, 153, 154, 167, 192
ownership limits. 220
Ozzie and Harriet. 109

P

Page, Patti. 70
Paley, William. 37, 109, 127
Palmer, Fred. 164
Pamida. 208
Parade of Bands. 102
Parker, Dr. Sam. 243
Parks, Bert. 97
Partick, Dennis. 198
"party line" type broadcasts. 26
Patterson, Ken. 122
Paul, Lillian. 32
Pawley, Bill. 111
payola. 126, 127
Peale, Dr. Norman Vincent. 41
Pearl Harbor. 64
Pearson, Drew. 70
Peden, Katherine. 63
Penetread. 78

Penney, John Cash 202
Penney, J.C. store 48
Pepper, Vince 96, 184
per inquiry (P.I.) business. 44
Perkins, Les 77
Perot, Ross. 225
Persons, Charlie. 82, 275
Persons, June 82
Petrillo, James Caesar 65, 66
Petroleum Telephone Company, Oil City, Pennsylvania 30
phone-in programs 157
Pierce, Webb 142
Pleasants, George 142
Ponca City News 24
population. 141, 176, 235-237
     1920s 8
     shifts 74, 107, 173
portable radio stations 23, 24
Porter, Paul. 75, 76
Portland (Oregon) Ballet Company. 233
Pot O' Gold 97
Potash, Warren 100
Powell, Bob. 151, 152
Powell, John. 84-87, 275
Powell, Stephen 152
Presley, Elvis. 125
"Press-Radio Wars" 53
"Printer's Devil, The" 7, 273
Prinz, Peter J.. 30
profits 141,154, 166-168, 195
Program Distributors, Jonesboro, Arkansas 42
program formats, 1995 survey. 240
programming. 156, 169, 179, 213, 216, 236
Progressive Network, The 130
Prohibition 25
promotions 78, 80, 156, 158, 193, 213
public address systems 49, 99
public affairs programming 183, 233
public service 157, 158, 234
Puffer, Eugene 249
Pulliam, Eugene. 226, 227
Pyles, C.C.. 46

Q

Quayle, Vice President Dan 226
Queen for a Day 73
Queensboro Corporation. 5, 6

quota units 38

R

"race music" 125
racial unrest 161
radar weather 89
Radio Advertising — The Authoritative Handbook 6
Radio Advertising Bureau (RAB) (formerly Broadcast Advertising Bureau)
100, 101, 111, 190, 191, 209, 229
Radio Digest 11, 27, 239, 272
Radio Electric Company 13, 30
Radio Guide 28
"radio gypsies" 143-146
radio households 64
Radio Ink 112, 279
Radio Network Association 190
"Radio Only Convention" 191
"Radio Programming Clinics" 90
Radio Radio 153
"Radio Sales Universities" 191
Radio Service Laboratories, Auburn, New York 30
Radio Shack 211
Radio Shop, The, Chelsea, Massachusetts 29
radio receivers
    first 4
Radio Sales Company, Blytheville, Arkansas 14
Radio Talk 230
Radio-Television News Directors Association 190
radiotelegraph transmitter 4
radiotelephony transmitter 4
Radio Wayne Awards 279
Raley's School of Beauty Culture, Harrisburg, Illinois 17
rate card 80
Rathert, R. 28
ratings 112, 164, 165, 204
Ray, Eula 216, 217
RCA 66
Readers Digest 26
Reagan, President Ronald 174-176, 183, 184, 219
Reagan's America 76
Rebel in Radio 67
recession 175, 182
Red Cross 234
Red Lion case 162
Red Network 43, 57, 58, 68
Reeves, Jim 142
Regional Broadcasters Association 122

Regional Reps 205
Reich, Ray 215
Reinsch, J. Leonard 128
"reinvented" radio 132, 209
religious broadcasting 88, 212
remote control studios 85, 116, 215
remotes 109
Republican Party 43, 219
revenue tables 44, 133, 154, 168
revenues 101, 102, 120, 132, 133, 141, 166, 201, 210
Review-Republican, The, Alliance, Ohio 98
Rhoads, B. Eric 279
Rice, John 225
Rice, Phyllis 224-226
Richards, Jack 55, 56
Riker, W.E. 28
Rivers, E.D. 53
Rivers family 168
Rivers, Jim 53
Rist, Frank J. 30
RKO-General 108
Robinson, Aaron 186, 187
Robinson, Betty 178
Robinson, Frederick 28
Robinson, Len 56, 246
Robinson, Paul 177, 178
Robson, Pat 238
Robson, Tom 238
Rock Around the Clock 125
rock 'n' roll 129
Roller Derby 110
Roosevelt, Franklin D. 43, 44, 49, 64, 65, 176
    landslide 21, 49
Root, Tom 198
Roper, Jim 248
Roper, Mark 248
Roper, Mary Lynn 248
Roper Poll 132, 237, 238
Rose Bowl, the 27
Rosedale, Hospital, Minneapolis, Minnesota 3
"Rosie the Riveter" 64
Round Hills Radio Corporation, South Dartmouth, Massachusetts . . . 29
Rounsaville, Bob 91-96, 168
royalties 9, 50, 51
RTC 182
Ruse, Paul 156
Russell, Betty 70
Rust, Bill 116

Ryan, William B. 100, 101

S

Safeway 202
St. Olaf College, Northfield, Minnesota 16
Samuels, Hartley 81, 82
Sanders, Ben 87-91, 156
Sanders, Betty 88, 89
Sanders, Bill 90
Sanger, Elliot 67
Sarnoff, David 127
satellite 83
Satellite Music Network 212, 216, 217
satellite programming 213, 228, 231, 237
Savage, Ralph 198
Schaeffer Music House, Oil City, Pennsylvania 30
Schulke, Jim 147
Schultz, Charles 183
Scofield, Charles 36, 105, 106, 173, 239
Scripps Howard Newspapers 49, 52, 53, 88
Sears 75, 202
Sears, Jerry 102
Seaton family 115
Seaton Newspapers, Hastings, Nebraska 53, 86
Sedgewick, Ginny 49
Sedgewick, Harry 46-49
Seehafer, Don 25
SESAC 89, 109
Shadow, The 57, 73, 108
Shake, Rattle and Roll 125
share-time 39, 40, 54
Sharp, Stuart 205
Shell Oil 78
Shepherd, Jerrell 155-158, 160, 161, 277
"shock jocks" 143
Shott, Hugh 38
Shott, Mike 38
Show of Shows 115
Showerer, Julius 30
Shulberg, Bob 6
Signal, The, Zanesville, Ohio 113
Signal Corps 110
Sikes, Al 218-220, 239
silent stations 200
Simpson, Barbie 111
Simpson, Betty 111
Simpson, Cary 110-112, 221, 279

Simpson, John 111
simulcast 147, 166
"Singing Troubadour, The" 18
$64,000 Question, The 97
Sky King 70
skywave 39
Small Business Administration 224, 225
Small Market Financial Data
    1945 table 68
Small Market Grosses
    1945 table 68
Small Market Radio Newsletter . . . . *i*, 222
Smith, Bob 142
Smith, Gov. Al 37
Smith, J. 29
Smith, Malcomb 109
Smith, Rev. J. Harold 88–90
Smithsonian magazine 64
Snider, Ted 208
Snow, Hank 142
"soft rock" 147
Solberg, Darrell 165
"song pluggers" 126
Sonrise Communications, Columbus, Georgia 198
Sons of the Pioneers 58, 70
Sorenson, Dean 26, 27, 116, 201, 221–223, 271
Sorry 41
Sosh, Lon 188
Sothman, Otto F. 30
Sound Off 233
Source, The 153
Southern Communications 215
Spanish programming 97
sports 48, 93, 96, 108, 109, 113, 121, 148, 153, 156, 158, 212, 216, 217
Sports, W. Don 248
"Sportscasters Club" 86
Squire, Lloyd 65
"stagflation" 167
Stakelin, Bill 100
stand-alone stations 98, 133, 148–150, 154, 188, 189, 212, 214, 235
Standard Rate and Data Service book 205
Stanton, Dr. Frank 98
Star, The, Miles City, Montana 53
Star Station format 212
State College of Washington, Pullman, Washington 16
"Station BOB," Carthage, Illinois 14, 15, 270
station prices and values 223, 224
Station Representatives Association 190

Steese, Don 250
Stefan, Karl. 7, 273
Stephenson, Hobert 65
Sterling, Christopher. 184
Stewart, Jim 252
Stop the Music 97, 131
Storer, George B. 17, 38, 57, 113, 130
Storz, Todd 129, 131, 276
Strand, Bill. 82
Stryker, Fern 57
Stubblefield, Nathan B. 243
Sturtz, Howie. 81
Sudbury, Harold 14
Summers, Bill. 96
Sun Oil Co.. 66
Sun, The, Vincennes, Indiana. 53
Sunday Morning 84
"Super" radio association 190, 192
"Supercenter" 207
Superman 73, 109
Supreme Court. 44, 52, 162, 202
Sutton, Art 252, 279
Sutton, Willie. 76
Sweeney, Kevin. 100
Sweetland, Lee 69
syndicated music. 157
syndication. 176
Systemation. 214-217

T

Take It or Leave It 97
talk radio 153, 212
Talley, Hayward 109, 110
Tate, Joseph R.. 17
Tate Radio Company, Harrisburg, Illinois 28
Taylor, Art 277
Taylor, Bill 145, 146, 249
Ted Mack's Amateur Hour 70
Teich, Walt. 156
Telegraph, The, Garden City, Kansas 53
telemarketing. 210
television 58, 62, 66, 73, 75, 80, 81, 84, 96-99, 101, 102, 105, 113, 113, 115,
127, 133, 142, 150, 154, 165, 183-186, 189-192, 212, 213, 219, 227, 231,
238
    color TV. 108, 115
    first television-voice phone transmission 31
    freeze on station building. 112

licenses. 108
    Low Power Television Stations 193
Tennessee Valley Authority. 93
Terry and the Pirates 70
Tescher, Kay and Ted. 174
Thelen and Ladd 30
This Incredible Century 41
Thomas, Arthur. 7, 273
Thomas, Bob 7, 274
Thomas Drugs, Thomasville, Georgia 56
Thomas, John Charles 142
Thomas, Lowell. 52, 66
Thomas, Rob 7, 274
Thornton, Chuck. 233
Thurston, Donald. 186
Tice, Olin 142
Time magazine 98, 129
Times Recorder, Zanesville, Ohio 113
Times Republican, Marshalltown, Iowa 53
Tinkle, Paul. 246
Titworth Music Shop, Union City, Texas. 31
Today. 109
Tom Mix. 73, 109
Tonight. 109
Top 40 . . . . 129, 131, 153, 276
tourism 178
Tower, Sen. John. 163
"Town Crier" 128
Tracy, Michael 219
transcription library 46
transistor radios. 125
transmitter. 45, 50, 116
transmitter monitoring 215
Transtar. 212
Trask, Blair. 214
"treasure hunts" 131
Treloar-Church Broadcasting Company 19
Treloar, Donald. 19, 20
Trinidad Broadcasting Co., Trinidad, Colorado. 28
Trinidad Creamery, Trinidad, Colorado 40
tri-opoly 228
Trivers, Steve. 189, 191
Trolard, Don 168
Trout, E. Dale 28
True Detective 73
Truman, President Harry S.. 74
Truth Or Consequences 97
Tubb, Ernest. 142

Tudor, Dave 230
Tumwall Electric Company, Fort Dodge, Iowa 29
20 Questions 73, 108
Twin Cities Barber College, Minneapolis, Minnesota 3
Tyler, John 212, 213

U

Ulrick, D.S. 32
Uncle Ezra's Radio Station 58
unemployment 41, 42, 106, 140, 141, 201
Unistar 212
United Paramount Theatre 108
United Press (UP)/United Press International (UPI) 52, 53, 117
United States Air Force Band 233
University of Arkansas, Fayetteville, Arkansas 15, 16
University of Kentucky 63
unlicensed stations 14, 15
U.S. Chamber of Commerce 162
U.S. Commerce Department 3, 10, 14, 20, 23, 218
U.S. Court of Appeals 52
USO 62
Using Radio in Sales Promotion 6

V

V.A. (Veterans Administration) benefits 75
Vagabonds, The 70
Valley, Tim 214
Van Houton, G.H. 32
"Vast Wasteland" 142
Vaughn, James D. 30
VHF 183
Vida Syncopators, The 3, 4, 35, 139, 269
Vietnam War 140, 161
Vincennes Sun, Vincennes, Indiana 226, 227
Vincennes University, Vincennes, Indiana 227
Vito, Lou 246, 279
"Voice of Egypt, The" 17
Volker, Paul 175
Voran, Abe 191, 192
Voy, Dennis 251

W

WABC, New York, New York 153
WABD, Fort Campbell, Kentucky 142
WABR, Winter Park, Florida 183

WAGE, Leesburg, Virginia 233
wage and price controls. 174
wages 140, 141
WAGS, Lexington, Massachusetts 29
WAKO-AM/FM, Lawrenceburg, Illinois 228
Walker, Charlie. 143
Wall Street. 41
Waller, Roy 16, 17, 30
Waller's Evening Broadcast Entertainers 16
Wal-Mart 180, 205-209, 225, 236
WALR, Cambridge, Ohio/Zanesville, Ohio. 17, 40, 113
Walters, Bud. 124
Walton, Sam 206-208
WAML, Laurel, Mississippi. 42
Wannamaker, John 204
WAOP, Otsego, Michigan 169
WAOS, Charlotte, North Carolina 189
WAOV, Vincennes, Indiana. 53, 226-229
WAQQ, Charlotte, North Carolina. 189
Waring, Fred and The Pennsylvanians 51, 64
Warner, Norton 158
Warren, Bill. 103, 253
Wasalewski, Vince. 185, 186
Wasmer, Louis 40
Wachtel, Rich 245
WATH-AM/FM, Athens, Ohio 164
WAVE, Hopkinsville, Kentucky 61
WAVG, Louisville, Kentucky. 61, 214
Wayne Hospital, Wayne, Nebraska. 30
WBAC, Cleveland, Tennessee 92-95, 168
WBAL, Baltimore, Maryland 39
WBAL-TV, Baltimore, Maryland 238
WBAR, Bartow, Florida 125
WBAR, Sisiht, Wisconsin 31
WBBM, Chicago, Illinois 39
WBBZ, Ponca City, Oklahoma. 23, 24
WBCU-AM, Union, South Carolina. 234, 252, 279
WBDX, Springfield, Vermont/Keene, New Hampshire 54
WBEJ, Elizabethton, Tennessee 94, 95
WBJZ, Alton, Illinois 109, 110
WBLK, Clarksburg, West Virginia. 53
WBLL, Bellefontaine, Ohio. 246, 279
WBMS, Union City, New Jersey 30
WBOC, Salisbury, Maryland 115
WBOC-TV, Salisbury, Maryland. 115
WBOG, Tomah, Wisconsin. 226
WBRL, Berlin, New Hampshire 151, 152
WBUX, Doylestown, Pennsylvania 142

WBWA, Washburn, Wisconsin 214
WBYS-AM/FM, Canton, Illinois 179, 241
WCAL, Northfield, Minnesota 16, 214
WCAZ, Quincy, Illinois/Carthage, Illinois 14, 15, 39, 270
WCBD, Zion, Illinois 9
WCCO, Minneapolis, Minnesota 3, 6
WCCY, Calumet, Michigan/Houghton, Michigan 39, 40, 53
WCDZ-FM, Martin, Tennessee 246
WCED, DuBois, Pennsylvania 85
WCFB, Tupelo, Mississippi 188
WCKR, Hornell, New York 247
WCKY, Cincinnati, Ohio 164
WCLA-AM/FM, Claxton, Georgia 248
WCMT-AM/FM, Martin, Tennessee 246
WCOA, Pensacola, Florida 57
WCOT, Olneyville, Rhode Island 30
WCPO, Cincinnati, Ohio 49
WCRS-AM, Greenwood, South Carolina 252
WCRW, Chicago, Illinois. 39
WCYN, Cynthiana, Kentucky 118, 119, 134, 135
WDAD, Indiana, Pennsylvania 53
WDBA, DuBois, Pennsylvania 234
WDEV, Waterbury, Vermont. 42, 64, 65
WDGY, Minneapolis, Minnesota 3
WDHR-FM, Pikeville, Kentucky 190, 247
WDIA, Memphis, Tennessee 97
WDKD, Kingstree, South Carolina. 142, 143
WDLB, Marshfield, Wisconsin 79-82, 276
WDME-AM/FM, Dover-Foxcroft, Maine 229-231
WDMJ, Marquette, Michigan 42, 53
WDVH, Gainesville, Florida 183, 184
WDXY, Sumter, South Carolina. 215
WDZ, Tuscola, Illinois/Decatur, Illinois 12, 28, 46, 120, 121, 213, 214
WEAF, New York 4-6
WEAT, Lake Worth, Florida 94, 95
weather 113
WEAV, Plattsburgh, New York 55
Weaver, Pat 109, 126
WEBC, Duluth, Minnesota 53
WEBE, Cambridge, Ohio/Zanesville, Ohio. 16, 17, 30, 40, 113
WEBQ, Harrisburg, Illinois. 17, 28, 38
WECZ, Punxsutawney, Pennsylvania. 111
WEDC, Chicago, Illinois. 39
weddings, broadcast of. 50
WEEI, Boston, Massachusetts 185
Weiss, Sam G. 55, 56
WEKR, Fayetteville, Tennessee 148
WEKY, Richmond, Kentucky 118

Welch, Fred 132
Welk, Lawrence 12, 102
We'll Meet Again 65
Welles, Orson 57
Wells, Bob 186
WELO, Tupelo, Mississippi 188
Welsh Company 163–165
WELY, Ely, Minnesota 82–84
Wendall, Harold 28
WENK, Fulton, Kentucky 186, 187
Wenona Legion Broadcasters, Wenona, Illinois 28
WERZ, Exeter, New Hampshire 233
Westcoast Broadcasting, Seattle, Washington 40
Westerhold, Jim 233
Westinghouse, Pittsburgh, Pennsylvania 4, 18
Westland Oil Station, Wolf Point, Montana 35
Westpfahl, Jamie 225, 226
Westwood One 212, 228, 277
WFAH, Alliance, Ohio 98
WFAN, New York 4, 5
WFAW, Fort Atkinson, Wisconsin 82
WFBE, Cincinnati, Ohio 49
WFHR, Wisconsin Rapids, Wisconsin 78
WFIS-Am, Fountain Inn, South Carolina 251
WFIW-AM/FM, Fairfield, Illinois 251
WFIW, Hopkinsville, Kentucky 29, 61
WFKY, Frankfort, Kentucky 77, 78
WFLQ-FM, French Lick, Indiana 251
WFML-FM, Washington, Indiana 227
WFOB, Fostoria, Oregon 234
WGAA, Cedartown, Georgia 92, 95
WGCB, Red Lion, Pennsylvania 162
WGCD, Chester, South Carolina 145, 146
WGEE, Green Bay, Wisconsin 9
WGLD, Greensboro, North Carolina 189
WGMR, Pennsylvania 111
WGN, Chicago, Illinois 57
WGOH, Grayson, Kentucky 234
WGOV, Valdosta, Georgia 53
WGRM, Clarksdale, Mississippi/Grenada, Mississippi/Greenwood,
Mississippi 54, 55, 168
WGRV, Greeneville, Tennessee 94, 95
WGUY, Dexter, Maine 231
WHAI, Greenfield, Massachusetts 55
WHAL, Shelbyville, Tennessee 94
WHAR, Clarksburg, West Virginia 162
WHAS, Louisville, Kentucky 58
WHBA, Oil City, Pennsylvania 30

WHBO, Bellefontaine, Ohio 30
WHBT, Harriman, Tennessee 142
WHDM, McKenzie, Tennessee 148
Wheaties 7
Wheeler, Carl S. 29
Wheeler, Dub. 206
WHEP-AM, Foley, Alabama. 252
"Wherever You Go, There's Radio". 101
Whig Journal, The, Quincy, Illinois 14, 15
WHIS, Bluefield, West Virginia. 38, 39, 53
White, George 178
White House 199
    radio in the 5
Whiteman, Paul 52, 69, 96
WHIZ, Zanesville, Ohio. 17, 40, 113-115
WHIZ-TV, Zanesville, Ohio 113-115
WHJB, Greensburg, Pennsylvania. . . . . *ii*
WHKP-AM, Hendersonville, North Carolina 247
WHLB, Virginia, Minnesota 53, 275
WHOO, Orlando, Florida 183
WHOP, Hopkinsville, Kentucky 61-64
WHOU, Houlton, Maine 230
WHOW, Clinton, Illinois 121, 125
WHRT, Hartselle, Alabama 212
WHUB, Cookeville, Tennessee. 65
WHUN, Huntington, Pennsylvania. 110
WIAR, Paducah, Kentucky 60
WIAS, Burlington, Iowa 28
WIBU, Poynette, Wisconsin 13, 31
WIBZ, Sumter, South Carolina 215
WICA, Ashtabula, Ohio 53
Wick, Bert 13, 49
WIEL, Elizabethtown, Kentucky. 148
WIGM, Medford, Wisconsin. 79, 80
Wilburn, Frank 28
Wilhight radio surveying firm 200
Williams Hardware Company, Streator, Illinois 28
Williams Insurance Agency, Devils Lake, North Dakota 13
Williams, Jim 5, 163-166
Willis, Col. Bill. 251
Wills, Gary. 176
Wilson, J.P. 30
Wilson, L.B. 164
WILY, Centralia, Illinois 65
Wimpy, Hoyt 49, 56, 168, 272, 273
WIN (Whip Inflation Now) 175
Winchell, Walter 70
WIRE, Indianapolis, Indiana 227

Wisconsin State Journal, The, Madison, Wisconsin. 13, 31
Wismer, Harry 70
WJAG, Norfolk, Nebraska. 7, 8, 30, 39, 53, 273, 274
WJAT, Swainsboro, Georgia 142
WJAZ, Chicago, Illinois 22
WJBC, La Salle, Illinois 28
WJBK, Detroit, Michigan 113
WJBL, Ladysmith, Wisconsin 250
WJBQ, Lewisburg, Pennsylvania. 54
WJBR, Omro, Wisconsin. 31
WJBU, Lewisburg, Pennsylvania/Somerset, Pennsylvania 54
WJCD-AM/FM, Seymour, Indiana. 214
WJDM, Elizabeth, New Jersey 124
WJEH, Gallipolis, Ohio. 123
WJMC, Rice Lake, Wisconsin 53
WJMS, Ironwood, Michigan 42
WJNZ, Greencastle, Indiana. 149
WJON, St. Cloud, Minnesota. 49
WJPW, Ashland, Ohio. 30
WKBB-FM, West Point, Mississippi 245
WKBE, Webster, Massachusetts. 29
WKBI, St. Marys, Pennsylvania. 111
WKBV, Brookville, Indiana 28
WKBZ, Ludington Michigan. 29
WKEE, Huntington, West Virginia 183
WKEN, Kenmore, New York. 30
WKNE, Keene, New Hampshire 54
WKOK, Somerset, Pennsylvania. 54
WKRP in Cincinnati 58
WKSR, Pulaski, Tennessee 94, 95
WKTQ-AM, Norway Maine. 246
WKZO, Kalamazoo, Michigan. 9
WKZX, Presque Isle, Maine 42
WLAG, Minneapolis, Minnesota 3
WLBC-TV, Muncie, Indiana 145
WLBH, Mattoon, Illinois. 125
WLBI, Wenona, Illinois 28
WLBM, LaGrande, Oregon 85
WLBQ, Atwood, Illinois 28
WLBR, Belvidere, Illinois 28
WLBT, Crown Point, Indiana 28
WLBW, Oil City, Pennsylvania. 30
WLBY, Iron Mountain, Michigan. 29
WLDG, Logan, West Virginia 53
WLDS, Jacksonville, Illinois 65, 97
WLDY, Ladysmith, Wisconsin. 250
WLEA, Hornell, New York 247
WLKR, Norwalk, Ohio 233

WLOU, Louisville, Kentucky 95
WLPN, Ashtabula, Ohio 30
WLS, Chicago, Illinois 38, 153
WLW, Cincinnati, Ohio. 57, 121, 122
WMAC, Cazenovia, New York. 30
WMAF, South Dartmouth, Massachusetts 29
WMBD-TV, Decatur, Illinois. 46
WMBO, Auburn, New York 30
WMCR-AM/FM, Oneida, New York 103, 253
WMFG, Hibbing, Minnesota 53
WMFN, Clarksdale, Mississippi/Grenada, Mississippi/Greenwood,
Mississippi 55
WMGR, Bainbridge, Georgia 142
WMJM, Cordele, Georgia 53
WMLO, Milton, Pennsylvania 250
WMMN, Fairmont, West Virginia 37, 38
WMOA, Marietta, Ohio 100
WMOU-AM/FM, Berlin, New Hampshire 151, 152
WMRF, Lewistown, Pennsylvania 114
WMRJ, Jamaica, New York 30
WMT, Cedar Rapids, Iowa 90
WMTS, Murfreesboro, Tennessee 142
WMVR, Sidney, Ohio. 142
WNAX, Yankton, South Dakota 8, 12, 30
WNBS, Murray, Kentucky 243
WNEW, New York, New York 96, 151
WNLA, Indianola, Mississippi. 187, 188, 277
WNOX, Knoxville, Tennessee 88
WOAI, San Antonio, Texas. 165
WOAN, Lawrenceburg, Tennessee 30
WOAW, Omaha, Nebraska 10
WOBT, Union City, Texas. 31
WOC, Davenport, Iowa 9
WOKZ, Alton, Illinois 109, 110
women in radio
    managers 66
    owners. 198
women in the work force 140
WOMT, Manitowoc, Wisconsin 25, 31
Wood, Barry 102
Wood, Gen. Robert 75
Woods, Dick (see Sedgewick, Harry)
WOR, New York, New York. 57, 122
WORD, Spartanburg, South Carolina 146
World Radio Allocation Conference (WARC). 123
World Series 73
World War I. 59
World War II . . 40, 53, 62-67, 69, 74, 75, 77, 85, 87, 92, 93, 101, 106, 110,

117, 120, 141, 151, 154, 155, 174, 199, 201, 207, 213

World's Fair of 1939 66

"World's Greatest Country Daily, The" 7

WOXO-FM, Norway Maine 246

WPA 61

WPAD, Paducah, Kentucky 42, 59-62, 188, 274, 277

WPAX-AM, Thomasville, Georgia. 49, 56, 168, 246

WPKE-AM/FM, Pikeville, Kentucky 190, 247

WPKO, Bellefontaine, Ohio 246, 279

WQAA, Parkersburg, Pennsylvania 30

WQDM, St. Albans, Vermont 42

WQDY-AM/FM, Calais, Maine. 142, 209

WQKC, Seymour, Indiana. 214

WQLR, Kalamazoo, Michigan 189

WQRX, New York, New York. 67

WQKE, Elizabethtown, Kentucky 148

WQXI, Atlanta, Georgia 94, 95

WRAK, Escanaba, Michigan 29

WRAY, Princeton, Indiana 112, 113

WRAY-TV, Princeton, Indiana 112, 113

WRBT, Vincennes, Indiana 228

WRBX, Roanoke, Virginia 39

WREN, Lawrence, Kansas 29

Wren, Jenny. 29

WRGA, Rome, Georgia 91

WRHM, Minneapolis, Minnesota 3

Wright, Charlie 179, 180, 241

Wright, Robert 192

Wright, Ruth. 179

WRJC-AM/FM, Mauston, Wisconsin. 249

WRNR-AM, Martinsburg, West Virginia. 245

WRNY, Coteysville, New York 30

WROB-AM, West Point, Mississippi 245

WRQB, Brewer, Maine. 231

WRSC, Chelsea, Massachusetts 29

WSAJ, Grove City, Pennsylvania 16

WSAZ, Pomeroy, Ohio. 9

WSB-TV, Atlanta, Georgia 127, 128

WSBC, Chicago, Illinois 39

WSCR, Chicago, Illinois. 9

WSLM-AM/FM, Salem, Indiana 233, 254

WSMI, Lietchfield, Illinois 110

WSON, Henderson, Kentucky 62, 63

WSSZ, Greensburg, Pennsylvania . . . . *ii*

WSTO-FM, Owensboro, Kentucky 227

WSZC-FM, Greenwood, South Carolina 252

WTAD, Carthage, Illinois/Quincy, Illinois 15, 88

WTAQ, Osseo, Wisconsin 9

WTAX, Streator, Illinois/Springfield, Illinois 9, 28
WTBM-AM/FM, Norway Maine 246
WTBO, Cumberland, Maryland 38, 66
WTCJ, Tell City, Indiana 214
WTCW, Whitesburg, Kentucky 142
WTIC, Hartford, Connecticut 39
WTIQ, Michigan 83
WTKZ, Huntington, West Virginia 9
WTMB, Tomah, Wisconsin 224-226
WTMJ, Milwaukee, Wisconsin 99
WTUF-FM, Thomasville, Georgia 246
WUZR, Bicknell, Indiana 228
WVAC, Norwalk, Ohio 233
WVEL, Pekin, Illinois 122
WVLK, Versailles, Kentucky 130
WVLY, Milton, Pennsylvania 250
WVMI, Mount Carmel, Illinois 112
WVOS-AM/FM, Liberty, New York 213, 244
WVOX, New Rochelle, New York 231
WWL, New Orleans, Louisiana 22
WWSR, St. Albans, Vermont 42
WWTC, Minneapolis, Minnesota. 3
WWWB, High Point, North Carolina. 189
WWYN, McKenzie, Tennessee 149
WWZN, Winter Park, Florida 183
WXLT, Ely, Minnesota 82
WXVW, Jeffersonville, Indiana 214
WXYZ, Detroit, Michigan 57
Wychor, Jim 123, 124, 190
WYEA, Ely, Minnesota 82
WYKR-AM/FM, Wells River, Vermont 249
Wylie, Cole E. 66
Wylie, Helen 66
Wynn, Ed 57, 130
WYSL, Buffalo, New York 131
WYTM, Fayetteville, Tennessee 148
WZDM, Vincennes, Indiana 227, 228
WZFR, Tomah, Wisconsin 226
WZLQ, Tupelo, Mississippi 188
WZPK, Berlin, New Hampshire 152
WZZB, Seymour, Indiana 214

X

XER, Mexico 22
Xerox 160

Y

Yarborough, Sen. Ralph. 130
Yeager, Sneed 76, 77
Young, Joe 148
"Young Sound" 147

Z

ZBM, Bermuda 66
Zenith Radio Corporation 22
Ziegfeld Follies of 1922, The 5